D1269633

The Sacred River

THE

$\mathcal{S}$ACRED

RIVER

Coleridge's Theory of the Imagination

BY JAMES VOLANT BAKER

INTRODUCTION BY RICHARD HARTER FOGLE

LOUISIANA STATE UNIVERSITY PRESS

COPYRIGHT 1957

BY THE LOUISIANA STATE UNIVERSITY PRESS

LIBRARY OF CONGRESS CARD CATALOG NO. 57-11543

PRINTED IN THE U.S.A.   FIRST EDITION

DESIGNED BY JEAN KYLE & ASSOCIATES: PAULINE MANNING

To Dorothy Davis Baker
In Appreciation

Acknowledgments

~~~~~~

The writer wishes to express his deep sense of obligation to the tireless sympathy and profound knowledge in the field of aesthetic theory of Professor Clarence D. Thorpe, who has patiently watched over the slow gestation of the present work from a much larger history of associational theory and theory of imagination, to the present shortened version, focused on Coleridge's theory itself. He also wishes to thank Professor T. M. Raysor, of the University of Nebraska, for bibliographical suggestions.

Librarians as a class of persons are among the most cooperative to be found. The writer wishes to express his sense of indebtedness and gratitude to the custodians of the British Museum and to the librarians of the Widener Library at Harvard; of the University of Michigan, including the custodians of the Rare Book Room; of the University of Nebraska; of the Anderson Library at the University of Houston; and of the Fondren Library at the Rice Institute.

He also wishes to express his gratitude to Robert Penn Warren for his critical essay on *The Rime of the Ancient Mariner*; to M. W. Bundy for his invaluable, though unfortunately never

vii

finished, history of the imagination; to Martin Kallich for his dissertation, *The Association of Ideas and Critical Theory in England*; to Kenneth Millar for his dissertation, *The Inward Eye: A Revaluation of Coleridge's Psychological Criticism*; to Walter Jackson Bate, particularly for his books *From Classic to Romantic* and his recent *Criticism: The Major Texts*; and once more to Professor Clarence D. Thorpe of the University of Michigan for his numerous articles on imagination and for his book, *The Aesthetic Theory of Thomas Hobbes*, which fills an important chapter in aesthetic theory. The writer wishes to thank Mr. T. S. Eliot for a kind letter of encouragement; Dr. Maurice Natanson of the New School for Social Research, New York City, for critical reading and the stimulation of his companionship; and Dr. Richard H. Fogle of Tulane University for helpful criticism and for his Introduction to the volume.

Finally, the author wishes to express his gratitude to the Research Institute of the University of Houston and to the United States Steel Corporation for their financial assistance in the completion and publication of this book.

J. V. B.

Table of Contents

Introduction

Professor Baker's rich and thorough study of the role of
the unconscious mind in Coleridge's theory of the poetic imagination should take up an important place in Coleridge scholarship. A supremely gifted introspectionist, Coleridge was a
pioneer in speculation upon the unconscious. As our author
remarks, his subject is "interesting at the present time and even
fashionable, in view of the no small interest in our day in the
creative process, in Freudian 'depth psychology,' in corrections
to Freud supplied by the neo-Freudians, in Gestalt psychology,
in the stream of consciousness and the Joycean type of fiction,
in the relation between the creative process and dreams, in
surrealist art and kindred topics." The value of Coleridge's
theory of the unconscious, however, is neither merely contemporary nor merely historical. For literary criticism it is
decidedly preferable to most contemporary psychologizing. As
the product of a poet and a philosopher, it is better balanced and
of greater critical value. It is this value that Professor Baker's
book explores.

"The unconscious," said Coleridge, "is the genius in the
man of genius," and the statement is a key to the treasure of
his critical thought. He has the peculiar faculty, indeed, of
focussing his entire meaning in such pregnant observations; a
believer in the Each and All, he was marvellously successful
at expressing the All in Each. If you touch upon any filament

of his closely woven web, the whole vibrates; if you follow the windings of any idea of his you are led inevitably to the central unity of his manifold system.

Another of his electrical sayings has been a rallying-cry for the most militant modern defenders of poetry. In the first chapter of the *Biographia Literaria* Coleridge affirms that poetry, "even that of the loftiest and, seemingly, that of the wildest odes, had a logic of its own, as severe as that of science; and more difficult, because more subtle, more complex, and dependent on more, and more fugitive causes." This is the origin of the subtle semanticisms of I. A. Richards, William Empson, and Cleanth Brooks. Even more important, however, is its influence as a defense of poetry as knowledge, a kind of discourse with claims to truth as valid as those of science. In the Twentieth Century, when poetry has been in danger of losing all intellectual prestige, Coleridge's trumpet-call has been as heartening as the ballad of Chevy Chase to Sir Philip Sidney, or Emerson's *American Scholar* to the young men of New England. It has encouraged the serious lovers of poetry, stimulating our famous New Critics to rebuild its fortress and stand at arms, so that Professor Murray Krieger has aptly renamed them The New Apologists for Poetry.

Coleridge's defense of poetic logic has a very definite bearing on Professor Baker's study of his theory of the unconscious, particularly as the passage is frequently and quite naturally misunderstood. Critics have interpreted Coleridge's "logic" too narrowly as an intellectual process, and have slighted the claims of feeling, of spontaneity—of all the elements, in fact, associated with the unconscious mind. For their purposes they have assumed that the composition of poetry is completely conscious, voluntary, and susceptible of rational explanation. Reacting against criticism that was damp, sentimental, and antirationalist, they have produced a criticism that is dry, ironic, and intellectualist. Their error is more respectable than the error they have superseded, but it is nevertheless a divagation from the true center. Investigations like the present study will help to correct it.

What Coleridge meant by "logic" in the *Biographia Literaria* passage is what he calls elsewhere "the logic of passion," and his reference to the difficulty and complexity of its causes is a reference to the unconscious, from which alone this logic derives its interest and vitality, and by means of which it can escape the circular futility of a self-displaying ingenuity that ends by dismaying and repelling us. Coleridge leaves the poet in his poetry, and thereby preserves it alive, whereas the intellectualist critic, in his natural and praiseworthy desire to endow poetry with the objectivity of science, banishes the poet and the creative source from the poetry, and thereby kills it in the separation.

The unconscious is, as Baker remarks, "the dark side" of Coleridge's theory of imagination, but it is also the light, itself invisible, in which poetry is manifested to us. This is to say that while a proper theory should explain all relevant facts, it will not explain itself. Like the statement that "a poem should not mean but be," it can only achieve the tautology of declaring that "I am what I am." To make the known intelligible there must be a realm of the unknown. From time to time its frontiers may be rolled back, and the *terra cognita* enlarged, but the *terra incognita* will remain as spacious as ever.

Coleridge's literary criticism is one long attempt to demonstrate concretely the structure and the processes of "the logic of passion," and thus to enlarge the sphere of the rational and the intelligible in criticism to the utmost expansion appropriate to them. His favorite critical terms are "propriety," "appropriateness," and "harmony." "The unconscious is the genius in the man of genius," and for Coleridge Shakespeare is the ideal man of genius, but all of his Shakespearean criticism is a demonstration that "Shakespeare's judgment is equal to his genius." His conscious knowledge and artistry balance his immense natural endowment, that in him which is simply given, and they are adequate to control and wield its mighty forces. Yet the deep mine of the unconscious, the subterranean fountains of the sacred river, remain unknown except to the imagination.

The Sacred River is one of those books which roll back the frontiers of darkness, while its author's literary experience and tact preserve him from the error of supposing that this darkness can—or should—be wholly dispelled. Professor Baker's thoroughness and erudition are greatly to be praised, as they appear in the comprehensive frame he provides for Coleridge, from his knowledge of psychological theories of the Seventeenth, the Eighteenth, and the Twentieth centuries. His scholarly competence, however, speaks for itself, and does not need the support of an introduction. One is more inclined to remark on a quality in his book that is for various reasons very uncommon in scholarship, that might be called sympathy, or insight, or genuine sensibility. The Coleridge scholar in particular, since he deals with a difficult problem, is often over-cautious, over-timid in asserting the value of his subject, prone to split hairs and pursue contradictions. But without impressionism, sentimentality, or any failure in due discrimination, Professor Baker has written what Coleridge termed a "genial" work of scholarship, which does justice to the worth of his subject.

RICHARD HARTER FOGLE

New Orleans, Louisiana
July 30, 1957

The Sacred River

In Xanadu did Kubla Khan
A stately pleasure-dome decree;
Where Alph, the sacred river, ran
Through caverns measureless to man,
*   Down to a sunless sea.*

~~~~~~

SOME BEARINGS

OF THIS STUDY

Coleridge, author of " The Ancient Mariner " and " Kubla Khan," master of atmosphere and musical suggestion, has never been taxed with lack of imagination, though he has been accused, and self-accused, of almost every other failure. Such a man, with his known propensity for searching self-analysis and introspection, probed into his own processes of creation and watched the quick forge of his own imagination at work. As a result, he produced a theory of imagination which has proved endlessly exciting to critics of poetry.

The cardinal fact about his theory of imagination is that for him, the imagination, so far from being merely spontaneous, unconscious, and passive, is active in the highest degree. The creative act calls the whole soul of man into activity. The essence of it is certainly not some form of automatic writing or surrealistic dream activity, unguided by the conscious intellect or will. The creative act, on the contrary, is a godlike act of power and causing-to-be, imagination being the divine potency in man. The creative act by which the poet writes the poem is similar to the creative act by which God ordered the world out of chaos; if the poet's creative act is not a creation *ex nihilo*, it is a process of organic becoming through which old materials are transformed into something absolutely new and also, very likely, strange.

Such was his theory, or the most famous statement of it, which climaxes the thirteenth chapter of *Biographia Literaria*. But does this theory always fit Coleridge's own experience of poetic creation? Here is part of his account of the composition of "Kubla Khan": "The author continued for about three hours in a profound sleep, at least of the external senses, during which time he has the most vivid confidence that he could not have composed less than from two to three hundred lines; if that indeed can be called composition in which all the images rose up before him as *things*, with a parallel production of the correspondent expressions, without any sensation or consciousness of effort." [1] His actual experience, in this perhaps exceptional instance, contradicted his theory.

This contradiction suggests the line of my inquiry. I propose to examine the role of the unconscious in Coleridge's theory of the imagination. To what extent did Coleridge allow for unconscious as well as conscious processes at work in poetic creation? This is the principal question which it will be my purpose to answer. Since it is rather generally admitted that associations are often made unconsciously, and since it is part of the thesis of Professor Lowes's *Road to Xanadu* that unconscious associations from Coleridge's vast reading in voyages and travels rose to the surface or threshold of consciousness and so played no inconsiderable part in the composition of "The Ancient Mariner" and "Kubla Khan," the scope of my inquiry will include the extent to which Coleridge admitted association of ideas as fecundating the poetic process.

[1] *Poems of Samuel Taylor Coleridge*, ed. Ernest Hartley Coleridge. (One-volume edition; London, 1912), 296. Hereafter this work will be referred to as *Poems*.

A theory of the creative imagination and an aesthetic of the imagination as a means to the criticism and appreciation of poetry are not easily separated, being the obverse and reverse of the same coin. The aim of the present study, however, is, so far as the two sides of Coleridge's theory of the imagination are separable, to concentrate on the former, the creative aspect of his theory. Did Coleridge recognize the passive side of the creative process, or did he overvalue and overstress the active side, the element of will and intellectual control? Or, did he, in his poetics, achieve a satisfactory balance between the two?

It may seem unnecessary to undertake a further study of Coleridge's theory of imagination at this time, when so many notable studies of it have already been made. Yet there is always *lebensraum* for fresh study, especially if that study is from a new approach. Lowes's work *The Road to Xanadu*, to which the writer, in common with every other student of Coleridge, is deeply indebted, is an inspired source book, invaluable to the study of the creation of the " Rime of the Ancient Mariner ' and " Kubla Khan." The thesis of that monumental study of the workings of Coleridge's imagination is partly stated in the following sentence: " We have to do . . . with one of the most extraordinary memories of which there is record, stored with the spoils of an omnivorous reading, and endowed into the bargain with an almost uncanny power of association." [2]

While Lowes is not slow to recognize the force of the shaping power, it is clear from the above quotation that the passive memory and secret links of association are credited with much of the magic of the poem. And though Lowes, from his vast learning, quotes often and incidentally from Coleridge's comments about the creative process, the object of his book is to account for the two poems, to get as close to the sources of

[2] John Livingston Lowes, *The Road to Xanadu* (Boston, 1927), 43. This work will hereafter be referred to as Lowes, *The Road to Xanadu*.

creation as it is possible to go without being the poet Coleridge. But Lowes does not pretend to give a systematic account of Coleridge's theory of the creative imagination, nor of the influences that may have shaped it.

Another study which might be thought to obviate the need of further investigation is *Coleridge on Imagination* by I. A. Richards. Perhaps one criticism of this book might be—and this is often true when two powerful minds meet—that it is more illuminating as I. A. Richards apropos of Coleridge than as straight exposition of Coleridge, Richards having a strong disposition to make Coleridge over in his own image as a psychological critic of the twentieth century armed with his own tools of Empsonist analysis. Similarly, when Coleridge writes about Hamlet, he reveals as much of himself as he does of the Prince of Denmark. While making this criticism, which is really a right-, rather than a left-handed, compliment to Richards, the writer wishes to express his deep sense of obligation to Richards for his many luminous insights, not only in the book just cited, but in the *Principles of Literary Criticism* and in *The Philosophy of Rhetoric*.

The more one thinks over one's indebtednesses, the more impossible it becomes to acknowledge them all. It will become evident, from the several references to Eliot later in his work, that the writer has thought of Eliot's poetry, Eliot's poetics, and Eliot's criticism as supplying interesting counterpoint and complement to, Coleridge's poetry, Coleridge's poetics, and Coleridge's criticism. It is possible the perfect English poetics will never be written, but if it could be, it might be a combination of the strongest elements in Eliot and Coleridge. Perhaps Eliot, having the advantage of coming later in time, has said the final word on the balance of unconscious and conscious elements in creation, but this is to anticipate. In any case Eliot's remarks on Coleridge are in the nature of generalizations or asides rather than of sustained study.

Three eminent critics of Coleridge—Lowes, Richards, and Eliot—have been searched and pressed for a solution to the problem. But the special concern here—the rôle of the unconscious in Coleridge's theory of imagination—has not, to the best of the writer's knowledge, been made the focus of any study.

A distinguished English poet, Stephen Spender, feels that the stored images of memory are the stuff out of which poetry is made:

> For memory is the root of creative genius. It enables the poet to connect the immediate moment of perception which is called "inspiration," with past moments in which he has received like impressions. This relating of the immediate impression with past ones enables the poet, through the moment, to strike a kind of chord across time, made up of notes which are similar impressions felt at different times and connected with one another in a simile within which all are contemporaneous.[3]

This striking quotation gives rise to the question of how far Coleridge himself would subscribe to a theory of imagination which relied heavily on memory.

The subject—Coleridge's theory of imagination, particularly the dark side of it, that is, the part played by the unconscious—may be said to be interesting at the present time and even fashionable, in view of the no small interest in our day in the creative process, in Freudian "depth psychology," in corrections to Freud supplied by the neo-Freudians, in Gestalt psychology, in the stream of consciousness and the Joycean type of fiction, in the relation between the creative process and dreams, in surrealist art and kindred topics. Without wishing to add any fictitious glamor or meretricious glitter to a genuine inquiry, the writer will say at the outset that Coleridge's imagination—his native

[3] Stephen Spender, *World Within World* (New York, 1951), 53.

endowment and his theory—has affinities with some of the most radical artistic developments of our own day; or, more concretely, that there are direct if underground connections between Xanadu and *Finnegans Wake*.

2

THE MATERIAL

IMAGINATION

In the first chapter the question was raised as to how far Coleridge would subscribe to a theory of imagination which relied on those passive links of association, those submarine marriages of ideas that occur in what—since the prefaces of Henry James and *The Road to Xanadu* of Lowes—it has become customary to call "the deep well." The purpose of the present chapter is to enquire at what time of life Coleridge was introduced to such theories, how much he knew about them, and whether he accepted them or grew critical towards them as his thought matured.

It was probably while he was an undergraduate at Cambridge that Coleridge was first introduced to associationist theory. At this time he entered into a period of intense intellectual excitement. His interests extended from politics and philosophy to the most recent scientific findings. He used his marvellous memory to repeat verbatim to an admiring crowd who foregathered in his rooms the latest political pamphlets hot from the press.[1] "His rooms at Jesus College were a veritable left-

[1] See the account of his rooms at Jesus College, Cambridge, by C. V. LeGrice quoted by Lowes, *The Road to Xanadu*, 43.

wing cell of those days." [2] An ardent supporter of the freedom of intellectual discussion, he sided warmly with Mr. Frend, a don who was deprived of his fellowship for his religious opinions. It was at this time that Coleridge dined with Godwin, wrote sonnets to Godwin and Priestley, and formed his violent enthusiasm for Hartley.

Coleridge had a real respect for Priestley, whom he refers to as "Patriot, and Saint, and Sage." [3] His sonnet to Priestley appeared in the *Morning Chronicle*, December 11, 1794.[4] The reasons for this respect were solid ones. Priestley was distinguished as a scientist; he had isolated oxygen in 1774. His eminence as a scientist lent his theological speculations prestige. "I regard," Coleridge wrote, "every experiment that Priestley made in Chemistry, as giving wings to his more sublime theological works." [5] Then, too, Priestley had the added prestige of being a martyr in the liberal cause. The Birmingham mob in 1791 had broken into his house at Fairhill, one mile from the city and destroyed nearly all of his books, papers, and apparatus. No wonder, then, that Coleridge eagerly read his works as they came off the press, books like his *Opticks* or his *History of the Corruptions of Christianity* (1782), which he withdrew from the Bristol Library, March 27, 1795.[6]

It was this Priestley, clothed with all the aura of scientist's and martyr's prestige, who was "the most enthusiastic and most articulate associationist of the eighteenth century." [7] Priestley

[2] Basil Willey, *Nineteenth Century Studies* (New York, 1949), 5.

[3] *Poems*, 123.

[4] *Ibid.*, 81.

[5] *Unpublished Letters*, ed. Earl Leslie Griggs (2 vols.; New Haven, 1933), I, 94-95. This will hereafter be referred to as *Unpublished Letters*.

[6] Paul Kaufman, "The Reading of Southey and Coleridge: The Record of Their Borrowings from the Bristol Library, 1793-98," *Modern Philology*, XXI (1923-24), 319.

[7] Martin Kallich, "The Association of Ideas and Critical Theory" (Doctoral

was to Hartley very much as, later, Huxley was to Darwin. Believing that Hartley had thrown more useful light upon the theory of mind than Newton did upon the theory of the natural world, he sought every opportunity to publicize Hartley's psychology. His best service was his abridgement of Hartley's *Observations on Man.*[8]

Another thinker indebted to Hartley through whom Coleridge could have indirectly become acquainted with Hartleian associational theory was William Godwin, whose *Political Justice*, published in 1793, influenced both Coleridge and Wordsworth when as young men they entered their rationalistic or necessitarian phase of thought. The Godwinian phase did not last long for either poet.[9] It is known for certain when Coleridge tired of Godwin, for conclusive evidence is found in the essays of *The Watchman*. For instance, Coleridge wrote: " I do consider Mr. Godwin's principles as vicious; and his book as a pandar to

Dissertation, Johns Hopkins University, 1945), 380-81. This work will be referred to as Kallich, " The Association of Ideas."

[8] The original edition of Hartley's *Observations on Man* appeared in 1749. Priestley published his abridgement as *Hartley's Theory of the Human Mind on the Principle of the Association of Ideas* (London, 1775). Scholars are of the opinion that the second edition of this abridgement (London, 1790) was probably the one known to Wordsworth. W. L. Sperry supposes that Wordsworth read Hartley in Priestley's second edition printed by J. Johnson, in whose shop Wordsworth "foregathered with his malcontent friends "— *Wordsworth's Anti-Climax* (Cambridge, Mass., 1935), 126-27. Coleridge knew Hartley's *Observations on Man*, as we shall presently see, both in the abridged and unabridged versions, greatly preferring the latter. The unabridged edition of Hartley certainly known to Coleridge was that in three volumes quarto published by the same liberal or radical bookseller, J. Johnson (London, 1791), and edited by David Hartley, Jr. Volumes I and II are identical with the first London edition of 1749; Volume III has the additional notes by Pistorius.

[9] Wordsworth's revulsion from the Godwinian system is recorded in *The Borderers* and *The Prelude*.

sensuality." [10] And in February, 1797, he wrote to Thelwall, "Thank Heaven! I abominate Godwinism!" [11]

No fact of Coleridge's intellectual history is better known than his enthusiasm for Hartley and the story has already been told in a scholarly manner by Professor Arthur Beatty.[12] At the risk, however, of repeating some of this material, it will be necessary to retell the salient points of this story once more, in order to discover to what extent Hartley may have influenced Coleridge's theory of imagination, and particularly how Coleridge reacted to Hartley's doctrine of association.

But first, that the cause of Coleridge's intellectual excitement may be appreciated, Hartley's system will be briefly described. Essentially the interest of it lies in its psychophysical parallelism, in its comprehension of psychosomatic unity. Mental events are understood to be events in the nervous system; Hartley builds upon the physiological-neurological foundation.

His *magnum opus*, the *Observations on Man* (London, 1749), is in three parts. The first part contains the neural basis, the physical doctrine of vibrations; the second contains his psychology; the third contains the metaphysical superstructure of Christian doctrine.

The first, physical doctrine of vibrations, need not detain us long, since Hartley's physiology is outmoded anyway. Sensation, according to him, produces an impression on the organism, creating a disturbance of the nerves; these disturbances are called vibrations. The nerves are thought of as solid rather than tubular

[10] *Watchman No. 5*, April 2, 1796. *Essays on His On Times*, ed. Sara Coleridge (3 vols.; London, 1850), I, 164.

[11] Letter dated from Stowey, Feb. 6, 1797, in *Letters*, ed. Ernest Hartley Coleridge (2 vols.; Boston, 1895), I, 215. Hereafter this work will be referred to as *Letters*.

[12] *William Wordsworth, His Doctrine and Art* (Madison, 1927). Professor Beatty tells the story of Hartley's influence on Coleridge as well as on Wordsworth.

or capillary; the disturbance in the nerves is a bombardment of particles, and the nerves act as conductors through which the movement is transmitted. Thus "sensations . . . leave certain vestiges, types, or images of themselves"[13] in the brain. These faint traces left in the brain are feebler, less intense vibrations, or in Hartley's curious terminology, "vibratiuncles."

The second part of Hartley's book, his psychology, rests firmly on his single law of association, which he enunciates as follows: "Any sensations A, B, C, &c., by being associated with one another a sufficient number of times, get such a power over the corresponding ideas [also called by Hartley vestiges, types, images] a, b, c, &c., that any one of the sensations A, when impressed alone, shall be able to excite in the mind b, c, &c., the ideas of all the rest."[14]

Simple ideas, the traces left from sensation, may combine under the power of association to form complex ideas[15] and the whole mind may become an infinitely complex network of interconnected associations, like a switchboard of a metropolitan telephone exchange. Moreover, a complex idea is more than the sum of its parts; it has unique quality not present in the component ideas taken separately. Not only this, but complex ideas may run into clusters.[16]

It is hard to convey, in a condensed summary, the scope of Hartley's work. He shows how, beginning with childhood, ideas come to be associated with words. He shows, as earlier psychologists had done, that association can be charged with emotion; indeed, he defines human passions and emotions as built

---

[13] David Hartley, *Observations on Man* (2 vols.; London, 1749), Proposition 8, I, 56. This work will hereafter be referred to as Hartley, *Observations on Man*.

[14] *Ibid.*, Proposition 10, I, 65.

[15] "Simple ideas will run into complex ones, by means of association," *ibid.*, Proposition 12, I, 73.

[16] *Ibid.*, Proposition 12, Case 5, I, 74-75.

up of aggregates or complexes of association.[17] He shows that imagination (a point of some importance for this study of Coleridge) is governed by association of ideas and images. He finds association at work also in reverie and dreams.[18]

What about the power of genius, the power of creativeness and invention? Hartley has his answer ready for this also; invention is dependent on memory's stock of images and ideas: " A strong and quick memory is necessary, that so (sic) the ideas of the poet or philosopher may depend upon, and be readily suggested by, each other. . . . And the nature of this faculty seems as reconcileable with, and deducible from, the power of association of the mind here explained, as that of any other." [19]

Hartley includes an aesthetic breviary, though it is only one corner of his vast work. As usual, he uses association to explain the pleasures derived from landscape, music, painting, and poetry.[20] He dwells, too, prophetically for Coleridge, upon the pleasures of imagination induced by opium.[21] In deriving aesthetic pleasure from association, though he undoubtedly has a point, he commits the usual fallacy of the eighteenth century: he substitutes that which simply aids and abets the sensuous imagination, for the structure, balance, or form of the aesthetic work itself, in which the pure aesthetic experience rests.

In his brief excursus into metaphor or figure of speech he is truly acute, reminding of Dr. Johnson's *discordia concors* and Keats's expression about surprising by a fine excess:

Now figurative words seem to strike and please us chiefly from that impropriety which appears at first sight, upon their applica-

---

[17] *Ibid.*, Proposition 89, I, 368.

[18] *Ibid.*, Proposition 91, I, 383.

[19] *Ibid.*, Proposition 94, I, 434-35.

[20] For example: " Musical sounds afford, like articulate ones, various instances of the power of association," *ibid.*, I, 321.

[21] *Ibid.*, I, 423.

tion to the things denoted by them, and from the consequent heightening of the propriety as soon as it is duly perceived. For when figurative words have recurred so often as to excite the secondary idea instantaneously,[22] and without any previous harshness to the imagination, they lose their peculiar beauty and force; and in order to recover this, and make ourselves sensible of it, we are obliged to recall the literal sense, and to place the literal and figurative senses close together, so that we may first be sensible of the inconsistency, and then be more affected with the union and coalescence.[23]

The above is a good discussion of the freshening effected by metaphor, which it is one of poetry's main objects to achieve.

It might be thought from this that Hartley values the imagination. But though he is not especially hostile to the imagination, he does not rate it highly: "It is evident that the pleasures of the imagination were not intended for our primary pursuit, because they are, in general, the first of our intellectual pleasures, which are generated from the sensible ones by association, come to their height early in life, and decline in old age." [24] Thus, Hartley "arranged for imagination's early demise" [25] and threw his long shadow over Wordsworth.

Hartley inevitably makes application of association of ideas to ethics. The trick, if one wishes to be morally guided aright,

[22] Hartley here is describing "faded metaphor."

[23] *Ibid.*, I, 429.

[24] *Ibid.*, Propositions 55, 56.

[25] The phrase stays in my memory. I cannot place the source. Hartley's breviary of aesthetic is utilitarian and oversimple—association accounts for appreciation in a manner as simple as this: the Red Lion Inn is appreciated by one of its guests because he once had a good roast beef dinner there (association). John H. Muirhead writes of it as follows: "There was no department in which the defects of the Hartleian philosophy were more glaring than in aesthetic theory. In the *Observations on Man*, imagination is dismissed in a short paragraph in a section devoted to 'Dreams.' The sense of Beauty is treated under the head of 'Pleasures and Pain of Imagination.'" John H. Muirhead, *Coleridge as Philosopher* (London, 1930), 195.

is to make the right associations of pleasure with virtue. This leads to an environmental approach to ethics; surround the child with the right environment, and he will make the right associations; his moral progress will be assured. This idea has a history and is written large in the speculations of the next one hundred years. It is found in William Belsham and in Godwin; in Robert Owen's proposals for the improvement of working people's morals by the improvement of their living conditions; in Bentham and the whole utilitarian school.

Such, then, is Hartley's imposing system, with its obsessional reliance on the one idea of association. In typically eighteenth-century fashion he has an ascending scale of being: from the pleasures and pains of primary sensation, man rises through the new compounds or complexes of association to the second level of imagination; above that, to ambition and self-interest; above that, to sympathy; and finally, to theopathy and the moral sense, so that, as Leslie Stephen puts it, "Vibratiuncles set up in the medullary substance of the brain are ultimately converted into the pure love of God." [26]

What was Coleridge's reaction? It was a case of love at first sight, an infatuation with Hartley. With brash assurance and in the first flush of discovery he wrote to Southey: "I am a complete necessitarian and understand the subject as well almost as Hartley himself, but I go farther than Hartley, and believe the corporeality of *thought*, namely, that it is motion." [27] It is

---

[26] *History of English Thought in the Eighteenth Century* (3rd ed.; 2 vols.; New York, 1902), II, 68-69. Hartley's rising scale is possibly a variation on the chain of being.

[27] Letter dated December 11, 1794. *Letters*, I, 113. The note of enthusiasm had been sounded even earlier in a letter to his brother George of November 6, 1794: "And after a diligent, I may say an intense, study of Locke, Hartley and others who have written most wisely on the nature of man, I appear to myself to see the point of possible perfection at which the world may perhaps be destined to arrive." *Ibid.*, I, 105.

hard to see how Coleridge is going *beyond* Hartley, or Hobbes either, for that matter; but he possibly meant, in the enthusiasm of the moment, that he was a more thoroughgoing materialist than Hartley himself. It looks as though, for a short time only, he completely accepted a mechanistic theory of mind; it would seem that in the red or radical heats of his undergraduate days, Coleridge flirted with a deterministic materialism. The only way in which he could go *beyond* Hartley would be in accepting the neural basis without the metaphysical superstructure ascending to theopathy and the love of God.

Critics have too readily assumed that Coleridge cared only about the first two parts of Hartley's system, the neurology and the psychology. They attribute to Coleridge the boredom they themselves would feel in having to plough through Hartley's theology. But to do so is to underestimate Coleridge. There is evidence that Coleridge read the theology and was profoundly impressed by it.[28] The acceptance of a mechanistic psychology, the necessitarian phase of Coleridge's mental development, was brief, a flash-in-the-pan. It was contrary to the native bias of his temperament which was platonic, mystical, and mythologizing. It was the latter part of Hartley's system which caused him to feel an abiding respect for Hartley as " that great master of Christian philosophy."

The familiar tribute to Hartley in " Religious Musings ":

> . . . he of mortal kind
> Wisest, he first who marked the ideal tribes
> Up the fine fibres to the sentient brain

proves Coleridge's acquaintance with Hartley's theory of vibrations. But to be familiar with this quotation only is to miss the

---

[28] H. N. Fairchild, " Hartley, Pistorius and Coleridge," *PMLA*, 62 (1947), 1016-17. The article is excellent and indispensable to an understanding of Coleridge's relations to Hartley.

seriousness with which Coleridge accepted the golden links of
Hartleian association which ascended from vibrations of the
nerves to the throne of God. In the same poem Coleridge has
an ascending passage climaxed by the lines concerning the soul's
attainment:

> God only to behold, and know, and feel,
> Till by exclusive consciousness of God
> All self-annihilated it shall make
> God its Identity: God all in all! [29]

In the *Poems* of 1797 Coleridge's note to line 44 reads: "See
this *demonstrated* by Hartley, vol. I, p. 114 and vol. II, p. 329."

If we look up Coleridge's reference, we find how closely he
has followed Hartley's thought: "Since God is the Source of
all Good, and consequently must at last appear to be so, i. e. be
associated with all our Pleasures, it seems to follow . . . that the
Idea of God . . . must, at last take place of, and absorb all other
Ideas, and He himself become, according to the language of the
Scriptures, All in All." [30]

The evidence of Coleridge's enthusiasm for Hartley is plain
and unmistakable. His friend Cottle, the Bristol publisher, tells
that he "generally contrived . . . to notice, in the warmest ecomi-
astic language, Bishop Berkeley, David Hartley, or Mr. Bowles." [31]
This statement of Cottle's refers to 1795 and suggests that, while
the star of Hartley was still in the sky, that of Berkeley was
beginning to rise into the ascendant. The gradual ousting of
Hartley by Berkeley is the next phase in Coleridge's intellectual

---

[29] "Religious Musings," ll. 41-44, *Poems*, 110-11. Fairchild points to the
paradox that the most mystical passage in the poem is inspired rather by
Hartley than Plotinus, *loc. cit.*, 1010-11.

[30] Hartley, *Observations on Man* (London, 1791), I, 114. The edition
to which Coleridge refers is that printed by Joseph Johnson, 3 vols., 4°.
Quoted by Fairchild in "Hartley, Pistorius, and Coleridge," *loc. cit.*, 1019.

[31] Joseph Cottle, *Early Recollections* (London, 1837), 21.

development. It will be proper to inquire what influence, if any, Berkeley's philosophy would exert on a theory of creative mind.

Coleridge's letters to comrade Thelwall, colored though they no doubt are by the character of his correspondent, are very revealing as to what was really going on in his mind at this time, and he wrote in December, 1796: "Now that the thinking part of man, that is, the soul, existed previously to its appearance in its present body may be very wild philosophy, but it is very intelligible poetry; [32] inasmuch as 'soul' is an orthodox word in all our poets, they meaning by 'soul' a being inhabiting our body, and playing upon it, like a musician enclosed in an organ whose keys are placed inwards. Now this opinion I do not hold; not that I am a materialist, but because I am a Berkeleyan." [33] There is, in this passage, considerable sympathy with and nostalgia for the Platonic mythology. Moreover, the "soul" is considered active. And Coleridge's phrase *not that I am a materialist* indicates that his materialist phase had passed.

At the end of a manuscript copy of *The Destiny of Nations* Coleridge wrote: "N. B.—Within twelve months after the writing of this Poem, my bold Optimism, and Necessitarianism, together with the Infra, *seu* plusquam-Socinianism, down to which, step by step, I had unbelieved, gave way to the daybreak of a more genial and less shallow system. But I contemplate with pleasure the phases of my Transition." [34] This would date Coleridge's emancipation late in 1797. Apparently, he threw away his necessitarianism, including his mechanistic theory of mind, very close to the time when he also threw away "his squeaking baby-trumpet of sedition."

[32] An interesting foreshadowing of the germ idea of Wordsworth's Immortality Ode.

[33] *Letters*, I, 195.

[34] Coleridge's *Poetical Works*, 1828, annotated copy. Quoted by Lawrence Hanson, *The Life of S. T. Coleridge: the Early Years* (London, 1938), 307.

The Godwin-Hartley-necessity phase of Coleridge's intellectual development lasted then, at most, from two to three years, 1794 to 1796, or, at furthest, 1797. But it would be entirely wrong to conclude that the influence of Hartley therefore ceased. It did nothing of the kind. In a mind as complex as Coleridge's, that which he still found valid or viable in a philosophy partly discarded would be grafted into the philosophy newly adopted.

Coleridge might abandon necessity or determinism as a satisfactory philosophy; he might give up a mechanistic view of mind; but association of ideas was a phenomenon that occurred in too many minds for its existence to be doubted. Moreover, Hartley's explanation in terms of neural traces, though suspect in its physiological detail, was as good a one as could be found. And the warm sincerity of Hartley's new approach to ethics, the moral earnestness with which he enlisted association in the cause of God, would not easily be forgotten and still commanded Coleridge's respect. " I now," Coleridge wrote, speaking of the time when he first settled at Stowey, " devoted myself to poetry and to the study of ethics and psychology; and so profound was my admiration at this time of Hartley's Essay on Man that I gave his name to my first-born." [35]

It is significant, perhaps, that Coleridge's next son was called Berkeley. Berkeley was the brilliant critic of Locke, who, so far from discarding innate ideas, and doubting whether any knowledge could be absorbed except through the cinque ports of the senses, made the evidence of the senses themselves dependent for any real existence upon being ideas in the mind of God. In vain Dr. Johnson might stub his toe against a stone; he might

[35] *Biographia Literaria*, ed. J. Shawcross (2 vols.; London, 1907), I, 121. This will hereafter be referred to as *Biographia*. Coleridge moved into a cottage at Nether Stowey on the last day of 1796. Coleridge's first child (a son) was born on September 19, 1796, and named David Hartley in honor of " that great master of Christian philosophy." Coleridge to Thomas Poole, September 24, 1796, *Letters*, I, 169.

continue to stub his toe until he did his foot a real injury, and the objective existence of rocks would remain as solid as before, and Berkeley's idealism be equally unmoved. For Berkeley never denied the solidity of rock nor the impressions of the senses as received by the man of common sense (typified by Dr. Samuel Johnson). Berkeley was merely pointing out, in a manner very close, actually, to Hobbes and Locke, that what rock in itself is independent of ourselves we can never know; our perceptions of rock and all events in our mind are mental. Coleridge, as is made plain by Hazlitt, thoroughly apprehended Berkeley's position and condemned Johnson's literal and clumsy attempt at rebuttal.[36] Berkeley conceived a universe in which stones and rocks and people like Dr. Johnson and much else besides existed *grace à Dieu*. Under all strata was the substratum or, as the mystics use the term, the ground of all existence and behind all data of the senses was the original datum, namely God himself.

Such a philosophy, of which the fundamental principle is *esse est percipi* (to be is to be perceived—nothing exists, or, at least, exists significantly, unless it be perceived in the mind of a sentient and percipient being) and in which all things exist within the creative mind of God, would tend, it may be inferred, to look upon the mind of man as creative in perception, active in creation. And this inference is, in fact, supported by Berkeley's own words. In the *Commonplace Book* in which he jotted down the germinal ideas for the *Principles of Human Knowledge* (1710) he observes, " Certainly we ourselves create in some wise whenever we imagine." [37]

This impression is confirmed by two modern exponents of Berkeley's philosophy who say:

---

[36] William Hazlitt, " My First Acquaintance with Poets," *The Complete Works of William Hazlitt*, ed. P. P. Howe (21 vols.; London, 1930-34), XVII, 113. This will hereafter be referred to as *Works of Hazlitt*.

[37] *Philosophical Commentaries, Generally Called the Commonplace Book of George Berkeley*, ed. A. A. Luce (London, 1944), 295.

The great fault of empiricism is that it makes of man a purely inactive mirror, on which the external world reflects itself: the sensations, passively received, give rise to human knowledge, without the intervention of any activity, or creative force on the part of the human mind . . . The mind, in knowing clear and distinct ideas, is at bottom receptive . . . On the contrary, for Berkeley (at least in the first stage of the New Principle) the function of perceiving is a creative function, so much so that it can be assimilated to divine creation.[38]

A good case can be made out for the contention that the real overthrower of Hartley in Coleridge's thinking was Berkeley rather than Kant—Kant merely, at a later stage, confirmed the overthrow. Berkeley is an exceedingly pulverising critic of the " inert senseless substance " which was Locke's abstraction of Matter; he demonstrates that " extension, figure and motion, are only ideas existing in the mind, and that an idea can be like nothing but another idea, and that consequently neither they nor their archetypes can exist in an unperceiving substance." [39]

Mr. Kenneth Millar, author of a very able dissertation on Coleridge's aesthetic ideas, observes that

Berkeley, who was Coleridge's favorite philosopher at least from 1796 to 1798, successfully demonstrated the subjectivity of spatial extension and thus cut off materialistic determination at its root. . . . Berkeley's basic criticism of materialism freed Coleridge from Hartley while Kant was still " most unintelligible " to him. The latter, no doubt, confirmed his views, and provided a logical apparatus to enforce them. But Berkeley had shown Coleridge, and possibly Kant, the way . . . It is not too much to say that Berkeley demolished the philosophic basis of Hartley's psychology before Hartley wrote it.[40]

[38] J. M. Hone and M. M. Rossi, *Bishop Berkeley* (London, 1931), 38-40.
[39] George Berkeley, *Principles of Human Knowledge*, Part I, Section 9, *The Works of George Berkeley*, ed. Alexander Campbell Fraser (4 vols.; Oxford, 1901), I, 262.
[40] Kenneth Millar, " The Inward Eye: A Revaluation of Coleridge's Psycho-

The same writer adds: "When Coleridge announced himself a Berkeleian, five years before he wrote his letters to Poole, he must have had some awareness of Berkeley's implications. I suggest that at the very least they help to account for Coleridge's early impatience with Locke and Hartley, and for his rather sudden acceptance of Kant." [41]

Proof positive exists that Berkeley was active in Coleridge's thinking in the years 1796 to 1798. There is the explicit avowal of Berkeley's system in the notebook of 1796, aimed directly against the Godwinian System of atheism and necessity. [42] And it is further known from the records of the Bristol Library that in the year 1798, when he was in the west of England before his departure for Germany, he had been reading Berkeley. [43] It is easy to agree that at this point: "Berkeley was to him the most fascinating of English philosophers, for, as he states, 'his premises granted, the deduction is a chain of adamant.' Not only this irrefutable logic, but also, and most of all, Berkeley's idealistic content made its appeal to Coleridge." [44] Nonetheless it is customary to say that the earlier Berkeley of the *Principles* was too close in his theory of perception to the empiricism of Hobbes and Locke for Coleridge's entire comfort and that he was more at home with the later Platonic Berkeley of the *Siris*, to whom *esse* is *concipi*, than with the earlier empirical Berkeley of the *Principles* to whom *esse* is *percipi*. [45]

logical Criticism" (Doctoral Dissertation, University of Michigan, 1951), 260-61. This work will hereafter be referred to as Millar, "The Inward Eye."

[41] *Ibid.*, 264.

[42] Folios 25ª to 25ᵇ, printed by Brandl, *Herrigs Archiv* XCVII (1896), 354. Cited by René Wellek, *Kant in England* (Princeton, 1931), 72.

[43] R. L. Brett, "Coleridge's Theory of Imagination," *English Studies* (London, 1949), 77.

[44] Claude Howard, *Coleridge's Idealism* (Boston, 1924), 19.

[45] Muirhead, *Coleridge as Philosopher*, 46. See, too, the reproduction of Coleridge's comment on the flyleaf of his copy of Berkeley's *Siris*, in Wilma L.

It seems incredible in any case that Coleridge could have long or seriously entertained a passive theory of imagination, leaving creative power in poetry at the mercy of chance association. Robert Penn Warren is of the opinion that "Coleridge was early moving towards his later views . . . As early as 1794, he was . . . thinking of the mind as an active thing, the 'shaping mind' and claiming it for himself, and if we grant the power of the mind in one sense we have broken the iron chain of necessity." [46] The same writer adds, "It seems that we have in these years a tortured churning around . . . and the necessitarian philosophy is only one possible philosophy in that agitated brew." [47]

It was on the dark evening of November 20, 1797, that Dorothy Wordsworth, her brother William, and Coleridge set out on the walking tour on which the *Rime of the Ancient Mariner* was planned. It will be recalled that part of the design of the *Lyrical Ballads* was to investigate how "we associate ideas in a state of excitement." [48] Nothing, however, could have been better calculated to confirm Coleridge in the belief in "my shaping spirit of imagination" (the loss of which he was soon to lament) than the experience of authentic power in completing *The Ancient Mariner* the following spring.

Kennedy, *The English Heritage of Coleridge* (New Haven, 1947), frontispiece. Kennedy is of the opinion that Coleridge was more beholden to Berkeley than Kant, *ibid.*, 90. In modern times, Berkeley has made a powerful appeal to the poet W. B. Yeats and the philosopher A. N. Whitehead. See, for instance, Whitehead's conclusion in his *Science and the Modern World* (Cambridge, 1933), 82-83, where he points out that Berkeley "made all the right criticisms" of the "reigning scientific scheme" and "laid his finger exactly on the weak spots" in the system of Newton and Locke.

[46] *The Rime of the Ancient Mariner*, ed. Robert Penn Warren' (New York, 1946), 80.

[47] *Ibid.*, 81.

[48] Preface to *Lyrical Ballads* (1800) in *Literary Criticism: Pope to Croce*, ed. G. W. Allen and H. H. Clark (New York, 1941), 201.

When Hazlitt made his first acquaintance with poets, particularly on the occasion when he accompanied Coleridge along the road from Wem to Shrewsbury (in January, 1798), he broached the subject of what later became his *Essay on the Principles of Human Action: Being an Argument in favour of the Natural Disinterestedness of the Human Mind. To which are added, some Remarks on the Systems of Hartley and Helvetius.*[49] Professor Beatty says that "the main thesis of this book is in substance one of the cardinal doctrines of Hartley, and the whole argument is impregnated with Hartleian influences, despite the fact that it is developed in conscious contradiction of the Hartleian theory."[50] Hazlitt felt that he made a discovery concerning the natural unselfishness of human nature. "I tried," he says, "to explain my view of it to Coleridge, who listened with great willingness, but I did not succeed in making myself understood."[51] The report is tantalizing, as it leaves us in the dark as to what Coleridge may have said about Hartley at this time. A strong hint as to Coleridge's probable state of mind is furnished by his contempt for Paley; it is clear that Coleridge, while he would accept the law of association as scientific fact, would not rest content in any mechanical system. Not for him a watchmaker's world.

Despite the fact that (as Hazlitt's essay makes apparent) the moon of Hartley was setting while the sun of Berkeley was rising on Coleridge's horizon, it would seem that Hartley was still a live issue. "Carlyon, our authority for Coleridge in Germany, details conversations belonging to the spring of 1799, which are thoroughly Hartleian in substance."[52]

[49] Published in 1805. It was, of course, one of several answers to Hobbes's opinion that self-interest is the motivating force in human nature.

[50] Beatty, *Wordsworth: His Doctrine and Art*, 102.

[51] "My First Acquaintance with Poets," *Works of Hazlitt*, XVII, 114. The same topic was brought up in conversation between Coleridge and Hazlitt some weeks later, *ibid.*, 121.

[52] Beatty, *Wordsworth: His Doctrine and Art*, 101. In support of his

Coleridge returned from Germany and arrived at Stowey in July, 1799. And at some time in this same year he heard a series of popular lectures delivered by Sir James Mackintosh in Lincoln's Inn Hall, London. Sir James asserted

> that the law of association as established in the contemporaneity of the original impressions, formed the basis of all true psychology; and any ontological or metaphysical science, not contained in such (i. e. empirical) psychology, was but a web of abstractions and generalizations. Of this prolific truth, of this great fundamental law, he declared HOBBS to have been the original *discoverer*, while its full application to the whole intellectual system we owed to David Hartley; who stood in the same relation to Hobbs as Newton to Kepler; the law of association being that to the mind, which gravitation is to matter.[53]

Mackintosh was a smooth popularizer of current psychological theory. The view, here so clearly presented, was the one which Coleridge came to detest. He regarded Mackintosh and his ilk as men of talent rather than of insight, and their empirical psychology as superficial.

Coleridge did not swallow the easy assumption that the mere absorption of grand scenery will of itself produce the sublime— the grandeur of mountain scenery will produce sublime feelings, but feelings are not works of art. The mind in creation must be the mind *active*. In a letter to Godwin of May, 1800, he indulges in some gentle leg-pulling: " I left Wordsworth on the 4th of this month. If I cannot procure a suitable house at Stowey I return to Cumberland and settle at Keswick, in a house of such prospect, that if according to you and Hume, impressions and ideas *constitute* our being, I shall have a tendency to become a god, so sublime and beautiful will be the series of my visual existence.[54]

statement, Beatty cites Clement Carlyon, M. D., *Early Years and Late Reflec-tions* (3 vols.; London, 1856), I, 33-34.

[53] *Biographia*, I, 67.

[54] Coleridge to Godwin, May 21, 1800, *Unpublished Letters*, I, 138.

The point is that this was written *before* he had unpacked that box of German metaphysical books, and *before* he is supposed to have come under the influence of Kant.

During his stay in Germany, and particularly during his residence at the university of Göttingen, he would most likely become aware of the great reputation in philosophy of Immanuel Kant at the German universities. He did not, it seems, study Kant seriously at this time, but some time after settling into his home, Greta Hall, near Keswick, in the English Lake District, in July, 1800, began the study of Kant in earnest. Kant's profound probing of epistemology, his transcendental analysis of the mind itself as the instrument by which phenomena are known, caused him to rethink the Hartleian system of psychology and to grow dissatisfied with it in a more conscious and reasoned manner than he had done before.

Early in 1801 Coleridge began the serious study of metaphysics. "Change of Ministry interests *me* not—I turn at times half reluctantly from Leibnitz or Kant even to read a smoking new newspaper, such a purus putus Metaphysicus am I become," he informed Poole.[55] Probably feeling the prick of conscience, and in an endeavor to show some tangible result of his stay in Germany, in February of 1801 he wrote to his patrons, the Wedgwoods, four letters of considerable length, which supply evidence that he had parted company with the British empiricists.[56] His intellectual effort, in these letters, is a technical comparison between Locke and Descartes, to the great advantage of the latter. Locke is assailed for inaccuracy in the use of terms. "In Mr. Locke there is a complete Whirl-dance of Confusion with the words *we, Soul, Mind, Consciousness,* & *Ideas.* . . .

---

[55] *Collected Letters of Samuel Taylor Coleridge,* ed. E. Leslie Griggs (2 vols.; Oxford, 1956), II, 380. This work will hereafter be referred to as *Collected Letters.*

[56] *Ibid.,* 381-84.

I . . . seem always in an *eddy*, when I read him, round & round, & never a step forward." [57] And Coleridge alludes contemptuously to " the trifling Chapter on Association " which Locke added to the fourth edition of the *Essay Concerning Human Understanding*.[58]

Sir Leslie Stephen claims that Coleridge was still a Hartleian even on the eve of his conversion by Kant, and that he " still sticks to Hartley and the Association doctrine." [59] Sir Leslie Stephen's opinion of Coleridge's position is this: " he is dissatisfied with Locke, but has not yet broken with the philosophy generally supposed to be on the Locke line." [60] It appears, at any rate, that Coleridge was ripe for a change; uneasiness with the general psychology of Locke and Hartley would not be incompatible with the acceptance of the fact of association; Kant accepted it, too, as a psychological fact, but not without profound accompanying criticism of the whole British school of empirical associationism.

In the spring of 1801 Coleridge entered upon a period of great intellectual excitement. It was in March of that year (the month after the lengthy letters to the Wedgwoods) that he made his triumphant announcement to Thomas Poole: " I have not only completely extricated the notions of time and space, but have overthrown the doctrine of association as taught by Hartley and with it all the irreligious metaphysics of modern infidels—especially the doctrine of necessity." [61] The announcement is made with all the fervor of religious conversion. Coleridge, like a cosmic Houdini, has escaped from the ironbound chest of necessity. " Extricated the notions of time and space " can only mean, according to Professor René Wellek,[62] that Coleridge at this time had begun the " intense study " of Kant. The reading of

---

[57] *Ibid.*, 383-84.   [58] *Ibid.*, 383.   [59] *Letters*, I, 351n.   [60] *Ibid.*
[61] Coleridge to Thomas Poole, March 16, 1801, *Letters*, I, 348.
[62] *Immanuel Kant in England*, 71-72.

Kant took hold of Coleridge's mind, as he himself said, "with a giant's hand." [63] Kant administered the *coup-de-grace* to Hartley.

Clearly what Coleridge liked in Kant was the ideality of space and time, the *a priori* ideas, the creativity of mind, in opposition to mechanic laws of association. In Kant's philosophy, the mind is no passive receiver of impressions. The nature of reality, the *Ding-an-sich*, the human mind can never know. But it cannot deal with mere disorder and imposes its own concepts of space and time upon the flood of impressions. Then, too, the fact that, no matter with what disproportionate oddness of length the sides of a triangle may be drawn, the two sides of any given triangle will forever be greater than the third, had an adamantine quality of assurance as of a truth from everlasting: this was an *a priori* idea, and it held true, even if no empirical world existed, even if no physical triangles attested or illustrated it.

Kant's whole philosophy, and this was no doubt why Coleridge delighted in it, was an answer to the system of Hobbes and Locke, and to that which had been grafted upon Locke, the associationism of Hume and Hartley. To account for synthesis in cognition, in express opposition to the associationism of Hume, was his prime object, starting as he did, from the assumption that there was that in knowledge which no mere association of experience could explain. To the extent, therefore, that his influence prevailed, all inquiries made by the English associationists were discounted in Germany.[64]

It was not only, however, in his theory of cognition that Kant supplied a criticism of the English associationists. He did so further in his treatise on aesthetics, the *Critique of Judgment*. Genius, Kant defined as the faculty of aesthetic ideas. The

[63] *Biographia*, I, 99.
[64] A. Wolf, "Associationism," *Encyclopedia Britannica*, 14th ed., II, 565.

imagination of genius is not necessarily tied down by the laws of association.

> If, now, imagination must in the judgment of taste be regarded in its freedom, then, to begin with, it is not taken as reproductive, as in the subjection to the laws of association, but productive and exerting an activity of its own (as originator of arbitrary forms of possible intuitions).[65]

Moreover:

> The imagination (as a productive faculty of cognition) is a powerful agent for creating, as it were, a second nature out of the material supplied to it by actual nature. It affords us entertainment where experience proves too commonplace; and we even use it to remodel experience. . . . By this means we get a sense of our freedom from the law of association (which attaches to the empirical employment of the imagination), with the result that the material can be borrowed by us from nature in accordance with that law, but be worked up by us into something else—namely, what surpasses nature.[66]

"Our freedom from the laws of association" seems evidently aimed at Hartley, Beatty, and Gerard.[67]

Kant's imagination has a threefold capacity. First of all, it is reproductive. It assists at the intuitive perceptual level the intake of the sensory manifold, but is tied down since it can only reproduce rearrangements of the data of experience. Secondly, it is productive, though not really free. It enables the mind to create concepts from the raw materials of sense data, acting as a sort of emissary or liaison officer between sensation and understanding. It is not really free because it is subservient to the purposes of the understanding. Finally, it is aesthetic, and, in this third capacity only, is both productive and free, able to arrange the

---

[65] Kant, *Critique of Aesthetic Judgment*, tr. James Creed Meredith (Oxford, 1911), 86.
[66] *Ibid.*, 176.   [67] *Ibid.*, 291. Editorial comment by Meredith.

elements of experience at its own pleasure, to organize them into meaningful wholes, and to be in the fullest sense of the word, creative.[68]

Not only was Hartley criticized by Kant in Germany; he was also criticized in England. Abraham Tucker, in his *Light of Nature Pursued*,[69] criticized him for regarding the mind as a passive receiver of impressions. Coleridge in 1803 proposed to write a prefatory essay on Hartley for a new edition of Tucker's *Light of Nature*, while Hazlitt did actually write an introductory essay for the new edition of Tucker's work. While Coleridge's essay remained among his numerous embryonic schemes never brought to birth, the fact that he planned it, in this connection of Tucker and Tucker's criticism, is significant of the direction his mind was taking.

His revulsion from Hartley, part of a revulsion against the whole school of seventeenth- and eighteenth-century mechanist psychologists, led to his forming his own theory of association, which he felt to possess deeper insight than Hartley's. He stated it, with the usual triumphant note, in a letter to Southey in 1803: "How flat, how wretched, is Hartley's solution of the phenomena (of memory). Believe *me*, Southey, a metaphysical solution that does not tell you something in the heart is grievously to be suspected as apocryphal. I almost think that ideas never recall ideas, as far as they are ideas, any more than leaves in a forest create each other's motion—the breeze it is that runs through them—it is the soul, the state of feeling." [70] Hartley, however, was aware of the emotional nature of association, as were Hume, Hobbes, Descartes, Spinoza; Coleridge was not so original as in the enthusiasm of the moment he supposed. He simply stated the truth in a more vivid way.

[68] Kant's threefold activities of the imagination have been explained and defined by Shawcross, *Biographia*, I, lviii and R. L. Brett, *loc. cit.*, 86.

[69] London, 1768.   [70] *Letters*, II, 428.

The subject of Hartley came up once more when DeQuincey found a dreamy-eyed Coleridge in Somerset in August, 1807. According to DeQuincey " Coleridge was so profoundly ashamed of the shallow Unitarianism of Hartley, and so disgusted to think that he could at any time have countenanced that creed, that he would scarcely allow to Hartley the reverence which is undoubtedly his due . . ." [71] He had indeed traveled far from his early enthusiasm.

It is not on the whole surprising, then, that when he came to write his own intellectual history, Biographia Literaria, which he finished at Calne, in Wiltshire, in 1815, he should be critical in his treatment of Hartley. But the importance of the whole subject of association for Coleridge may be gauged from the fact that he devotes three chapters to it. [72]

Chapter V of Biographia is a condensed history of association from Aristotle to Hartley. Sir William Hamilton had a low opinion of Coleridge's accuracy in this chapter, stating bluntly that it is " a plagiarism and a blundering plagiarism from Maass." [73] Shawcross's notes in the standard edition of Biographia confirm the impression of inaccuracy and indebtedness to Maass. " There is no question," Shawcross says, " of any deep intellectual affinity between Maass and Coleridge . . . But he agrees with Coleridge in his approval of the Aristotelian, and disapproval of the Hartleian psychology of association, and it

[71] Thomas DeQuincey, Recollections of the Lake Poets, ed. Edward Sackville-West (London, 1948), 34.

[72] Chapters V, VI, and VII.

[73] Sir William Hamilton in his Note D** appended to his edition of Thomas Reid's Works (2d ed.; Edinburgh, 1849), II, 889-90. In the 1848 edition of Biographia it is pointed out that Coleridge draws upon the Versuch über die Einbildungskraft of J. G. E. Maass (1797), an annotated copy of which was found among Coleridge's books. Maass (1766-1832) was for many years Professor of Philosophy at Halle.

is from Maass' confutation of Hartley and interpretation of Aristotle that Coleridge has most largely borrowed." [74]

Now, it is regrettable, of course, that Coleridge was not at all times accurate, and we could have wished that he had been more honest in making a completer acknowledgment of indebtedness to Maass,[75] but Coleridge, after all made no pretence of attention to scholarly minutiae. He had a creative mind, and if he makes minor or even major slips in accuracy, he compensates us with positive insights. His sins, therefore, are easily forgiven, for we have an abundance of scholars who can set right his inaccuracies, but we do not have an abundance of minds with insights like his. Moreover, Coleridge's account of association in *Biographia* is not so shoddy as Hamilton would have us believe. It has the merit of pointing to the great names in association theory, Aristotle, Aquinas, Vives, Hartley.

To come then to Coleridge's account of association: he finds that one can trace " the first, . . . fullest and most perfect enunciation of the associative principle " in " the writing of Aristotle," particularly the *De Anima* and the *De Memoria*:

> In the first place it is to be observed that Aristotle's positions on this subject are unmixed with fiction. The wise Stagyrite speaks of no successive particles propagating motion like billiard balls, as Hobbes; nor of nervous or animal spirits . . . that etch and re-etch engravings on the brain, as the followers of Des Cartes . . . ; nor of an oscillatory ether which was to effect the same service for the nerves of the brain considered as solid fibres, as the animal spirits perform for them under the notion of hollow tubes, as Hartley teaches—nor finally (with yet more recent dreamers), of chemical compositions by elective affinity . . . Aristotle delivers a just theory without pretending to an hypothesis.[76]

Coleridge continues his exposition: " The *general law* of

---

[74] *Biographia*, I, 230-31.
[75] He does allude to Maass, *Biographia*, I, 74.   [76] *Biographia*, I, 71-72.

association, or, more accurately, the *common condition* under which all exciting causes act, . . . according to Aristotle is this. Ideas by having been together acquire a power of recalling each other; or every partial representation awakes the total representation of which it had been a part." [77] To be sure, Aristotle has several laws of association, but this, according to Coleridge, is the underlying principle. " In association then consists the whole mechanism of the reproduction of impressions, in the Aristotelian Psychology. It is the universal law of the *passive* fancy and *mechanical* memory; that which supplies to all other faculties their objects, to all thought the elements of its materials." [78]

Having stated this fundamental principle, Coleridge proceeds to the criticism of Hartley, which occupies the two succeeding chapters of *Biographia* (VI and VII). Having first shown how completely Hartley's theory of vibrations was superseded by the later studies of eighteenth-century physiologists, Coleridge proceeds to demonstrate the essential unity of Hartley's system. In this, Coleridge had a better grasp of that system as a whole than some more recent commentators have had, who see that system as composed of two irreconcilable halves. For instance, J. H. Muirhead argues: " the Second Part of Hartley's treatise is devoted to an exposition of natural and revealed religion from an entirely different point of view from that of the First Part, and enables the writer to pose as the defender of faiths, of which his scientific theory has destroyed the intellectual foundations." [79] Not so, says Coleridge, and rightly, for association is worked into Hartley's system from top to bottom. Remove the foundation and the whole structure topples:

It is fashionable to smile at Hartley's vibrations and vibratiuncles; and his work has been re-edited by Priestley, with the omission of the material hypothesis. But Hartley was too great a man, too

---

[77] *Ibid.*, 72.   [78] *Ibid.*, 72-73.   [79] *Coleridge as Philosopher*, 42.

coherent a thinker, for this to have been done, either consistently
or to any wise purpose. For all other parts of his system, once
removed from their mechanical basis, not only lose their main
support but the very motive which led to their adoption. Thus
the principle of contemporaneity, which Aristotle had made the
common condition of all the laws of association, Hartley was con-
strained to represent as being itself the sole law. For to what law
can the action of material atoms be subject, but that of proximity
in place? And to what law can their motions be subjected, but
that of time? Again, from this results inevitably, that the will, the
reason, and the judgment, and the understanding, instead of being
the determining causes of association, must needs be represented as
its creatures, and among its mechanical effects." [80]

Here is Coleridge's basic objection to Hartley's system.

In Chapter VII of *Biographia* Coleridge pursues his attack
on what he considers the " blind mechanism " of the mind as
Hartley conceived it. He attacks the assumption that " the will,
and with the will, all acts of thought and attention are parts
and products of this blind mechanism, instead of being distinct
powers, the function of which is to control, determine and
modify the phantasmal chaos of association." [81] This passage
has been quoted because it is perhaps the clearest and most
effective statement of his anti-Hartleian thesis.

Coleridge then substitutes a law of association of his own for
Hartley's law; the point to be observed is that Coleridge's law
involves active choice. He says:

Contemporaneity, then, being the common condition of all the
laws of association, . . . the true practical general law of association
is this: that whatever makes certain parts of a total impression more
vivid or distinct than the rest, will determine the mind to recall
these in preference to others equally linked together by the common condition of contemporaneity, or (what I deem a more appropriate and philosophical term) of continuity. [82]

[80] *Biographia*, I, 76.   [81] *Ibid.*, 81.   [82] *Ibid.*, 86-87.

It will be noted that Coleridge has substituted selectivity of interest, emotional heightening, and, in his case doubtless, perception of possible value as poetic imagery, as potent causes of recall; the perceived significance, as in the case of Vinteuil's little phrase, is the trigger of recollection.

Coleridge's view receives the support of William James. James thought that consciousness displays interest and attention. It is selective; it is voluntary; some topics arouse our interest; others do not. Our minds are receptive to some subjects, go more than halfway to meet and welcome them, while others are relegated to limbo. Our minds are not a blank or a *tabula rasa*, but are already somewhat conditioned by our previous experience:

> This reinforcement of ideas and impressions by the pre-existing contents of the mind was what Herbart had in mind when he gave the name of apperceptive attention to the variety we describe. We easily see now why the lover's tap should be heard—it finds a nerve centre half ready in advance to explode. We see how we can attend to a companion's voice in the midst of noises which pass unnoticed though objectively much louder than the words we hear. . . . The boys at school, inattentive to the teacher except when he begins an anecdote, and then all pricking up their ears, are as easily explained.[83]

James adds this proviso: "Attention *creates* no idea; an idea must already be there before we attend to it. Attention only fixes and retains what the ordinary laws of association bring 'before the footlights' of consciousness."[84]

Nevertheless, by choosing what we attend to, we do in a sense create our world of impressions. Or, as Hamlet puts it, "there is nothing either good or bad, but thinking makes it so."[85]

Psychology of recall of the Hartleian type has been under fire recently from the Gestaltist school and once more Coleridge's

---

[83] *The Principles of Psychology* (2 vols.; New York, 1890), I, 450.
[84] *Ibid.*   [85] *Hamlet*, II. ii. 245-46.

sureness of psychological intuition receives additional confirmation. I. A. Richards explains:

> How far experience is receivable would seem to depend in the first place upon the interests, the impulses, active in the experience. Unless similar interests recur its revival would seem to be difficult. The original experience is built upon a number of impulses; it came about only through these impulses. We may even say that it is those impulses. The first condition for its revival is the occurrence of impulses similar to *some* of these . . . Most revival is distorted because only some of the original impulses are repeated, new impulses being involved and a compromise resulting . . . It is a first principle of psychology that the partial return only of a situation may reinstate the whole, and since most impulses have belonged in the past to many varied wholes there must evidently be much rivalry as to which wholes do actually recur. What seems to decide the dispute more than anything else is the character of the original connections between the parts. As has been recently emphasized by the exponents of *Gestalt-psychologie*, mere original contiguity or simultaneity is comparatively powerless to control revival.[86]

Miss Kathleen Coburn of Toronto, the editor of Coleridge's notebooks, like Richards, connects Coleridge with *Gestalt* psychology, and thus succinctly summarises the progress of his psychological thinking:

> After a brief flirtation with mechanical Associationism, the Behaviourism of his day, he developed views along the lines of a *Gestalt* psychology, denying that man is the mere sum of his parts, and insisting on a totality, an organism,
>
> > Dark fluxion, all unfixable by thought
> > A phantom dim of past and future wrought.[87]

Support for Coleridge, too, comes from another quarter. Suzanne K. Langer, in her book *Philosophy in a New Key*, a

---

[86] *Principles of Literary Criticism* (London, 1926), 182-83.

[87] *Inquiring Spirit: A New Presentation of Coleridge from his Published and Unpublished Writings*, ed. Kathleen Coburn (New York, 1951), 27.

work which belongs to a school of thought of which Ernst Cassirer's *Philosophy of Symbolic Forms* is the grand example, says:

> Ideas are undoubtedly made out of impressions—out of sense messages from the special organs of perception and vague visceral reports of feeling. The law by which they are made, however, is not a law of direct combination. Any attempt to use such principles as association by contiguity or similarity soon runs into sheer unintelligible complication and artifice. Ideation proceeds by a more potent principle, which seems to be best described as a principle of symbolization. The material furnished by the senses is constantly wrought into *symbols*, which are our elementary ideas.[88] . . . The fact that the human brain is constantly carrying on a process of symbolic transformation of the experimental data that come to it causes it to be a veritable fountain of more or less spontaneous ideas.[89]

Surely Coleridge, if he were alive today, would receive this theory of the mind with a shout of joy and recognition.

Any vitalistic or organic theory of life is likely to have little truck with mechanical associationism; one is reminded at this point of the general objective that Bergson set for himself: "The duty of philosophy it seemed to me was to lay down the general conditions of the direct, immediate observation of oneself by oneself." [90] He wished to intuit consciousness directly without any imposed forms, and consequently speaks of "a psychological theory, associationism, which I brushed aside." [91]

I have not finished with the subject of association, for I wish to postpone consideration of what Coleridge called the "streamy nature of association," his awareness of association in dreams,

[88] Suzanne K. Langer, *Philosophy in a New Key* (New York, 1948), 33.
[89] *Ibid.*, 34.
[90] Henri Bergson, *The Creative Mind*, tr. Mabelle L. Andison (New York, 1946), 29.
[91] *Ibid.*, 31.

to the appropriate time and place, when I consider Coleridge's awareness of the unconscious, and to what extent he admitted collaboration between conscious and unconscious powers of mind in the act of creative imagination.

For the time being it is enough that considerable evidence has been brought forward to show that Coleridge was well informed about the association of ideas. He was more than informed; he had brought the highest kind of intelligence to bear on current associational theory and had put his finger on its weak spot. He had clearly perceived that a law of association cannot in itself or alone explain the creation of the ordered whole, the organic unity, of a work of art. He had discovered ontological rather than Hartleian grounds for association, grounds in the major motivation of the poet's being. Not any stick or straw, iota or trifle, would be stashed away with the potential of recall, but many an apparently inconsequent trifle might be so stored providing it were activated by a living interest, providing it were real grist to the poetic mill.

3

~~~~~~

ORGANISM AND

THE MACHINE

i

Associationist Views of
Imagination in the Eighteenth Century

Few subjects were more thoroughly canvassed during the eighteenth century than the creative power, called by various names, such as wit, fancy, imagination, invention. Two schools of thought developed, the one conveniently labeled " mechanist," the other, gaining force as the century advanced, named " vitalist." Coleridge's vigorous part in the controversy is the subject of the present chapter. The vehemence, almost violence, with which he entered the lists will help to explain why he defined fancy (labeled " mechanical " and confined to passive association) in sharp opposition to creative imagination. First, it will be convenient to sketch the opinions of the " mechanist " school. Descartes, in the earlier half of the seventeenth century, wished to make a clean break in philosophy; he wanted to wash his brain of all preconceptions and start afresh. He was in the main a mathematician, though he had lively biological interests also, using dissection to discover the secrets of the body and the nervous system. Having discovered a mode of mathematical reasoning in which geometry was combined with algebra, and thus satisfying himself that the two were essentially one, he wrote his *Discours de la Méthode* (1637). All ideas other than those which were clear and distinct were excluded; clearness and distinctness, he made the test of validity. Cartesian rationalism engendered a mental climate which blew rather cool, and, indeed, cold, towards the imagination. The mounting wave of speculation in the late eighteenth century on such subjects as instinct, intuition, imagination, feeling, the sublime, and the indefinable may be ascribed in part to a reaction from Cartesian mathematics and Cartesian logic.

The Cartesian system is a dualism. Basically, only two things exist, namely, thought and extension. The two things of which he can be certain, having arrived at the *cogito ergo sum* criterion of certainty, are matter and mind. Man has a soul as well as a body, and this soul is just as truly substantial; its substance is not matter with the attribute of extension, but mind with the attribute of thought.

Whether, having created this dualism, Descartes at the same time created a fatal dichotomy is a question worth raising. It is possible that there is some connection to be seen between Eliot's famous "dissociation of sensibility" and the Cartesian dualism. However this may be, to Descartes belongs the honor of perceiving the problem and of stating the question, whether or no he provided a satisfactory answer. The crux of the problem was this: how was thought to come to terms with matter? Where would be the *liaison* and point of contact between them? A name it already had, but where would "soul" or thinking substance have a local habitation in the body?

He solved the problem as best he could. Without arriving at the modern conception of psychosomatic unity, he is one of the first philosophers to state the interaction between body and mind in a modern way, showing how sensations will cause excitements in the nervous system, and the movements which are thus excited in the brain by the nerves, variously affect the soul or mind, which is intimately connected with the brain; and conversely, thoughts, though intellectual at their source, in passing into the nerves and acquiring the excitements of the imagination and the animal spirits, affect the body. And where did he locate the soul? He pitched upon the pineal gland.

The Cartesian theory of memory and association is essentially one of neural traces, though his curious terminology of " animal spirits " obscures that fact. This is the way in which Descartes explains how we recover what we wish to remember:

> . . . When the soul desires to recollect something this desire causes the gland, by inclining successively to different sides, to thrust the spirits toward different parts of the brain until they come across that part where the traces left there by the object which we wish to recollect are found; for these traces are none other than the fact that the pores of the brain, by which the spirits have formerly followed their course because of the presence of this object, have by this means acquired a greater facility than the others in being once more opened by the animal spirits which come towards them in the same way.[1]

Habit, or the repetition of the traces, wears a smoother path.

Descartes trusted only that kind of knowledge which met his test of being clear and distinct; imagination was suspect because it was involved with sensation and emotion. The evidence of the senses could not be relied upon, for it was tricky, and it was often hard to know where dream began or sensation ended. Using " intuition " in a strictly Augustinian and nonromantic sense, he thus defined it:

---

[1] *Les Passions de l'Ame*, Part I, Article 42, *The Philosophical Works of Descartes*, tr. Elizabeth S. Haldane and G. R. T. Ross (2 vols.; Cambridge, 1911), I, 350.

By intuition I understand, not that fluctuating testimony of the senses, nor the misleading judgment that proceeds from the blundering constructions of imagination, but the conception which an unclouded and attentive mind gives us so readily and distinctly that we are wholly freed from doubt about that which we understand. Or, what comes to the same thing, *intuition* is the undoubting conception of an unclouded and attentive mind, and springs from the light of reason alone.[2]

An historian of modern philosophy in France puts the matter picturesquely and forcefully:

Let us remember Descartes' oft-repeated caution to " cast off all the impressions of the senses and imagination and trust to reason alone." There are not two kinds of evidence: one which tells us that the sun shines, that honey is sweet, that lead is heavy; and another which informs us that if equals be added to equals, the sums are equal. Only the latter proposition is self-evident; the former statements, in spite of any prepossession to the contrary, are not so.[3]

Descartes is often written about as though he had a quarrel with the imagination. This, however, is probably to go too far. Indeed, he is capable of paying imagination very handsome compliments, attributing to it insights more movingly expressed than in the writings of the philosophers; he had no quarrel with the imagination where it operated in what he conceived to be its right domain, namely in poetry and the arts.[4] Thus Croce's remark, " The French philosopher abhorred imagination . . . and though not utterly condemning poetry, he allowed it to exist only in so far as it was guided by intellect. . . . He tolerated it but that was all," [5] and his further remark, " Cartesianism was

[2] *Rules for the Direction of the Mind, ibid.*, I, 7.
[3] Lévy-Bruhl, *Modern Philosophy in France* (Chicago, 1899), 22.
[4] See for instance the quotation from *Œuvres de Descartes*, ed. Charles Adam and Paul Tannery (13 vols.; Paris, 1894-1913), X, 184. Quoted by A. Boyce Gibson, *The Philosophy of Descartes* (London, 1932), 35.
[5] Benedetto Croce, *Aesthetic*, tr. Douglas Ainslie (London, 1922), 204.

incapable of an Aesthetic of imagination," [6] require some quali-
fication.

Descartes himself should not be blamed for all the excesses
of the Cartesians. As explained above, his system was a dualism.
The lofty part of the Cartesian system which dealt with the
abstractions of the intellect and the substance of the soul was
neglected by them; being, perhaps, what Coleridge later called
"pollarded men," they seized upon the roots and trunk, neglecting the upper branches. They accepted the body as a machine
with a nervous system, but denied the existence of a "soul."
Their excesses consisted in applying the Cartesian method of
logic to organic studies and nonmathematical problems with
which it was not fitted to deal.

In England, Hobbes, who came late in life to philosophy by
way of mathematics, and who, through sojourn in Paris, was
well-acquainted with Cartesianism, was radical in his materialism, conceding the existence of nothing except matter and
motion. Thought, of course, existed for Hobbes, but not as
independent substance.

Many opinions of Hobbes resemble those of Descartes, however. This psychology began with sensation. He believed that
sensation was caused by motion impinging on the body and
nervous system, which the nervous system registered in the
brain,[7] and to which (as in Newton's laws of mechanics) the
nervous system responded in a reflex action to protect itself with
a force equal to that of the original stimulus. Such impressions
left traces in the brain which Hobbes called "phantasms." He
uses the terminology consecrated by classical and medieval usage;

---

[6] *Ibid.*, 205.

[7] See for instance Hobbes's account of the action of the optic nerve in
Human Nature, Ch. II, Sec. 8 in *The Works of Hobbes*, ed. by Sir William
Molesworth (London, 1839-45), IV, 6. This will hereafter be referred to
as Molesworth.

imagination is identified with memory and, indeed, he can define it in the Aristotelian way as "nothing but decaying sense." [8] These phantasms or images were originally preserved in the sequence or order of the original impressions received by the senses, but as time went on, the phantasms were cut loose from their moorings and became disarranged, "so that when by length of time very many phantasms have been generated within us by sense, then almost any thought may arise from any other thought . . ." [9]

Hobbes is aware of the principle of association, so that one phantasm may readily suggest another. The basic term which Hobbes uses for the creative power is fancy; it is fancy which has the power of selecting and combining among the phantasms. Fancy is often compared by Hobbes to a spaniel; it has a good nose, a quick scent, is fond of ranging over the fields of memory for the appropriate quarry. Dryden readily adopted the sporting metaphor, as one too good to lose. Fancy is a good hound, but has to be brought to heel by his master, judgment. The three faculties, reproductive imagination, active fancy, and restraining judgment cooperate in the work of invention. Fancy is a power quick at seeing analogies in things apparently unlike; judgment, on the other hand, is an analytic power, noting differences. Great inventive power or genius is allied to quickness of fancy; a power of rapid ranging and a quickness in making associations are essential to it. There seems to be little distinction in Hobbes between wit and fancy. Wit is judged by the rapidity with which associations are made. Wit consists in "celerity of imagining." [10]

[8] *Leviathan*, Part I, Ch. II; Molesworth, III, 4.

[9] *Elements of Philosophy*, IV, Ch. XXV; Molesworth, I, 397-98. Note also Hobbes's suggestive phrase, "the perpetual arisings of phantasms," *ibid.*, I, 399.

[10] *Leviathan*, I, Ch. VIII; Molesworth, III, 56. For a good discussion of the creative imagination see C. D. Thorpe, *The Aesthetic Theory of Thomas*

Though Hobbes's philosophy calls for nothing, essentially, except matter and motion, his psychology of the imagination is not so mechanical or grossly materialistic as might be supposed. Indeed the one region or nook of Hobbes's universe in which subtlety of shadowy suggestion is possible is in the mind. Coleridge's view which makes the mind as seen by Hobbes a green baize table under a hard light, with clicking billiard balls, is, of course, a caricature.[11] Hobbes noticed that in the free play of reverie the stream of thought was not always as inconsequent and incoherent as might be surmised, for " in this wild ranging of the mind, a man may oft-times perceive the way of it, and the dependence of one thought upon another." [12] Here the suggestibility of one thought or image by another is more than hinted. Usually close to Aristotle in his psychology, Hobbes has pregnant things to say about the physiological causes of dreams; [13] indeed, in some of his remarks on dreams he is distinctly Freudian, recognizing a connection between dreaming and sexual desire.[14] He sharply distinguishes between the connectedness of logical discourse and the incoherence of dreams. And with his usual shrewdness he points out that when a writer has a design, it is desire that " brings in all the phantasms that are means conducing to that end." [15]

To sum up, then, Hobbes, in spite of his mechanical theory, makes the mind creative and uses association of ideas as an aid to creativity. Association provides the cohesion in the storehouse

Hobbes (Ann Arbor, 1940). Thorpe draws attention to the importance of Hobbes's great tribute to the imagination in the " Answer to Davenant."

[11] Coleridge speaks of " successive particles propagating motion like billiard-balls," Biographia, I, 71.

[12] Leviathan, Part I, Ch. III; Molesworth, III, 13.

[13] Leviathan, Part I, Ch. II; Molesworth, III, 7-8.

[14] See for example his remarks about "dreams of lust " in Human Nature, Ch. 3; Molesworth, IV, 9-10.

[15] Elements of Philosophy, Ch. XXV; Molesworth, I, 398.

of memory. This was Hobbes's great originality and his particular contribution to our subject.

Another English philosopher, John Locke, raised the profoundest question of epistemology. That question concerns the source of our knowledge. Are we to hold with Plato that the source of our knowledge is from the realm of ideas somewhat dimly recovered by us in the world of the senses, like people searching for coins clearly stamped with the divine image by the light of guttering candles? Or are we, with Locke, to deny the existence of innate ideas (this, of course, was Locke's originality) and to claim that the sole origin of our ideas is through the inlets of the senses?

The question raised by Locke is more than a question of epistemology. It is a question involving also the foundations of psychology. Is the human mind in any true sense creative of its ideas? Is it no better than a camera lens or like a lake which lazily reflects mountains and clouds, or flags and flapping sails? "The eye," says Wordsworth, "cannot choose but see," and the mind cannot choose but reflect, apparently, that which is given to it to reflect in the givenness of experience. Can it in any true sense originate, or does it merely work up the givenness of experience into its own shapings? Locke did not deny creativity to the mind—how could he? But he looked somewhat askance at the vagaries of the imagination.

The vast influence of Locke's sensationalist psychology hardly, at this time of day, needs stressing. That influence is written large in the history of French eighteenth-century philosophy. His influence on English thought is equally marked and has been carefully traced in such works as Kenneth MacLean's *John Locke and English Literature in the Eighteenth Century* [16] or Basil Willey's *The Seventeenth Century Background*,[17] which

[16] New Haven, 1936.   [17] London, 1942.

has chapters on "Locke and Poetry" and "On Wordsworth and the Locke Tradition."

The subject of association was also advanced by Locke, who added a chapter "Of the Association of Ideas" to the fourth edition of his *Essay Concerning the Human Understanding* (1700). Locke has a curiously new approach. He makes no reference to Aristotle or Hobbes. It happened that Locke added the new chapter at a time when he was engaged upon his *Examination* of Malebranche, and when he was impressed by what Malebranche had described as *chance* association of ideas, answering in the mind independently of the will.[18] Locke, the cool rationalist, regarded such chance associations as a source of irrationality. His purpose in his additions on association is to promote the cause of mental health; he is not interested in chance or uncommon associations as an aid to creativity. Yet it was Locke, rather than Hobbes, who was widely read; Locke did far more than Hobbes to publicize the theory of association.

The next important contribution to the subject was Hume's *Treatise* of 1739. In Hume we have the by-now familiar psychology: sensations leave impressions, impressions fade into ideas, and ideas, though they may be ordered, tend, with length of time and the multiplied rain of new ones, to grow confused. The mind, therefore, becomes like a kaleidoscope, in which ideas may be shaken up into new and sometimes brilliant combinations. This is what Hume means by his phrase "liberty of the imagination to transpose and change its ideas." [19] Hume makes very great play with association; fundamentally he has an associationist psychology. He regards association as "a gentle force "; " were ideas entirely loose and unconnected, chance alone

[18] C. W. Hendel, *Studies in the Philosophy of David Hume* (Princeton, 1925), 100.

[19] David Hume, *Treatise of Human Nature*, ed. T. H. Green and T. H. Grose (London, 1875), I, 318.

would join them "; the laws of association provide cohesion and prevent the contents of the mind from becoming a chaos. He definitely makes the connection between imagination and association of ideas. "Our imagination runs easily from one idea to any other that resembles it" is a characteristic remark.[20] He even goes so far as to speak of the swift associating activity in the imagination as "genius" or "a kind of magical faculty in the soul"[21] that combines ideas by means of resemblance.

His *Enquiry Concerning Human Understanding* (1748) was regarded by him as a simpler, more popular treatment of his earlier work, the *Treatise* of 1739. It contains much of the same material. He again emphasizes association of ideas and remarks in language reminiscent of Hobbes that "even in our wildest and most wandering reveries, nay in our very dreams, we shall find, if we reflect, that the imagination ran not altogether at adventures, but that there was still a connection upheld among the different ideas."[22] Imagination is not arbitrary in its activity; it works, it combines ideas, with the help of the laws of association.

The Humean imagination is essentially a combining or compounding one: "Nothing is more free than the imagination of man; and though it cannot exceed that original stock of ideas furnished by the internal and external senses, it has unlimited power of mixing, compounding, separating, and dividing these ideas in all the varieties of fiction and vision."[23]

Hume is aware that association is often emotional, not always intellectual. On this point he says: "'Tis evident there is an attraction or association among impressions, as well as among ideas; tho' with this remarkable difference, that ideas are asso-

---

[20] *Ibid.*, I, 319.   [21] *Ibid.*, I, 331.

[22] David Hume, *Enquiry Concerning Human Understanding*, ed. L. A. Selby-Bigge (Oxford, 1902), 23.

[23] *Ibid.*, 47.

ciated by resemblance, contiguity and causation; and impressions only by resemblance." [24] Association is all the stronger when it is double, when it is association of ideas plus impressions. He cites Addison's *Spectator* Number 412 as an example of double association of emotions and ideas, and of how the two reinforce one another. He uses double association to explain aesthetic pleasure in the sublime and in tragedy.

Though Hobbes's psychology of invention and Hume's are essentially alike, both founded on sensation (nothing in the mind except what the senses put there), Hume has made several important advances. Hobbes does not use the term association; he speaks instead of "trains" of related thoughts or images. Hobbes has causes of association, but they are to be collected from scattered passages in his work; he does not tabulate them or set them out distinctly. That association operates as a powerful aid to the fancy is a plain inference to be made, especially in what Hobbes says about fancy roving over the ordered files of memory; it is, however, inferred rather than stated. In Hume, the word association is used. The laws of association are set down in orderly exposition both in *Treatise* and *Enquiry*. And nothing is left to inference; it is plainly stated that association is the magic secret of genius. Hume thus pointed the way to Gerard and a host of other aestheticians.

Kallich states that "Hume conceives association as something almost purposeful, especially as the guide of the artistic imagination." [25] It is as though association had the materials imagination needed predigested or assimilated, ready for use in building the aesthetic body or design. Ideas are not stored away refrigerated, insular, or in isolation; past and present experience is related. To a sensitive or alert person, the present stimulus touches off

[24] *Treatise of Human Nature*, II, 82.
[25] Kallich, "The Association of Ideas," 150-51.

a wealth of associations; there is in the poet or genius "a perpetual readiness or power of associative response." [26]

Hume did not go uncriticized. One of the bitterest of his critics was Thomas Reid, who, anticipating the criticism of Coleridge, indignantly comments that under Hume's system man is but a puppet without a mind and all of human nature is reduced to the mechanical association of ideas and emotions. [27]

That may be so, but, nevertheless, Hume had an enormous influence in changing the whole thinking of his century about imagination from negative to positive. As Taylor points out, most

> eighteenth-century philosophers retained the traditional Aristotelian psychology and considered the faculty of imagination to be a source of error. . . . Reason was conceived to work most accurately in isolation from the imagination. . . . For Hume, however, the function of imagination is to give real images of past perceptions which we can relate to present ones. Instead of the wild product of dreams, deliriums, deceptions and hallucinations, the imagination in Hume's conception normally has an issue of real ideas, true perceptions. . . . Though the imagination, considered as a kind of fancy, may seem free to juggle ideas in a variety of ways, Hume discovered that actually it operates in a regular manner, according to certain conditions of human nature and natural instinct. Seventeenth-century philosophers, critics and essayists emphasized the arbitrary or abnormal function of imagining; Hume considered it a natural function of the mind, and the most important faculty which man possesses. [28]

Hume appreciated imagination as a creative force, though he did not surround it with a mystic halo.

Hume, too, marks a considerable advance over Locke, whose

[26] Walter Jackson Bate, *From Classic to Romantic* (Cambridge, Mass., 1946), 112.

[27] Kallich, "The Association of Ideas," 145.

[28] Harold Taylor, "Hume's Theory of the Imagination," *University of Toronto Quarterly*, XII (1942-43), 180-81.

attitude to imagination, as we have seen, was predominantly distrustful. Locke had simple ideas combining into complex ideas, but association formed no part of the process. With Hume, on the contrary, simple ideas formed into complex ones *through* association. The artistic associationist imagination, both free and not free (not free in that it was governed by association, free in that it was not tied down to the order of the original impressions in the memory, free, too, in that it was not too much regulated by the intellect) was Hume's great and original contribution to aesthetic theory.[29]

No subject interested the eighteenth century more than the passions. The boundary between the passions, Hume realized, was often thin to the point of extinction, and they have a resonance, for their frame " is not like a wind instrument, which, in running over all the notes, immediately loses the sound when the breath ceases; but rather resembles a string instrument, where, after each stroke, the vibrations still retain some sound. . . . Each stroke will not produce a clear and distinct note of passion, but the one passion will always be mixed . . . with the other." [30] One can almost hear in this passage the overtones of Coleridge's Aeolian harp; as so often in reading eighteenth-century poetry, philosophy, or aesthetics, one can hear the early pipings and orchestral preludings of the romantic movement.

No Chinese artist or poet would care for literal realism, for to leave something unsaid, to leave something for the imagination, is the essence of their art. Hume, too, understood this principle. "Nothing more powerfully excites any affection," he said, "than to conceal some part of its object, by throwing it into a kind of shade which, at the same time that it shows enough

---

[29] This summary is based on an excellent summary of Hume's contribution in Kallich, " The Association of Ideas," 165-66.

[30] Hume, " Dissertation on the Passions " (1757), *Works* (1854), IV, 191. Quoted by Bate, *From Classic to Romantic*, 153.

to prepossess us in favor of the object, leaves still some work for the imagination." [31] The man who could write with this amount of discernment in aesthetics is not to be dismissed as a dry Scotsman whose forte was skeptical logic or common sense, nor is he to be supposed a simple mechanist.

He is often accused of having pulverized or atomized the mind into its separate impressions. Coleridge is one of those who so accused him. He is regarded with awe as one who reduced the impressive structure of St. Peter's or St. Paul's—the sublime façade of classical reason with the omnipotent dome—into calcined dust, a powder of chalky particles. Even he himself was somewhat appalled at what he had done. And his somewhat dubious achievement still remains. Auguste Comte acknowledged Hume to be his master, and Hume's system, or the logical positivism built on Hume, is the dominant philosophy of our time.

Hume's associationist imagination became so firmly planted as aesthetic gospel that a poet sensitive to current ideas (like Akenside) accepted it as a matter of course in his *Pleasures of Imagination* (1744). Didactic poetry has a cactus-like quality, and versified associationist psychology of the imagination produces this spiny passage:

> . . . Let the mind
> Recall one partner of the various league,
> Immediate, lo! the firm confederates rise [32]
> . . . .
>
> By these mysterious ties the busy power
> Of memory her ideal train preserves
> Entire; or when they would elude her watch,
> Reclaims their fleeting footsteps from the waste
> Of dark oblivion; thus collecting all

[31] Quoted by Bate, *ibid.*, 157. Source not given.

[32] *The Pleasures of Imagination*, III, 318ff. Akenside's pedigree might be described as by Addison out of Hume.

> The various forms of being to present
> Before the curious aim of mimic art
> Their largest choice [33]

In a note to this passage (III, 348ff.), Akenside observes, "The act of remembering seems almost wholly to depend on the association of ideas." In the *Pleasures* association is thus fundamental to his concept of imagination; he maintains that association of ideas in the memory is an invaluable aid to imagination.[34]

When Hartley's *Observations on Man* was published (London, 1749), it served only to reinforce the associationist imagination of Hume. For Hartley, like Hume, had complex ideas formed out of simple ideas by means of association. For him, too, the imagination was inventive because it was quick to make associations. Hartley, in a way, was sounder than Hume, for, whatever the vagaries of his particles in ether and vibratiuncles, he had a neural base, and his single law of association was the form in which associationism was accepted in the late eighteenth century.

From then on there was a spate of theorizing on genius and the creative imagination. Little of it is original, however, and nearly all of it is based on the associationist imagination of Hume. It is simply repetition in one form or another. As Professor Sherburn observes, "Talk about 'genius' and 'imagination' certainly increased. These were the good words. *Genius* had

---

[33] *Ibid.*, III, 348ff.

[34] The young Coleridge was much attracted to Akenside, but it was to the mystical strain in Akenside's poetry, the correspondence between the mind of man and nature, the theme of the mind and nature fitted to each other—*The Pleasures*, III, 278-311. He concluded the second of the *Conciones* with one of Akenside's most transcendental passages [*The Complete Works of Samuel Taylor Coleridge*, ed. W. G. T. Shedd (New York, 1884), II, 303. This will hereafter be referred to as *Works*, ed. Shedd] and approved Akenside in a letter to Thelwall: "But why so violent against metaphysics in poetry? Is not Akenside's a metaphysical poem? Perhaps you do not like Akenside? Well, but I *do*, and so do a great many others. Why pass an act of *uniformity* against poets?" May 13, 1796, *Letters*, I, 163.

by mid-century supplanted *wit* as the creative force in an author's mind." [35] For instance, Joseph Warton, in his dedication to his *Essay on Pope*, announced that "it is a creative and glowing IMAGINATION, *acer spiritus ac vis*, and that alone" that can entitle a writer to the name of poet.[36]

First of this stream of writers on genius was William Sharpe, who, in *A Dissertation on Genius* (London, 1755), notes that "the necessary differences in the accidental association of ideas" is one of the chief causes of variety in genius. His thesis is that genius is an acquired second nature, established by habit and hard work.[37]

One of the clearest and most methodical of the many writers about genius was William Duff. Duff thought that the most important ingredient of genius is imagination, but that other qualities such as judgment and taste are needed to temper it. He defined imagination as "that faculty . . . which, by its plastic power of inventing new associations of ideas, and of combining them with infinite variety, is enabled to present a creation of its own." [38] He distinguishes between philosophical genius and poetical genius. "Original Philosophic Genius is that which is distinguished by regularity, clearness, and accuracy . . . Original Genius in poetry is that whose essential properties are a noble irregularity, vehemence, and enthusiasm." [39] Enthusiasm had

[35] George Sherburn, "Opinions of Critics," in *A Literary History of England*, ed. Albert C. Baugh (New York, 1948), 980.

[36] Hoyt Trowbridge, "Joseph Warton on the Imagination," *Modern Philology*, XXXV (1937), 73-87, esp. 82-84.

[37] For a pioneer essay on the school of genius see Paul Kaufman, "Heralds of Original Genius," in *Essays in Memory of Barrett Wendell* (Cambridge, Mass., 1926), 191-222.

[38] William Duff, *An Essay on Original Genius* (London, 1767), 7. Duff tends, in anticipation of Wordsworth and Coleridge, to name the associative power, fancy—John Bullitt and W. J. Bate, "The Distinction between Fancy and Imagination in Eighteenth-Century English Criticism," *Modern Language Notes*, LX (1945), 8-15.

[39] Quoted by Sherburn, "Opinions of Critics," *loc. cit.*, 981.

been a word used in a pejorative sense by Swift; now the enthusiast, Joseph Warton, and others, had made the word a term of praise. We are almost on the threshold of *Sturm und Drang*.

In this series of writings on genius a *ne plus ultra* is reached by Alexander Gerard. With him the associative imagination of Hume receives its apotheosis. Genius for him is essentially the power which utilizes association of ideas and images for the creation of new forms and combinations. He specifically acknowledges his debt to Hume. Like Hume, he has double association of ideas and emotions. In his *Essay on Taste* (1759) he explains concerning genius that:

> the first and leading quality of genius is invention, which consists in a great extent and comprehensiveness of imagination, in a readiness of associating the remotest ideas that are any way related. In a man of genius, the uniting principles are so vigorous and quick, that whenever any idea is present to the mind, they bring into view at once all others that have the least connexion with it. As the magnet selects, from a quantity of matter, the ferruginous particles which happen to be scattered through it, without making an impression on other substances; so imagination by a similar sympathy, equally inexplicable, draws out from the whole compass of nature such ideas as we have occasion for, without attending to any others. . . .[40]

The force in the mind, which in Hume had been likened to the gravitational pull of Newton's celestial mechanics, in Gerard is a magnetic force. Quickness and range in the associating power are made the essence of genius.

In his later elaborate work, the *Essay on Genius*, Gerard follows the same tack. The criterion of genius is invention. Imagination is the inventive power of the mind and "it can

[40] Alexander Gerard, *An Essay on Taste* (3rd. ed.; Edinburgh, 1780), 163-64. Gerard is very well read; at this point he refers in a footnote to the associationist passages in Akenside's *Pleasures*, III, 348-410.

transpose, vary, and compound our perceptions into an endless
variety of forms." [41] Perceptions are united through laws of
association and it is this power of association within the imagination that is the ultimate source of genius.[42] Lightning quickness
of association is the power in which genius excels: " This activity
of imagination by which it darts with the quickness of lightning
through all possible views of the ideas which are presented,
arises from the same perfection of the associating principles,
which produces the other qualities of genius." [43] Clearly, Gerard
is simply repeating the theory of the associative imagination of
Hume; the distinguishing feature of his treatise is the wealth
of literature that he cites. Marini, Montaigne, and Sterne together with Ariosto and Spenser, are censured as examples of
undisciplined luxuriance of fancy or association gone wild.

After setting forth the laws of association, of which, for the
purpose of aesthetic creation, he finds resemblance to be the
chief, he concludes: " there are innumerable handles by which
imagination may seize such ideas as it has occasion for. Genius
has, in some men, great force and compass: but a vigorous con-
struction of the associative principles is sufficient to account
for it, however great it be; for if they be vigorous, any one perception may introduce a great multitude of others." [44] Thus
Gerard accounts for the fecundity of genius which has open to
it " an almost infinite variety of combination." [45] The converse
is also true: " If none of the associating principles be strong,
there can be no genius." [46]

Gerard is not original, but he is systematic: as Kallich observes,
he is " the first important critic to expound systematically the
relationship between genius and associationism." [47]

---

[41] *An Essay on Genius* (London, 1774), 30-31.

[42] " In this operation of the imagination, its associating power, we shall,
on careful examination, discover the origin of genius—" *ibid.*, 41.

[43] *Ibid.*, 57.   [44] *Ibid.*, 185.   [45] *Ibid.*, 196.   [46] *Ibid.*, 242.

[47] Kallich, " The Association of Ideas," 339.

Parallel to the school of associationism in Great Britain was the school of materialist or mechanist psychologists in France. It might be more correct to say that a materialist psychology based on the neural system or the physical half of the Cartesian philosophy was typical of the French psychologists of the late seventeenth and eighteenth centuries; associationism was regarded by them as an importation from England. This mechanist point of view is seen even in the title of LaMettrie's work, *L'Homme Machine*. Condillac, who owed much to Hobbes and Locke, derived all ideas from sensation or experience. His epistemology advanced, indeed, to an empirical extreme: Locke had admitted two sources of ideas, sensation and reflection. Condillac insisted in his *Traité des sensations* that the only source of our ideas is sensation.[48] Thus his tendency is to make the mind more passive, more dependent on sensation, than it is in Locke. Condillac, too, explained knowledge, to a great extent, by the single principle of association (*liaison*) of ideas. Like Locke, he distrusted it, and thought that the acquirement of a philosophical analytic intelligence could only come through a process of disassociation. He thought that poetical intelligence worked in the same way; he gave the creative power to intellect or reason, *not* to the passive imagination. In this respect his view cannot be reconciled with those of Hume and Gerard.

D'Alembert maintained, with Locke and Condillac, that our direct knowledge comes to us through the senses; in other words, that it is to our sensations alone we owe our ideas.[49] Helvétius, the genial financier, in his work *De l'esprit* (1758), drew the conclusion that, if we are what our sensations make us, then improvement of man's lot can come through education, through control of his environment.[50] The crowning work of the French

[48] Lévy-Bruhl, *Modern Philosophy in France*, 273.
[49] *Ibid.*, 213.
[50] Helvétius' environmentalist thinking colored Godwin's *Political Justice*;

materialist school is *Le Système de la Nature* (1770) by Baron
D'Holbach. D'Holbach is a more thoroughgoing materialist
than anyone, except, perhaps, La Mettrie; the term "soul" is
scouted as having no meaning; all our intellectual faculties are
accounted for as changes produced by motion in the brain.[51]

Whether Coleridge knew these French philosophers in great
detail may be questioned. He does mention Condillac by name
and quotes him specifically in his course of philosophical lectures
given in London in 1819.[52] Once he reached philosophical
maturity and contemplated with complacency (too much complacency, perhaps) the phrases of his transition, his hostility to
what he called "dogmatic materialism" or "empirical dog-
matism" remained constant.

The point is that Coleridge, in attacking the mechanist psychology, was no Don Quixote warring against imaginary wind-
mills; he was not hurling missiles at a straw man or Aunt Sally.
He had against him the weight of philosophical opinion, the
prevailing psychology, both in Britain and France. To be sure,
he was not alone, for other kindred minds reacted from the
materialism of D'Holbach with strong disgust, notably Goethe
and Rousseau. Blake, too, though in a backwater or eddy away
from the main stream of European thought, revolted no less
strongly against the mechanist climate of opinion of the
eighteenth century.

Coleridge acted like a man alerted by an alarm, like a man
who felt all he held precious to be in danger. The reason that
he attacked the mechanist psychology in general was that it
threatened the element of mystery in religion, for if "soul"

similar thinking is at the back of Beccaria's treatise *On Crimes and Punishments.*

[51] Lévy-Bruhl, *Modern Philosophy in France*, 231.

[52] *The Philosophical Lectures of S. T. Coleridge*, ed. Kathleen Coburn
(New York, 1949), 363. This will be hereafter referred to as *Philosophical
Lectures*, ed. Coburn.

went, religion was undermined. The reason that Coleridge attacked the mechanist psychology of association in particular was that it, likewise, laid sacrilegious hands upon a mystery, the great mysterium of genius or original creative power. For the new psychology offered a natural explanation of creative power; if it could be accounted for by a few simple laws of association, then genius itself could be explained, or even explained away. What happened then to the numinous imagination, divine in origin, and august with the majesty of the great I AM? If imagination came trailing laws of association, where were the clouds of glory?

ii

The Vital Sources of Coleridge's Theory

It might be well, at this point, to inquire who were the philosophers of Coleridge's mature allegiance, what were the sources from which he drew the vitalism of his theory of imagination to oppose to the mechanism of Hobbes, Locke, and Hume; where did he recruit his strength to carry on his warfare?

To begin with, the deepest roots of Coleridge's theory of imagination are to be sought for in the Bible and in a highly imaginative childhood. Not for nothing was he the son of a minister; he was preaching all his life. The titles of his works, for instance, *Lay Sermons*, confirm it. In that remarkable series of autobiographical letters which he wrote to his friend, Thomas Poole, he tells how, curled up in the windowseat of his father's vicarage, he lost himself in the world of the *Arabian Nights* and *Robinson Crusoe*. The mature Coleridge valued the imagination as a means of ingress into a spiritual world in which all the manifold of sensuous experience was ultimately reducible to the One, the unchanging and the eternal. " My mind feels as if it ached to behold and know something *great*, something *one* and *indivisible*." From the winter evening when, as a boy of eight, he had listened entranced to his father's discourse about the night sky, and from the time of his reading of fairy tales, "my mind," he says, "had been habituated *to the Vast*, and I never regarded *my senses* as in any way the criteria of my belief. I regulated all my creeds by my conceptions, not by my sight, even at that age." Those, he adds, who are only educated through the senses "seem to want a sense which I possess. . . . The universe to them is but a mass of little things." [53] Thus early the interior imaginative life was more important to Coleridge than the sad, real, existential world of contingence and absurdity. We can imagine him in the churchyard of his father's church in Devon, racing up and down, "acting over" whatever he read upon the docks and nettles.

The Bible was a permanent influence on Coleridge's mind. More than once in his writings he compares the Greek and Hebrew imagination to the strong advantage of the latter. A striking illustration of this is given in a letter to Sotheby (September 10, 1802), where Coleridge compares the Greeks with the Hebrews in their poetization of nature:

It must occur to every reader that the Greeks in their religious poems address always the Numina Loci, the Genii, the Dryads, the Naiads, etc., etc. All natural objects were *dead*, were hollow statues, but there was a Godkin or Goddessling *included* in each. In the Hebrew poetry you find nothing of this poor stuff, as poor in genuine imagination as it is mean in intellect. At best, it is but fancy, or the aggregating faculty of the mind, not imagination, or the *modifying* and coadunating faculty. This the Hebrew poets appear to me to have possessed beyond all others, and next to them the English. In the Hebrew poets each thing has a life of its own, and yet they are all [one][54] life. In God they move and live and

[53] *Letters*, I, 16.
[54] The text has "our," but "one" would seem to be Coleridge's intended meaning.

have their being; not *had*, as the cold system of Newtonian theology represents, but have.[55]

Thus early (in 1802) did Coleridge insist on imagination as a unifying power, having analogies with divine creation.

When we come to a consideration of what influence Plato may have had on Coleridge, it should be pointed out that a deep cleavage, a sharp ambiguity exists in Plato's treatment of the imagination. On the one hand he looked upon imagination with suspicion and distrust (in the *Timaeus* locating it in the liver) and regarded it as a pander to the passions and the appetites. The arts, not only plastic arts of painting and sculpture, but the arts of epic and tragedy as well, are regarded as at a third remove from reality. The poets are banished from the Republic on the ground that their mimic representations are all too tempting and that they water and stimulate the passions, for Plato slurs art with a pornographic assumption. Critics have made attempts to explain away his banishment of the poets on the grounds that he really did not mean it, that he really sympathized with the arts, and so forth; there should, however, be no misunderstanding on this point. He banished the poets—regretfully, perhaps, in the case of Homer—but he banished them. Yet, on the other hand, the poet who can translate idea into symbol and myth, as Plato himself did in the allegory of the cave, is not only not banished, but is one of the Republic's most honored citizens. I find no evidence at all that Coleridge accepted the implications of the former part of Plato's theory, but his embracement of the second part (that imagination bodies forth ideas and archetypes) was, as we shall have occasion to see, Coleridge's profound conviction.

The generally held opinion among scholars and students of Coleridge's thought is that he was a born Platonist, though some

[55] *Letters*, I, 405-406.

would qualify, and call him a romantic Platonist. As good an
example as any (there are many more) of his Platonism is the
following: " There are two essentially different schools of philosophy, the Platonic and Aristotelian. To the latter but with
a somewhat nearer approach to the Platonic, Immanuel Kant belonged; to the former, Bacon and Leibnitz; and, in his riper
and better years, Berkeley. And to this I profess myself ad-
herent." [56] Coleridge's mature allegiance to Plato is not in any
doubt, the age at which Plato began to influence him is the
only matter in question. Evidence for Coleridge's knowledge
of Plato and Plotinus is partly his own statement. In *Biographia
Literaria*, in which he traces his own intellectual development,
he mentions " the early study of Plato and Plotinus." [57] " Early
study" probably refers to school and Cambridge. It is not
stretching probability greatly to suppose that a Grecian at Christ's
Hospital and a brilliant student at Cambridge with an omnivorous appetite for reading would early come into contact at
first or second hand, either in the original or in translation, with
the thinking of Plato.

Coleridge himself puts the opposition between Plato and
Aristotle about as strongly as it can be put: " Every man is
born an Aristotelian or a Platonist. I do not think it possible
for any one born an Aristotelian to become a Platonist; and I
am sure no born Platonist can ever change into an Aristotelian." [58]
While it is true that Aristotle became a sharp critic of Plato's

[56] Letter to J. Gooden, Jan. 14, 1820. *Unpublished Letters*, II, 264-66.
It is hard to think that Coleridge is right about Bacon, in view of Bacon's
sharp criticism of the Platonic ideas in *The Advancement of Learning*.

[57] Another, and perhaps even better, example of Coleridge's Platonism is
his remark, " Whether Ideas are regulative only, according to Aristotle and
Kant, or likewise Constitutive, and one with the power and Life of Nature
according to Plato and Plotinus . . . is the highest *problem* of Philosophy
and not part of its nomenclature." Appendix E of the *Statesman's Manual*
(1816), *Works*, ed. Shedd, I, 484.

[58] *Table Talk* (July 2, 1830), *ibid.*, VI, 336.

theory of ideas, and further that Aristotle answered Plato's criticism of the poet in Book X of the *Republic* with a justification of the social value of tragedy in his *Poetics*, it should be said that in some fundamental respects Aristotle himself was a good Platonist and never forgot the lesson of the master. The point of agreement is that neither philosopher denied the valid existence of universals; the point of divergence is that for Plato the ideas (not concepts, though they are only grasped through concepts) are existent in an eternal empyrean of being, while Aristotle, with a shift of emphasis, due perhaps to his scientific, and, indeed, biological interest and to a different temperament, saw the idea or form as form shaping from within the materials of experience. When Coleridge's theory of imagination is examined, especially in its root metaphor of organic unity, it will be found to be Aristotelian to a considerable degree.[59] Coleridge accepted the classic principle that it is the poet's business to deal with universals. "I adopt with full faith," he said, "the principle of Aristotle, that poetry as poetry is essentially ideal, that it avoids and excludes all accident . . ."[60] In his theory of imagination Coleridge was doing what he had a genius for doing, achieving an amalgam, in this case of Platonism and Aristotelianism, but of Aristotelianism on the side where it touched Platonism, that is, in the theory of universals, modifying the Platonism, however, with the notion of organic or shaping form. The poet like Shakespeare, according to Coleridge, creates the concrete universal;[61] he achieves the paradoxical feat of

[59] "The late Irving Babbitt recognized the fact that Coleridge's poetic was basically Aristotelian, though he coupled this perception with his customary disparagement of the theory of imagination." Millar, "The Inward Eye," 20. Millar has reference to *Coleridge's Shakespearean Criticism*, ed. T. M. Raysor (2 vols.; Cambridge, Mass., 1930), II, 326n.

[60] *Biographia*, II, 33.

[61] It was the gift of Shakespeare " to have the *universal*, which is potential in each *particular*, opened out to him . . . " Lecture VII (1818), *Coleridge's Miscellaneous Criticism*, ed. T. M. Raysor (Cambridge, Mass., 1936), 44.

uniting in the same dramatic character the highly individual or personal with the universal or typical.

In passage after passage of Coleridge's criticism, we find this wholly classic insistence upon going to the principle behind the surface of things. The poet's aim, he thought, is less to "copy nature" than to "create forms according to the severe laws of the intellect." "A poet," he said, "ought not to pick nature's pocket: let him borrow, and so borrow as to repay by the very act of borrowing. Examine nature accurately, but unite from recollection; and trust more to your imagination than your memory." [62] In his excellent critique of Wordsworth's poetry, he complains of a "*matter-of-factness* in certain poems." [63] He finds Wordsworth laborious and pedestrian in his representation of objects, adding, "To this *accidentality* I object, as contravening the essence of poetry, which Aristotle pronounces to be . . . the most intense, weighty and philosophical product of human art; adding, as the *reason*, that it is the most catholic and abstract." [64] Coleridge was always opposed to literal copying with the fidelity of a Norman Rockwell.

Should a detail be employed, it should be the significant detail that suggests the very essence of an experience. "The presence of genius," he maintained, is not shown by

> elaborating a picture: we have had many specimens of this sort of work in modern poems, where all is so dutchified, if I may use the word, that the reader naturally asks why words, and not painting, are used. . . . The power of poetry is, by a single word, perhaps, *to instil energy into the mind, which compels the imagination to produce the picture.* Prospero tells Miranda,

> One midnight,
> Fated to the purpose, did Antonio open
> The gates of Milan; and i' the dead of darkness,

---

[62] *Table Talk* (September 22, 1830), in *Works*, ed. Shedd, VI, 345-46.
[63] *Biographia*, II, 101.   [64] *Ibid.*

> The ministers for the purpose hurried thence
> Me, and thy *crying* self.

Here, by introducing a single happy epithet, "crying," . . . a complete picture is presented to the mind, and in the production of such pictures the power of genius consists.[65]

It should not be assumed, however, on account of the Aristotelian element in Coleridge's theory of the imagination that Coleridge deceived himself into thinking that no vital difference existed betwen Plato's and Aristotle's philosophy. He did nothing of the kind. On the contrary, he accused Aristotle of having too earthbound a mind to rise to the full height of Plato's philosophy, for certainly the scientific region of cognition *via* the concept and the abstraction was not what Coleridge understood by the Platonic realm of ideas. He makes the opposition between the Aristotelian and Platonist sharp and distinct:

> They are the two classes of men . . . The one considers reason a quality or attribute; the other considers it a power. I believe that Aristotle never could get to understand what Plato meant by an idea. . . . With Plato ideas are constitutive in themselves.
>
> Aristotle was, and still is, the sovereign lord of the understanding;—the faculty judging by the senses. He was a conceptualist, and never could raise himself into that higher state which was natural to Plato, and has been so to others, in which the understanding is distinctly contemplated, and as it were, looked down upon from the throne, of actual ideas, or living, inborn, essential truths.[66]

Even at school, Coleridge had been fascinated by Neo-Platonism. The classic passage by Lamb, full of nostalgia for the days of youth and promise, though familiar, is so important for an understanding of Coleridge that it will bear repeating:

> Come back into memory, like as thou wert in the dayspring of thy fancies, with hope like a fiery column before thee—the dark

---

[65] *Shakespearean Criticism*, ed. Raysor, II, 174.

[66] *Table Talk* (July 2, 1830), *Works*, ed. Shedd, VI, 336.

pillar not yet turned—Samuel Taylor Coleridge—Logician, Meta-physician, Bard!—How have I seen the casual passer through the Cloisters stand still, intranced with admiration (while he weighed the disproportion between the *speech* and the *garb* of the young Mirandula), to hear thee unfold, in thy deep and sweet intona-tions, the mysteries of Jamblichus, or Plotinus (for even in those years thou waxedst not pale at such philosophic draughts), or reciting Homer in his Greek, or Pindar—while the walls of the old Grey Friars re-echoed to the accents of the *inspired charity-boy!* [67]

H. N. Fairchild, usually critical of Coleridge and inclined to regard him as an escapist, is of the opinion that "the Neo-platonism was far more congenial to his visionary, believing nature, it was more deeply secluded from actuality, and it provided a means of acquiring a reputation for Orphic wisdom among the boys." [68] To inquire into the meaning of existence, however, is not to seek an escape: quite the reverse is true. Quite possibly, with that gift for extraordinary talk which he always possessed, he was at the time something of an exhibitionist; it probably elevated his sense of his own importance to be able to spout passages from mystical writers like Iamblichus in the original Greek. It held schoolboys enthralled and astounded bystanders. But while this is allowed for, Coleridge must have begun, even then, to pick up some emanations from the Plotinian philosophy.

Quite possibly while at school (but this is not proved) he may have known the translations of Plotinus and Proclus by Thomas Taylor "the Platonist." [69] He read Taylor's works later, and

[67] Charles Lamb, "Christ's Hospital Five and Thirty Years Ago," *The Works of Charles Lamb*, ed. E. V. Lucas (6 vols.; New York, 1913), II, 24-25.

[68] *Religious Trends in English Poetry* (3 vols.; New York, 1949), III, 265.

[69] Thomas Taylor, 1758-1835. On Taylor, who also influenced Wordsworth, Blake, and Shelley, see F. B. Evans, "Thomas Taylor, Platonist," PMLA, LV (1940), 1060-1079. John H. Muirhead observes concerning Thomas Taylor's translations: "These deserve more notice in any history of British idealism

Taylor's translations continued to come off the press while Coleridge was at Cambridge.

The *fons et origo* of Coleridge's vitalistic and dynamic theory of imagination is to be sought for in Plato's *Ion*, the theory of inspiration as divine drunkenness, coupled with what is almost the first adequate theory of a genuinely creative imagination, Plotinus's statement in the *Enneads* that the poet or sculptor does more than reproduce, but actually shapes his material giving it a character according to an idea in his mind:

> This essence or character was not in the material, but it was in the conceiving mind, even before it entered into the stone. But it was in the artist not by virtue of his having eyes, but by virtue of his imagination (τέχνη). And this beauty, already comprehended in his imagination, was far greater. For it went not out of him, but abode with him and gave birth to a lesser beauty. . . .
>
> The arts do not merely copy the visible world but ascend to the principle on which nature is built up; and, further, many of their creations are original. For they certainly make good the defects of things, as having the source of beauty in themselves. Thus Pheidias did not use any visible model for his Zeus, but apprehended him as he would appear if he deigned to show himself to our eyes.[70]

I. A. Richards is entirely right when he says, " Plotinus is a source for much in Coleridge." [71] At crucial points in *Biographia* Coleridge quotes him, especially in the great passage on the philosophic imagination in chapter XII.[72]

---

than they have hitherto received. They include, from Plotinus, Ennead I, book 6, Concerning the Beautiful (1787); An Essay on the Beautiful from the Greek of Plotinus (1792); Five Books of Plotinus (1794); from Plato, the *Phaedrus, Cratylus, Phaedo, Parmenides,* and *Timaeus* (1792-93)"— *Coleridge as Philosopher*, 38 n.

[70] *Enneads*, 5.8.1. Quoted by I. A. Richards, *Coleridge on Imagination* (New York, 1935), 26-27.

[71] *Ibid.*, 27.

[72] *Biographia*, I, 166-67. Coleridge there quotes *Ennead* 5.5.8. Again

Plotinus has a theory of perception, which may be summarized to the effect that the drinking-in by the senses, for instance, the eyes, is no mere sponge-like absorption, but involves a selectivity of interest; the mind, therefore, is creative even in perception.[73] This is the foundation for Coleridge's theory of the primary imagination, which he holds to be " the living Power and prime Agent of all human Perception, and as a repetition in the finite mind of the eternal act of creation in the infinite I AM." [74] Such a passage can make no sense whatever unless it is read in the light of Coleridge's theory of divine interchange or creative communion between the perceiving subject—the conscious I—and the perceived object, nature, in which divinity is immanent or transcendent. The heart of Coleridge's thought about imagination is the essential identity of the productive power in nature and the creative power in man.

For instance, Coleridge in *The Friend* speaks of the instinct:

by which in every act of conscious perception, we at once identify our being with that of the world without us, and yet place ourselves in contradistinction to that world. Least of all can this mysterious predisposition exist without evolving a belief that the productive power, which in nature acts as nature, is essentially one (that is, of one kind) with the intelligence, which is in the human minds above nature." [75]

Wordsworth had the same idea, very possibly derived from Coleridge, *via* Plotinus:

How exquisitely the individual Mind
. . . to the external World
Is fitted:—and how exquisitely, too—
. . .
The external World is fitted to the Mind;

Coleridge quotes Plotinus in *Biographia* I, 173. He there refers to *Ennead* 3.8.3.
    [73] *Enneads*, 4. 6. 2.   [74] *Biographia*, I, 202.   [75] *Works*, ed. Shedd, II, 449.

> And the creation (by no lower name
> Can it be called) which they with blended might
> Accomplish:—this is our high argument.[76]

Similarly he tried to preserve

> A balance, an ennobling interchange
> Of action from without and from within;
> The excellence, pure function, and best power
> Both of the object seen, and eye that sees.[77]

Nor do Coleridge and Wordsworth envision any mere flirtation between the poet and landscape, rather a sacred marriage between the poet and nature, or deep calling to deep. In a letter to Sotheby of 1802 Coleridge said, "The poet's heart and intellect should be *combined*, intimately combined and unified with the great appearances of nature, and not merely held in solution and loose mixture with them." [78] Such creative union and intercourse between poet and nature is also characteristic of Emerson and Thoreau.

A document of the first importance for Coleridge's theory of the poetic imagination is the poem "The Æolian Harp," composed August 20th, 1795, at Clevedon, Somersetshire. Here the lines of importance are:

> O! the one Life within us and abroad,
> Which meets all motion and becomes its soul,
> A light in sound, a sound-like power in light,
> Rhythm in all thought and joyance every where—
> . . .
> And what if all of animated nature
> Be but organic Harps diversely fram'd,
> That tremble into thought, as o'er them sweeps
> Plastic and vast, one intellectual breeze,
> At once the Soul of each, and God of all.[79]

---

[76] Preface to the *Excursion*.

[77] *Prelude*, XIII, 375-78. This thought, one of the chief articles of transcendental faith, is found strongly expressed in Emerson.

[78] *Letters*, I, 404.   [79] *Poems*, 101-102.

These lines were favorites with Coleridge and he often subsequently quoted them; he would hardly have done so, were they not often present to his mind and important to him.

At first sight it must seem that the Æolian harp is the wrong image or symbol to convey an activist theory of the mind, for this Æolian harp is passive, depending on the wind to give it music. Nevertheless, his poem "The Æolian Harp" expresses a vitalistic theory of imagination, derived from early reading of Plotinus; the divine *pneuma* or breath breathes its vitality through the universe, and the poet, though apparently passive, has the divine inspiration breathed into him. He swells like the buds of spring and puts forth creative leaf. Coleridge never swallowed the Plotinian doctrine of emanations, but the Plotinian doctrine of the unity of the One and the many was the ground of all his thinking. His theory of the imagination is embedded in this transcendental faith.

After his temporary wobble, his brief infatuation with rationalism, he returned with all the more force to the study of Plato, Plotinus, to mystics such as Law, Boehme and Fox, to philosophers like Berkeley, critic of Locke from a subjective idealist position. That Coleridge belongs no longer in the mechanist camp is made evident by a letter written to citizen Thelwall on November 19, 1796:

> I do not like history. Metaphysics and poetry and 'facts of mind,' that is, accounts of all the strange phantasms that ever possessed 'your philosophy'; dreamers from Thoth the Egyptian to Taylor the English Pagan, are my darling studies.[80]

Coleridge's "darling studies" are worlds away from Condillac and Hume; a strong current towards dreams and the occult is whirling him along. His liking for "Taylor the English Pagan" shows his continued taste for the Neo-Platonists.

---

[80] *Letters*, I, 181. Cf. "I love Plato, his dear *gorgeous* nonsense," Coleridge to Thelwall, Dec. 31, 1796. *Letters*, I, 211.

It is a well-known fact of intellectual history that while Aristotle probably remained the dominant philosopher of the schools during the Renaissance period, there was a distinct revival of Plato and Neo-Platonism at that time, witness the Platonic Academy in Florence and, in England, Spenser's Hymns. Coleridge specifically mentions that he studied the commentaries on Plato by Marsilius Ficinus.[81] During the Renaissance period Platonism and Neo-Platonism were not too clearly distinguished. In any case Coleridge would be drinking at the same kind of fountain so far as a theory of inspiration is concerned.

The Renaissance produced thought of a very mixed character; the Bible, Plato, the Aristotelian philosophy of the schools, the first findings of scientific method, together with alchemy and magic could be mixed and stirred into a grand *olla podrida* in the weirdest way. Such writers as Paracelsus and Jacob Boehme, whose works, however strange and, indeed, unreadable they may appear to a modern scientific mind, are nevertheless significant in a history of imagination. Jacob Boehme, particularly, the shoemaker of Görlitz, was an uncompromising thinker of tremendous force. Coleridge acknowledged a liberation of his mind as a result of reading him.

Boehme, perhaps, has more claim to be called a "*Gottbetrunkener Mann*" than Spinoza, to whom Novalis applied the epithet. Boehme's system is in a sense Plotinian, for in it the world is an emanation from God. But with Boehme it might rather be called a potent ejaculation of God's creative force, for it is improbable that any other thinker has a more vitalistic conception of creation than his. His is indeed a God-impregnated universe:

Ainsi, le Père est une source-fontaine d'où jaillissent les forces, d'où elles s'écoulent, fluides dont la synthèse organique forme le *salliter* divin, une sorte de protoplasme dynamique (organique)

[81] *Biographia*, I, 94.

qui vit, se meut et engendre de soi-même et en soi-même les formes des êtres créés.[82]

Moreover, the sky for an intuitive thinker, a poet, like Boehme is more than the sky; in a sense God is visibly present there, and it is a symbol of his living presence.[83] The whole universe becomes a symbol-language, and Boehme, we find upon examination of his work, proves to be a symbolic thinker of great power.[84]

Boehme's universe being so saturated with imagination and his vitalism so pervasive, it is easy to believe Coleridge's statement, with reference to Jacob Boehme and his commentator William Law, that

> to have passed them over in an historical sketch of my literary life and opinions, would have seemed to me like the denial of a debt, the concealment of a boon. For the writings of these mystics acted in no slight degree to prevent my mind from being imprisoned within the outline of any single dogmatic system. They contributed to keep alive the *heart* in the head; gave me an indistinct, yet stirring and working presentiment, that all the products of the mere reflective faculty partook of DEATH, and were as the rattling twigs and sprays in winter, into which a sap was yet to be propelled from some root to which I had not penetrated, if they were to afford my soul either food or shelter.[85]

The bedrock, then, of Coleridge's mind was the Bible, Plato and Plotinus—in other words, Christian Platonism. His central belief was a theory of the One and the Many, the unifying Life within all appearances. His brief excursus into adherence to mechanism of mind (Hartley) and necessity (Godwin) was a temporary wobble, as we have seen, from which he quickly

[82] Alexander Koyré, *La Philosophie de Jacob Boehme* (Paris, 1929), 116.
[83] *Ibid.*, 109.
[84] Boehme's philosophy will be taken up again later in connection with Coleridge's theory of the reconciliation of opposites.
[85] *Biographia*, I, 98.

righted himself to the Christian Platonism from which, at heart, he had never wavered.

His Plotinian view of the imagination was reinforced by reading Coleridge did during his formative period. His idealistic and transcendental psychology of creation was well on its way even before the friendship with Wordsworth began to ripen. That the mind of the poet is active in perception, active in creation—except, possibly for the brief Hartleian spell in December, 1794 and early in 1795—seems to have been continuously Coleridge's view. Even in June, 1795 the counter-action to Hartley set in. Coleridge, we know, made a great deal of use of the Bristol Library and we find that from the 15th May to 6th June 1795 and again in November and December of that year he had taken out Cudworth's *True Intellectual System*.[86] From this book he would have discovered the essentially Plotinian doctrine that the mind is creative in perception; the doctrine was akin to his own later doctrine of the primary imagination.[87]

The significance of the Cambridge Platonists to Coleridge's intellectual development is that they were the men who first offered criticism of the mechanist system of Hobbes. Their significance, further, for a theory of the imagination is that, in opposition to Hobbes, and in keeping with a vitalistic interpretation of plastic nature, in which the divine ideas or forms were constantly evolving, their psychology was vitalistic. Cudworth, for instance, thought that the mind is never purely passive; some obscure kind of intellection is present even in sensation. Sensation is a mixed state, neither autonomous activity nor pure passivity, but an interaction of the two. That there should be

[86] Paul Kaufman, "The Reading of Southey and Coleridge: The Record of their Borrowings from the Bristol Library, 1793-98," *Modern Philology*, XXI (1923-24).

[87] For a good brief treatment of the significance of the Cambridge Platonists for Coleridge's theory of imagination, see R. L. Brett, "Coleridge's Theory of Imagination," *loc. cit.*

such a meeting-place between the active and passive is, as J. A. Passmore points out, "bound to be an embarrassment to any sort of dualistic theory." [88] The point of embarrassment might well have been the focus of interest. But for Cudworth, whose psychology was classical, any cogitation mixed with sensation, any cogitation that was not pure intellection, was suspect. For him, who wore his Platonism with a Cartesian difference, the only reality consisted in clear and distinct ideas.

The pioneer study of the influence of the Cambridge Platonists upon Coleridge is *Coleridge's Idealism* by Claude Howard. [89] The thesis of Howard's book is as follows:

> It will appear, I believe, from the following treatment of Coleridge's relation to the English Platonists . . . that his idealism would not have been essentially different in its final form if he had not come in contact with German transcendentalistic thought. Although the formal basis of Coleridge's idealism is adopted from Kant's analysis of the human mind, yet even this analysis had been anticipated in all its fundamental points by the less elaborate and more theological English Platonists whom Coleridge had diligently studied. [90]

To be sure, a parallel exists between the criticism of Hobbes offered by the Cambridge Platonists and the criticism of Hume offered by Kant, but the thesis that the Cambridge Platonists to some degree "anticipated all the important results of Kant's critical philosophy" [91] is one not very easy to maintain. Coleridge, in fact, with his usual acuity, has gone straight to the point, and has shown in his criticism of the Cambridge Platonists why they failed to satisfy him the way that Kant did:

> What they all wanted was a pre-inquisition into the mind, as part organ, part constituent, of all knowledge, an examination of the

[88] J. A. Passmore, *Ralph Cudworth* (Cambridge, England, 1951), 30.
[89] Boston, 1924.
[90] Claude Howard, *Coleridge's Idealism* (Boston, 1924), 24.
[91] *Ibid.*, 31.

scales, weights, and measures themselves, abstracted from the
objects to be weighed or measured by them; in short, a transcendental aesthetic, logic, and poetic.[92]

Our conclusion is as follows: The Plotinian bias of Coleridge's
mind is very strong indeed. This means, in terms of a theory
of the imagination, that the artist literally creates, makes malleable matter comply with divine ideas. There is absolutely
nothing mechanistic about such a process. Coleridge might make
mistakes in his Greek accents, but he could read the *Enneads*
in Greek. And even if he had been unable to read Greek, he
could still read Plotinus in the translations of Thomas Taylor.
His other reading tended to confirm the Plotinian bias; the reading of the Cambridge Platonists, of Bruno and Jacob Boehme,
would all reinforce what companionship with Wordsworth certi-
fied by living example; that imagination is " THE VISION AND THE
FACULTY DIVINE." [93]

A philosopher of such historical importance as Spinoza, and
one, moreover, who had a good deal to say about imagination,[94]
is likely to have impinged at some point or other on Coleridge's
thinking. It was at that period in his life when he hibernated
to study psychology and philosophy in the cottage at Nether
Stowey (he cultivated philosophy much better than he cultivated
the garden) that Coleridge engaged in the serious study of
Spinoza: Spinoza and Berkeley ran parallel in his interest con-
temporaneously. It is to be inferred that the name of Spinoza
came up in the conversations between Coleridge and Wordsworth from the " Spy Nozy " episode which Coleridge relates

[92] *Works*, ed. Shedd, V, 267.

[93] Quoted by Coleridge at the point where he asserts that this faculty is
eminently possessed by Wordsworth, *Biographia*, II, 45.

[94] See Willard Clark Gore, *The Imagination in Spinoza and Hume: A
Comparative Study in the Light of Some Recent Contributions to Psychology*,
Chicago, 1902.

with so much humor.[95] Certainly Spinoza hove into sight at a
crucial period, when Coleridge, much tossed about, was looking
for roads or anchorage:

> I retired to a cottage in Somersetshire at the foot of the Quantock,
> and devoted my thoughts and studies to the foundations of religion
> and morals. Here I found myself all afloat. Doubts rushed in;
> broke upon me "from the fountains of the great deep" and fell
> "from the windows of heaven." The frontal truths of natural
> religion and the books of Revelation alike contributed to the flood;
> and it was long ere my ark touched on an Ararat and rested.[96]

We are somewhat baffled at the ouset of this investigation,
since our purpose is to inquire how Spinoza's philosophy might
affect Coleridge's theory of imagination. But we find that Coleridge's interest in Spinoza—and this happens very frequently
with Coleridge—was primarily theological:

> For a very long time, indeed, I could not reconcile personality
> with infinity; and my head was with Spinoza, though my whole
> heart remained with Paul and John. Yet there had dawned on
> me, even before I had met with the Critique of Pure Reason, a
> certain guiding light. If the mere intellect could make no certain
> discovery of a holy and intelligent first cause, it might yet supply
> a demonstration, that no legitimate argument could be drawn
> from the intellect *against* its truth.[97]

Not only at Nether Stowey, but again, upon his return from
Germany, we find Coleridge "sunk in Spinoza." [98] He grasped
the central point of Spinoza's philosophy, namely, that everything is comprised in the substance of God, and that every event
is both in the mind of God and simultaneously a physical event,
this being the essence of Spinoza's psycho-physical parallelism.
Coleridge's understanding is verified in the following passage:

> Body . . . might in the Cartesian sense be defined as space and

---

[95] *Biographia*, I, 126-27.   [97] *Ibid.*, I, 134.
[96] *Ibid.*, I, 132-33.   [98] *Unpublished Letters*, I, 126-27.

extension, with the attribute of visibility. As Descartes at the same time zealously asserted the existence of intelligential beings, the reality and independent self-subsistence of the soul, Berkeley-anism or Spinosism was the immediate and necessary consequence. Assume a plurality of self-subsisting souls, and we have Berkeley-anism; assume one only (*unam et unicam substantium*) and you have Spinosism, that is, the assertion of one infinite, self-subsistent, with the two attributes of thinking and appearing. Cogitatio in-finita sine centro, et omniformis apparitio.[99]

In further substantiation of Coleridge's knowledge of Spinoza, it may be said that he made marginal notes to the *Ethics*. A good deal of Coleridge's energy is expended in *Biographia* in denying that he (Coleridge) is a pantheist and he felt pantheism to be the danger in accepting Spinoza's philosophy.[100] But it seems to me that he protests too much, and there is little doubt that, in the days of his early association with Wordsworth, Spinoza attracted him greatly.

The attraction, or, to use the Goethean term, affinity, which Spinoza exerted on some of the major romantic minds raises the question why it occurred. Possibly the explanation is that a man who conceives the intellectual love of God—the *amor intel-lectualis Dei*—as Spinoza did is likely to be attractive to idealistic thinkers,[101] even if they will not submit themselves to the rigors of his geometric thinking. They lick the frosting off his system; in other words, they devour that which appears " transcendental " —in the Emersonian rather than Kantian sense—even if they ignore the logic, much less go through the laborious steps by which the logic was forged, proposition by proposition, into

[99] *Aids to Reflection* (New York, 1854), 313n.
[100] See the interesting quotation from Coleridge's Opus Maximum (in 3 vols. Ms. in the possession of the Rev. G. H. B. Coleridge) in Lawrence Hanson, *Coleridge the Early Years*, 305.
[101] See Coleridge's tribute to Spinoza, *Biographia*, II, 217, where Coleridge quotes from the *Ethics*, Part V, Prop. 42.

a chain.[102] Stallknecht suggests that Coleridge romanticized Spinoza into something like a Renaissance Neo-Platonist, largely ignoring his determinism.[103]

At first sight there is little foothold for a romantic thinker among the bleak Dolomites of Spinoza's Alps. Spinoza is apparently cold and hostile to the imagination for the same reasons that moved Descartes to distrust it, namely, its involvement with the emotions. Spinoza's account of the emotions includes the association of feelings and the association of images. He believes that the intellect and the bodily emotions or corporeal imagination interplay or reinforce each other's powers, at the same time sternly warning the conceptual thinker to beware of the " imaginations by which the mind is deceived." [104] How, then, account for the attraction?

Probably the answer is that Spinoza, as was true of Plato, had a complex theory of the imagination, and the animal imagination was not all that his philosophy included. In Spinoza, as in Bruno and other thinkers, Coleridge would meet with the concept of *natura naturans*,[105] namely, God manifested in his creative aspect endlessly prolific of forms. It is here, of course, that Spinoza reinforces all the other influences that we have noted. Spinoza, moreover, in his commentaries on the Bible, grants insight to the prophetic vision.

Lionel Trilling has expressed this aspect of Spinoza's thinking very luminously in the following passage:

---

[102] Sterling P. Lamprecht gives an illuminating account of Spinoza's geometrical manner considered as a mode of exposition rather than as strict logical proof in *Our Philosophical Traditions* (New York, 1955), 240-42.

[103] N. P. Stallknecht, *Strange Seas of Thought* (Durham, North Carolina, 1945), 176; Fairchild, *Religious Trends in English Poetry*, III, 295n.

[104] David Bidney, *The Psychology of Spinoza* (New Haven, 1940), 237, who quotes *Ethics IV*, Prop. 1, *schol.*

[105] H. A. Wolfson, *The Philosophy of Spinoza* (2 vols.; Cambridge, Mass., 1934), I, 253-54.

Even though the word of God is written in all hearts, there have been some who have understood it better than others and such men were the prophets. Their superiority consisted not in their unusually perfect minds but in their unusually lively imaginations, for by methods of apprehension not scientific but intuitive, they grasped the truth in metaphor, parable, and allegory. From these men, then, we learn nothing of natural or intellectual phenomena, but from their poetic insights we may derive a profound knowledge of morality. . . . Further, all language is basically figurative, the Hebrew tongue even more figurative than most languages, and the knowledge of the imagination cannot express itself save in the allegorical or metaphorical way.[106]

Coleridge also had great respect for the philosopher Leibniz. It was not that he was interested in the windowless monads, but that Leibniz was a sharp critic of Locke. Coleridge's respect had been earned because Leibniz had undercut Locke's " there is nothing in the mind which was not before in the senses" by adding " *praeter ipsum intellectum*—except the mind itself." In other words, Leibniz recognized acts of mind; he designated the mind active; he saw that the manner of our knowing is determined by the nature of our knowing-instrument, the mind The mind is active, grasping experience under its own forms.[107]

To make a river as long and broad as the Orinoco or Mississippi, so long and broad that at times it seems a reach of the sea, many streams converge. So, too, in Coleridge's thinking about the imagination, which was lifelong and, at times, profound, many streams of influence flow together. Berkeley's powerful influence on Coleridge's theory has already been mentioned in connection with that crucial period of Coleridge's development when as a young man in his twenties he dug in to read philosophy and think about poetry in the damp and

[106] *Matthew Arnold* (New York, 1939), 325.
[107] For Coleridge's respect for Leibniz see *Biographia*, I, 93-94 and *Philosophical Lectures of S. T. Coleridge*, ed. Coburn, 383-84.

narrow cottage at Nether Stowey. The Berkeleian influence, it
has been shown, would serve to reinforce the Leibnizian, for
Berkeley, too, was countermining Locke and in the same direction; Berkeley and Plotinus unite in a theory of creative perception, meaning by this, that the experiencing sensitivity picks
out from experience whatever it feels to be significant, rather
than being a passive mirror which has no choice except to reflect
whatever confronts it. If *esse est percipi*, the accent is on the
perceiver rather than the perceived.[108] The later, and as Coleridge thought, maturer Berkeley of the *Siris*—the Berkeley who
affirmed that Plato's writings " are the touchstone of a hasty and
shallow mind "[109]—would do nothing except strengthen the
Platonic and Plotinian tendency of Coleridge's thought.

It was Kant's great function in Coleridge's intellectual history
that he furnished him with the psychology that superseded the
soundly-rooted-in-physiology but otherwise superficial one-track
psychology of Hartley. Kant's dynamic psychology, which offered
a similar criticism of Locke and Hume as that offered by Leibniz
—the mind orders experience under its own forms—and his
theory of the productive imagination, the aesthetic imagination
creatively free, appealed to Coleridge as far superior to Hartley's
system by which the mind is passively at the mercy of association
among its own impressions.

The present discussion of Kant's influence on Coleridge's
theory of the creative mind will be somewhat brief, and by way
of review, since the subject has been already raised in connection
with the influences that overthrew Hartley. It may be sufficient
here to point out that the reason for Coleridge's veneration of
Kant was that he saw in him the final and complete theoretician

---

[108] Berkeley is often, though quite unjustly, accused of being a solipsist.
Berkeley would have been the first to admit the limited validity or the limited
area of his own field of perception. In his system, however, God is inevitably
the Arch-Solipsist or All-Perceiver.

[109] *Siris*, 332, in Berkeley, *Works*, ed. A. C. Fraser, II, 494.

and analyst of our knowing faculty. Coleridge accepted the
Kantian terms (though sometimes modifying them in *The Friend*
for his own purposes) and particularly he accepted Kant's
account of the imagination as mediator between sense and understanding:

> Of the discursive understanding, which forms for itself general
> notions and terms of classification for the purpose of comparing
> and arranging *phenomena*, the characteristic is clearness without
> depth. It contemplates the unity of things in their limits only,
> and is consequently a knowledge of superficies without substance.
> So much so indeed that it entangles itself in contradictions in
> the very effort of comprehending the idea of substance. The com-
> pleting power which unites clearness with depth, the plentitude
> of the sense with the comprehensibility of the understanding, is
> the imagination, impregnated with which the understanding itself
> becomes intuitive and a living power.[110]

It should be said that Coleridge was no superficial reader of
Kant and we are fortunate in possessing his marginal comments
to Kant's works.[111] One of the most penetrating and vital of
those marginalia is that in which he criticizes Kant's account
of the relation between the sense-manifold and the categories
of the understanding; he seems to feel that, though superior to
Locke's, Kant's psychology was still too imbedded in empiricism:

> How can that be called a *mannigfaltiges* ὕλη which yet contains
> in itself the ground why I apply one category to it rather than
> another? The mind does not resemble an Aeolian harp, not even
> a barrel-organ turned by a stream of water, conceived as many
> times mechanized as you like, but rather, as far as objects are
> concerned, a violin or other instrument of few strings yet vast
> compass, played on by a musician of genius.[112]

---

[110] *The Statesman's Manual*, Appendix B, in *Works*, ed. Shedd, I, 460-61.
[111] The numerous marginalia to Coleridge's copies of Kant are preserved in
the British Museum.
[112] Quoted by John H. Muirhead, *Coleridge as Philosopher*, 91-92.

This passage is of no small interest, since it shows the continued presence in Coleridge's mind of the theme of his early poem, "The Aeolian Harp," and his realization that, though the Aeolian harp might be a good symbol of the trembling sensitivity of the poet, and his responsiveness to the breeze, it otherwise fitted his creative re-forming of experience extremely poorly. It should be clear by now, if a word may be coined, that Coleridge was no *passivist* where the mind is concerned.

Finally, around 1804, Coleridge found a congenial philosopher in Schelling. No light dabbler in philosophy, he read everything Schelling published,[113] particularly his *Ideen zu einer Philosophie der Natur* (1797),[114] and his opus, *Der Transcendentale Idealismus* (1800).[115] The leading ideas of Schelling which contributed to the formation of Coleridge's theory of imagination were as follows. First, in the *Philosophy of Nature*, Schelling taught that nature in its totality is striving towards consciousness. "All nature is dual; the magnet with its union of opposite polar forces is the symbol of the life and productivity of nature. In an essay *On the World-Soul* (1798), Schelling developed the idea of an animated nature pervaded by an organizing principle, which originates and maintains the conflict of contending forces." [116] In the *Transcendental Idealism*, he found a creative nexus or synthesis between the perceiving subject or ego and the vitally-productive object, nature. Such an idea was already familiar to Coleridge, in the theory of mind-nature interanimation which he had worked out with Wordsworth in a Plotinian context. Schelling worked it out in systematic detail and made the aesthetic faculty or imagination the prince of human powers, because in that the fruitful union of subject and object was

[113] See the impressive list of all the works by Schelling annotated by Coleridge in Coleridge's *Philosophical Lectures*, ed. Coburn, 464-65.
[114] *Ideas Regarding a Philosophy of Nature.*
[115] *Transcendental Idealism.*
[116] William Turner, *History of Philosophy* (Boston, 1928), 557.

most nearly realized. Nature in the organ of aesthetic perception achieved consciousness at last and creative freedom. Add to this complete recognition of the human imagination as creative, in happy union with organic and inorganic nature, creating according to living principles of growth and reproduction, the concept of the reconciliation of opposites, of consciousness and unconsciousness; add also that Schelling as a philosopher went through a phase of devotion to Boehme; and it will be seen that the Schellingian philosophy did nothing but buttress and confirm the vitalistic-dynamic tendencies already inherent in Coleridge's theory of imagination. Schelling's thought was so nearly parallel to Coleridge's that when the stream of it ran into a confluence with Coleridge's stream, it could join the latter and scarcely cause a ripple.

The sources of Coleridge's theory of imagination should not be sought in German philosophy alone. Like Wordsworth, he had strong and vigorous roots in the eighteenth-century. It has already been remarked that that century produced a large body of speculation on the creative power of imagination. At the head of that stream of speculation and influencing all the rest of the century stands Addison.

Addison is the first man in the history of English literature and philosophy to write a systematic treatise on aesthetics. Reference is made, of course, to his series of papers in the *Spectator*, the preliminary paper, *Spectator* 409, and the series of *Spectators*, 411-421. He drew the psychological basis for his theory of imagination from the philosophers Hobbes, Locke, and Descartes. In the forming of this basis, Addison was eclectic, a synthesizer of other men's systems. The aesthetic sensitivity was Addison's own. The Addison who wrote, concerning the immediacy of aesthetic pleasure, " It is but an opening the eye and the scene enters "; [117] or who wrote " the ideas of both senses recommend

---

[117] *Spectator* 411, ed. G. Gregory Smith (4 vols.; London, 1907), IV, 57.

each other," [118]—surely an early intimation of synaesthesia; or
the Addison who wrote feelingly and movingly concerning the
sublime: "Look upon the outside of a dome, your eye half
surrounds it; look up into the inside, and at one glance you have
all the prospect of it; the intire Concavity falls into your eye
at once " [119]—it was the Addison who wrote in this manner who
may be supposed to have influenced Coleridge. It was Addison
who could see, as Hobbes did not, that aesthetic pleasures are
divorced from practical interests.

Very strong claims have been advanced for Addison. "It is
not too much to say," affirms one historian, "that in the suggestive papers on the Imagination Addison laid the foundation of
the whole Romantic aesthetics in England." [120] Professor E. F.
Carritt regards him as a primary influence on Kant. [121] He further
says, "It has always seemed to me that Addison foreshadowed
Wordworth's and Coleridge's theories of the Imagination and
Sublimity. . . ." [122] Foreshadow he certainly did, though when
a comparison is made between Addison's theory of imagination
and Coleridge's, the great advances made by Coleridge become
apparent. Professor C. D. Thorpe notices

> the appearance of concepts in Romantic aesthetics virtually foreign
> to Addison's view: as, for example, Coleridge's idea of organic
> form and his theory of the secondary imagination as an esem-
> plastic power operating on the materials of experience subsequent
> to reflective and subconscious processes. [123]

[118] *Spectator* 412, *Ibid.*, IV, 62.

[119] *Spectator* 415, *Ibid.*, 72-73.

[120] J. G. Robertson, *The Genesis of the Romantic Theory in England*
(Cambridge, 1923), 241.

[121] "Effects in England of Kant's Philosophy," *The Monist*, XXXV (1925),
322-23.

[122] "Addison, Kant, and Wordsworth," *Essays and Studies*, XXII (1937),
27.

[123] "Addison's Contribution to Criticism," in *The Seventeenth Century:
Studies in the History of English Thought and Literature from Bacon to
Pope*, by Richard Foster Jones, et al. (Stanford, 1951), 327.

Coleridge's unifying and modifying power is more cogent, more potent, than Addison's conventional compounding power. Even on this point, however, Addison could say, " Imagination has in it something like Creation." If, on the whole, Addison's theory of imagination as perceptive response is much more impressive than his theory of the active imagination, that, after all, is only to be expected from one with the temperament of a spectator.

The new critics are more impressed with Addison's limitations than with his merits. T. S. Eliot, for example, finds him "a conspicuous example of . . . embarrassing mediocrity," adding, " It is perhaps as well to warn you that Addison is a writer towards whom I feel something very like antipathy." [124] The ground of this antipathy is " the smugness and priggishness of the man." [125] He has been called the " first of the Victorians." Cleanth Brooks finds that he " represents a retreat of the imagination—a retreat that may be traced ultimately to Hobbes." [126]

If the reasons other than personal distaste are sought for, it will be found that Addison's limitations are felt to be these: First, he limited the poet to a conventionally beautiful or poetic subject-matter. Secondly, his account of aesthetic response as simply a pleasure in the recognition and arousal of associations is not very satisfying. Thirdly, Addison's view of metaphor, as simply *appliqué* or stucco or illustration, rather than functional to the poetic meaning, does, in truth, represent a retreat of the imagination.[127] But then, the retreat was not Addison's par-

[124] *The Use of Poetry and the Use of Criticism* (Cambridge, Mass., 1933), 51.

[125] *Ibid.*

[126] *Modern Poetry and the Tradition* (Chapel Hill, 1939), 11.

[127] On the status of metaphor in the eighteenth century there exists an unpublished dissertation by Scott George, " The Eighteenth Century Philosophy of Metaphor " (Vanderbilt University, 1943). This is referred to and partly summarized by Florence Marsh, *Wordsworth's Imagery: A Study in Poetic Vision* (New Haven, 1952), 112-13.

ticularly, nor can he be blamed for it; it was a general retreat, a retreat due to several causes, among them the rhetorical tradition, the vast prestige of the sciences, and Cartesian rationalism.

Professor Thorpe concedes Addison's limitations, but nevertheless asserts the importance of his aesthetic:

> Viewed as a systematic presentation of final theory, the essay is as imperfect as can be and is susceptible to all manner of captious or strictly logical criticism. But viewed as a set of tentative pronouncements charged with dynamic suggestion and exemplifying a method of almost illimitable possibilities of development, it is worthy to be classed as one of the great critical documents of all time.[128]

The same writer has magnificently expressed Addison's pervasive influence throughout the eighteenth century:

> Wherever we go in eighteenth century criticism, whatever the specific subject of speculation, we almost invariably find that Addison had been there. If it is Hutcheson on beauty and aesthetic response, we find parallels to or echoes of Addison's " Pleasures of the Imagination; " if it is Burke on taste and sublimity and beauty, Young and Tucker on original genius, Hume and Gerard, and Kames, Blair, and Alison on taste, imagination, sublimity and novelty, the association of ideas and original genius, we are again in the presence of theory partially developed or at least adumbrated in the *Spectator* papers.[129]

Addison has a commanding position in the history of both English and European criticism. It is not a question of specific influence on Coleridge that can be pinned down; it is rather a question of something deeper than influence. It is rather a matter of concern with similar questions, the psychological approach, the sense that the imagination is that which matters in art, whether it be creation or aesthetic response. Addison

---

[128] Thorpe, " Addison's Contribution to Criticism," *loc. cit.*, 324.
[129] *Ibid.*

stimulated a whole century to interest in the imagination; he created a climate in which questions about the psychology of the imagination were considered important. " It is perhaps more accurate," Thorpe believes, to describe Addison's gifts to the romantics "in terms of inheritance, a process which in a way is of more honor to the progenitor as an indication of deeply ingrained viable qualities than is influence, which may be only a temporary and surface affair." [130] Of this inheritance Coleridge was one of the chief beneficiaries.[131]

Following Addison, the psychological study of imagination proceeded further. In contrast to the theories of regular or mechanical association, a new tendency arose to regard imagination in man in the light of an analogy with organic growth in nature. It is usual to call this tendency vitalism and to refer to it as the vitalistic or organic theory of imagination. Coleridge touched this vitalistic movement at many points. His English roots go back (as already noted) to the Cambridge Platonists. They, in turn, influenced Shaftesbury, who in his famous invocation to nature, apostrophized it as divine. Shaftesbury, in his turn, influenced Akenside, who spread the gospel of the divinely-impregnated nature inspiring the poet with its pageantry of cloud-shapes and mountain forms. Coleridge, it is known, was attracted to the mystical phase or aspect of Akenside. He was enthusiastic over Collins's " Ode on the Poetical Character," which made poetry divine, wild and impassioned in origin.[132]

Nobody has understood Coleridge's eighteenth-century roots better than Professor Fairchild who writes:

---

[130] *Ibid.*, 329.

[131] See Thorpe, " Addison's Theory of the Imagination as ' Perceptive Response,' " *Michigan Academy Papers* (Ann Arbor, 1936), XXI, 509-30. Thorpe establishes Addison as Coleridge's precursor.

[132] " Collins's *Ode on the Poetical Character*—that part of it, I should say, beginning with ' The band, as faery legends say, Was wove on that creating

As Coleridge knew very well, an essentially transcendental view of creative imagination had been expressed by Watts, Dennis, Aaron Hill, Young, Akenside, Byrom, and Collins. More than most of his contemporaries, however, Coleridge was equipped to interpret the eighteenth-century cult of genius in the light of Neoplatonic and other more or less mystical ideas which had fertilized its roots . . . When he thought of creative genius, he thought of Spinoza's *amor intellectualis*, of Plotinus' association of the divine Nous with the mind of man, and of Boehme's identification of imagination with a godlike creative will.[133]

As the eighteenth century advanced, there was an increasing reaction against neo-classical reason in favor of intuition and imagination. Vitalism gained ground in parallel advance in England and in Germany. Herder's conception of spiritual power as the basic principle of physical nature contributed to the theory of imagination; it is possible that Coleridge learned from him his fundamental principle of organic unity. The poet, it was believed, wrote in a spirit of cooperation with nature, in a mode analogous to natural processes, as the sap rises in the trees.

Margaret Sherwood, interpreting Herder's *Fragmente* (1766-67), says that:

To Herder, more than to any other single thinker, we owe those conceptions whereby the life of man . . . as expressing itself in language, in literature, in myth, in religion, is interpreted, not through rationalistic conceptions . . . , but in terms of life, of growth, development . . . In the ceaseless working of nature as we observe it in leaf and flower we discern the very laws that govern the productive powers of man . . . Here is the key to Herder's whole life work.[134]

---

day ' has inspired and whirled *me* along with greater agitations of enthusiasm than any the most impassioned scene in Schiller or Shakespeare."—*Letters*, 196.

[133] Fairchild, *Religious Trends in English Poetry*, III, 295.

[134] *Undercurrents of Influence in English Romantic Poetry* (Cambridge, Mass., 1934), 124-25.

The same author observes, " His conception of one life throughout the universe, animated by indwelling spirit, is in striking
contrast to Holbach's view in his *System of Nature* (1770),
that nothing exists save matter and motion." [135] Herder's organic
vitalism may have left its mark on Coleridge's thinking on imagination, or, on the other hand, may simply be symptomatic of
the intellectual climate in which Coleridge, too, was living.
Herder's influence on Coleridge should not be overestimated,
for, on the whole, he had a low opinion of Herder as a thinker.[136]

The current vitalism is seen strikingly in Edward Young's
Conjectures on Original Composition (1759). "An Original,"
writes Young, "may be said to be of a vegetable nature; it rises
spontaneously from the vital root of genius; it grows, it is not
made: Imitations are often a sort of manufacture wrought up
by those mechanics, art and labour, out of preëxistent materials
not their own." [137] And he adds, " There is something in poetry
beyond prose-reason; there are mysteries in it not to be explained." [138] Men have dormant, unsuspected abilities and
writers sometimes surprise themselves with powers of which
they were unaware.[139] In this passage Young trembles on the
brink of the unconscious; he almost, but not quite, has that idea.

Another vitalist was Abraham Tucker, concerning whose
Light of Nature Pursued, Coleridge and Hazlitt were both, as
we have seen, much interested. Tucker had the usual associationist psychology, but he grafted some new ideas upon the old
stock. He made a sharp distinction between the mind as patient
and the mind as agent, though he admitted that the mind (as in

[135] *Ibid.*, 133.

[136] See G. A. Wells, " Man and Nature: an Elucidation of Coleridge's
Rejection of Herder's Thought," *The Journal of English and Germanic
Philology*, LI (July, 1952).

[137] " Conjectures on Original Composition," in *Criticism: The Foundations
of Modern Literary Judgment*, ed. Mark Schorer *et al.* (New York, 1948), 13.

[138] *Ibid.*, 16.   [139] *Ibid.*, 20.

Aristotle's *reminiscentia* or deliberate recall) could be both agent and patient in the same act.[140] The mind is passive in perception and in reverie. "I think," Tucker observes, "we may look upon the passivity of understanding as fully established. But active power alone, says Mr. Locke, is properly power . . ." [141] Creative power in which the mind exerts itself is something more than passivity. Tucker is extremely critical of Hartley for regarding the mind only or chiefly as a passive receiver of impressions. But Tucker's chief claim to originality and to importance is that he regarded the fusion or melting of ideas together as producing a compound of new and unique quality, just as hydrogen and oxygen in forming the compound water lose the separate properties of hydrogen and oxygen.[142] In much the same way, as Bate observes, "the Gestalt or 'configurationist' psychology emphasizes the new and irreducible unity of any 'pattern' of phenomena." [143] The imagination functioned in producing new and organic wholes.

It is very possible that Tucker influenced several of Coleridge's statements on imagination in *Biographia*, especially in those passages where Coleridge is speaking of the cooperation between active and passive powers, for Tucker's thinking is particularly clear and incisive on this point. He regards the mind as a unity which cannot operate successfully without cooperation between active and passive. He, in the traditional manner, reserves imagination as the name for the passive or absorbing powers of the mind; and, in a most interesting passage, where he brings Plato's fable of the chariot up to date, regards imagination (the horse) as inferior to reason (the rider). Reason, however, must provide a gentle and intelligent guidance, for it can get nowhere without the strength of the horse. "Man," says Tucker, "has

[140] *The Light of Nature Pursued* (2 vols.; London, 1852), I, 14.
[141] *Ibid.*, I, 17.
[142] *Ibid.*, I, 127-28.   [143] *From Classic to Romantic*, 120.

been incompletely defined a rational animal; he is rather, to use Mr. Woolaston's words, sensitivo-rational, therefore must regard both parts of his constitution; for one can do nothing without the other." [144]

Tucker here shows a singularly modern and sensible approach. His view of the mind is well balanced. To be sure the mind has extraordinary and frequently untapped resources. It has a maze of associations, and the manner in which these associations are interwoven and the number of possible combinations is mathematically almost "infinite." Nevertheless, little will result from all this, unless the active, creative power of the mind exert itself. Unless the diver dives after them, the pearls will remain in the oysters and the oysters remain on the ocean floor.

The vitalistic climate of the late eighteenth century is illustrated in a very interesting way in Maurice Morgann's provocative essay on Sir John Falstaff. Shakespeare is credited, in his power of creating character, with "a comprehensive energy of mind." [145] The characters he creates are organic wholes, and Shakespeare knows intuitively what influences a given nature or personality will most freely absorb or imbibe.[146] There is nothing whatever mechanical or stamped from outside in Shakespeare's character creations; Shakespeare *worked from within*:

> It was not enough for Shakespeare to have formed his characters with the most perfect truth and coherence; it was further necessary that he should possess a wonderful facility of compressing, as it were, his own spirit into these images . . . This was not to be done from *without*; he must have *felt* every varied situation, and have spoken thro' the organ he had formed. Such an intuitive comprehension of things and such a facility, must unite to produce a Shakespeare.[147]

---

[144] Tucker, *The Light of Nature Pursued*, I, 202.
[145] *Essay on the Dramatic Character of Sir John Falstaff*, 1777, ed. William A. Gill (London, 1912), 58n.
[146] *Ibid.*, 59-60n.   [147] *Ibid.*, 61n.

Shakespeare, Morgann adds, is "an author whose mimic creation agrees in general . . . perfectly with that of nature."[148] Not only are Shakespeare's characters natural, i. e. resembling human nature, but his method of creating character is a process resembling organic growth, or process of getting inside the organism and growing with it, of being it, suffering with it, knowing where its shoe pinches, a total immersion in it from birth.

Morgann assigns to creative imagination a *je ne sais quoi*, a something mysterious, certainly not explicable in mechanical terms:

> Poetry delights in surprize, conceals her steps, seizes at once upon the heart, and obtains the sublime of things without betraying the rounds of her ascent; True Poesy is *magic*, not *nature*; an effect from causes hidden and unknown. To the Magician I prescribed no laws; his law and his power are one; his power is his law. Him, who neither imitates, nor is within the reach of imitation, no precedent can or ought to bind, no limits to contain.[149]

So great was the prevalence of vitalism that even a member of the "mechanist" or associationist school, like Gerard, has to concede an organic power to imagination:

> To collect the materials, and to order and apply them, are not to genius distinct and successive works. This faculty bears a greater resemblance to *nature* in its operations, than to the less perfect energies of art. When a vegetable draws its moisture from the earth, nature by the same action by which it draws it in, and at the same time, converts it to the nourishment of the plant; it at once circulates through its vessels, and is assimilated to its several parts. In like manner, genius arranges its ideas by the same operation, and almost at the same time, that it collects them.[150]

To be sure, Gerard is here talking about the assimilative rather than the creative power of genius, but he writes of it in vitalistic terms.

[148] *Ibid.*, 61-2.   [149] *Ibid.*, 71.   [150] *An Essay on Genius*, 63-4.

As Professor Louis I. Bredvold has shown,[151] a vein of Platonism runs through the eighteenth century, and is especially to be found in the theory of the creation of the ideal and universal, rather than the atypical and particular, which Sir Joshua Reynolds held up as a goal before the students in his *Discourses*. The goal he holds before them is, in part, pure classicism, but as regards classicism and romanticism, Sir Joshua is Janus-faced, looking both ways, and holding the scales even in a balance of compromise. It is interesting to notice the change as his *Discourses* continue; as the century wore on, he came more and more to prefer genius to talent, Michelangelo to Rafael, and imagination to Cartesian reason. He confessed at last to a preference for imaginative force over the merely graceful.

His Platonism may be noticed in his Ninth Discourse, in which he tells his students that

> the Art which we profess has beauty for its object; this is our business to discover and express; the beauty of which we are in quest is general and intellectual; it is an idea that subsists only in the mind; the sight never beheld it, nor has the hand expressed it; it is an idea residing in the breast of the artist, which he is always labouring to impart, and which he dies at last without imparting.[152]

Sir Joshua did not believe that meticulous copying or playing the sedulous ape were sufficient. The young painter who should go to Italy

> and spend his whole time there in copying pictures, and measuring statues or buildings (though these things are not to be neglected), would return with little improvement. He that imitates the Iliad,

---

[151] "The Tendency toward Platonism in Neo-Classical Esthetics," *ELH: A Journal of English Literary History*, I (1934).

[152] Longinus *On the Sublime* and *Sir Joshua Reynolds Discourses on Art* with an Introduction by Elder Olson (Chicago, 1945), 239. Hereafter referred to as *Reynolds' Discourses*.

says Dr. Young, is not imitating Homer. It is not by laying up in
the memory the particular details of any of the great works of
art, that any man becomes a great artist, if he stops without
making himself master of the general principles on which these
works are conducted.[153]

Nor did Sir Joshua believe that much study plus a happy
readiness of association would automatically produce masterpieces
of art. The following of art required "the painter's entire
mind." [154] The artist must not avoid what Rossetti once called
"fundamental brainwork." As Reynolds shrewdly observed,

> a process of endless apparatus, a bustle of infinite inquiry and
> research, or even the mere mechanical labour of copying, may be
> employed to evade and shuffle off real labour—the real labour of
> thinking.[155]

Reynolds's remarks on this subject of would-be artists who spend
their lives "in planning methods of study without ever beginning " [156] calls to mind some lines from Auden's sonnet "The
Preparations " from his sonnet sequence known as "The Quest":

> All had been ordered weeks before the start
> From the best firms at such work; instruments
> To take the measure of all queer events,
> And drugs to move the bowels or the heart.
>
> A watch, of course, to watch impatience fly,
> Lamps for the dark and shades against the sun;
> Foreboding, too, insisted on a gun
> And colored beads to soothe a savage eye.
>
> In theory they were sound on Expectation
> Had there been situations to be in;
> Unluckily they were their situation.[157]

Reynolds so far accepted the contemporary associationist psychology that he believed the mind tends to become like that

---

[153] *Ibid.*, 270.   [154] *Ibid.*, 269.   [155] *Ibid.*   [156] *Ibid.*, 274-5.
[157] *The Collected Poetry of W. H. Auden* (New York, 1945), 251.

which it habitually contemplates, as the dyer's hand is subdued to what it works in; the mind that habitually contemplates the vast and sublime, expands to the sublime; the mind that habitually concerns itself with the picayune and petty, contracts to the petty. It therefore becomes the duty of the artist who wishes the health of his imagination (as Addison, too, insisted) to employ the associative process to his advantage, rather than being a slave to its alliance with chance and fashion.[158] The recognition of imagination as a sovereignly creative and synthesizing power was implicit, as Miss Kennedy says, in his understanding of the creative imagination of Michelangelo.[159]

Reynolds arrived finally in one of his last discourses (the thirteenth, delivered in 1786) at a view of the imagination as an intuitive power, and it is here that he touches hands with the romantics and with Coleridge:

> I observe as a fundamental ground common to all the arts . . . that they address themselves only to two faculties of the mind, its imagination and its sensibility.
>
> All theories which attempt to direct or to control the art upon any principles falsely called rational, which we form to ourselves upon a supposition of what ought in reason to be the end or means of art, independent of the known first effect produced by objects on the imagination, must be false and delusive. For though it may appear bold to say it, the imagination is here the residence of truth . . .
>
> There is in the commerce of life, as in art, a sagacity which is far from being contradictory to right reason, and is superior to any occasional exercise of that faculty; which supersedes it; and does not wait for the slow progress of deduction, but goes at once, by what appears a kind of intuition, to the conclusion.[160]

More interesting still, Reynolds arrived at the theory of a reservoir or pool of intuitive perception, "the result of the

[158] W. J. Bate, *From Classic to Romantic*, 90; *Reynolds' Discourses*, 305.
[159] Wilma L. Kennedy, *The English Heritage of Coleridge of Bristol*, 90.
[160] *Reynolds' Discourses*, 292-3.

accumulated experience of our whole life " [161] and this " habitual reason," of which he speaks, was taken over by Coleridge, who credited " myriad-minded " Shakespeare with this reservoir or fund of insight. " A man endowed," said Reynolds,

> with this faculty [of intuition] feels and acknowledges the truth, though it is not always in his power, perhaps, to give the reason for it; because he cannot recollect and bring before him all the materials that gave birth to his opinion; for very many and very intricate considerations may unite to form the principle . . .
>
> This impression is the result of the accumulated experience of our whole life, and has been collected, we do not always know how, or when. But this mass of collective observation, however acquired, ought to prevail over that reason which, however powerfully exerted on any particular occasion, will probably comprehend but a partial view of the subject; and our conduct in life as well as in the arts is, or ought to be, generally governed by this habitual reason: it is our happiness that we are enabled to draw on such funds. If we were obliged to enter into a theoretical deliberation on every occasion before we act, life would be at a stand, and art would be impracticable.[162]

Blake's violent reaction to Reynolds as the prince of academic stuffed shirts is well known; probably it is to be explained as a clash of personalities, the reaction of a fiery temperament at a cool academician. For Blake, in his marginalia to Reynolds' *Discourses*,[163] wrote, " This Man was Hired to Depress Art." Coleridge and Wordsworth reacted in a very different manner. The former praised Reynolds as an " artist, whose writings are

[161] *Ibid.*, 293.

[162] *Ibid.* Reynolds's view here quoted anticipates modern thinking on the subject of the superiority of the funded wisdom of the mind in its deeper, quieter levels, or in dreams, opposed to the flashy opportunism of the waking intelligence, distracted or frustrated by noise, telephone calls, interruptions, or the *ad absurdum* reduction of everything to unlimited silliness, which seems to be the aim, an aim quite completely achieved by certain programs on television.

[163] Edition, London, 1798.

scarcely less valuable than his works," [164] and Wordsworth re-
spectfully cited him by name in the advertisement to the *Lyrical
Ballads* of 1798, to the effect that an accurate taste in poetry,
like the city of Rome, was not formed in a day. It is not fanciful,
therefore, to suggest that Reynolds's view of imagination as an
immediacy of intuitive insight, drawing to itself "the accumulated experience of our whole life," could, among many other
influences, have helped to form Coleridge's theory.

In fact, the theory of instinctual reservoir and the steady
possession of insight, is found, much as Reynolds stated it, both
in Wordsworth and Coleridge. Wordsworth believed that the
absorbed experiences of a lifetime are turned over and over in
the mind, and examined in a sort of meditative chewing of the
cud. Art of any excellence, he said, is produced only

> by a man who, being possessed of more than usual organic sensi-
> bility, had also thought long and deeply. For our continued influxes
> of feeling are modified and directed by our thoughts, which are
> indeed the representatives of all our past feelings.[165]

The interaction of thought and feeling (feeling the recipience
of sensation and thought the philosophic mulling over the meaning of the received percipience) produces the fund of instinctual
wisdom. Keats, too, perhaps, had something of the same thought
in mind when he observed "the innumerable compositions and
decompositions which take place between the intellect and its
thousand materials before it arrives at that trembling, delicate,
and snail-horn perception of beauty." [166] Coleridge, certainly,
affirmed that Shakespeare

> no mere child of nature; no automaton of genius; no passive
> vehicle of inspiration . . . first studied patiently, meditated deeply,

---

[164] *Biographia*, II, 26.

[165] Preface to *Lyrical Ballads* (1800), *loc. cit.*, 202.

[166] *Letters*, ed. M. B. Forman (London, 1935), 129.

understood minutely, till knowledge, become habitual and intuitive, wedded itself to his habitual feelings, and at length gave birth to that stupendous power, by which he stands alone . . .[167]

iii

Coleridge's Attack on the Mechanists

It was from this platform, then, with this formidable body of philosophical opinion behind him, ranging from Platonism to the vitalism of the late eighteenth century, that Coleridge mounted his guns against the mechanists.

Every serious student of Coleridge soon becomes aware of his hostility to the mechanistic psychology and to the materialistic or matter-and-motion theory of the universe of which it formed a part. But the extent and depth of that hostility do not become apparent until the whole corpus of Coleridge's published work is examined; when the evidence is all in, when the poems, the letters, *The Watchman, The Friend, Biographia, The Statesman's Manual*, the MS. Logic, the *Aids to Reflection*, the *Shakespearean Lectures*, the *Philosophical Lectures* are sifted, it is extraordinary how all this sizable body of work is unified by that hostility and how large a percentage of Coleridge's total output and energy as a writer is directed to that lifelong campaign.

Obviously, so powerful a motive could have a bearing on the manner in which Coleridge defined the imagination, the more so, since mechanistic psychology and associationism were nearly synonymous terms.

Coleridge admired Descartes with distinct reservations. He liked Cartesian rationalism and the Augustinian intuition, for here he was on familiar ground; he specifically says that he

---

[167] *Biographia*, II, 19-20.

welcomed the "*Cogito quia sum, et sum quia Cogito.*" [168] He had the penetration to realize that the Cartesian skepticism was methodological, that its ultimate purpose was not negative but constructive. "This purification of the mind," he realized, "is effected by an absolute and scientific scepticism, to which the mind voluntarily determines itself for the specific purpose of future certainty." [169]

In criticism of a philosophic system, he almost invariably went to the heart rather than the periphery. Thus, he does not take issue (which he might well do) with the Cartesian treatment of imagination, but instead pounces for criticism upon the weakest point of the Cartesian system, the treatment of human and animal bodies as machines, and the mathematical-mechanical explanation of life itself.

Surely, Coleridge felt, there are more things in heaven and earth than are dreamed of in the Cartesian system. While he saw the value of abstraction for calculation, he took a position similar to that of a modern poet and critic, John Crowe Ransom in *The World's Body*, that scientific fictions or abstractions, valuable as they are for scientific purposes, are far from being the complete description of reality:

> Let the Mechanic or Corpuscular Scheme, which in its absolute-ness and strict consistency, was first introduced by Des Cartes, be judged by its results. By its fruits shall it be known.
>
> In order to submit the various phenomena of moving bodies to geometrical construction, we are under the necessity of abstract-ing from corporeal substance all its positive properties, and obliged to consider bodies as differing from equal portions of space only by figure and mobility. And as a fiction of science it would be difficult to overvalue this invention. It possesses the same merits in relation to geometry that the atomic theory has in relation to algebraic calculus. But in contempt of common sense, and in

---

[168] *Biographia*, I, 94-95.   [169] *Ibid.*, I, 176-77.

direct opposition to the express declarations of the inspired historian (Gen. i.) and to the tone and spirit of the Scriptures throughout, Des Cartes propounded it as truth of fact: and instead of a world created and filled with productive forces by the almighty *Fiat*, left a lifeless machine whirled about by the dust of its own grinding; as if death could come from the living fountain of life; nothingness and phantom from the plenitude of reality, the absoluteness of creative will.[170]

Not only did Coleridge object to the indiscriminate application of mechanism, but he clearly saw some of the ridiculous consequences of the application of Cartesian mathematicism to problems which it could never solve. In the course of philosophical lectures which he delivered in the spring of 1819 at the Crown and Anchor tavern in the Strand, "a new light," he said

was struck by Harriot and Descartes, with their contemporaries, . . . and the restoration of ancient geometry, aided by the modern invention of algebra, placed the science of mechanics on the philosophic throne. How widely this domination spread, and how long continued, if indeed even now it can be said to have abdicated its pretensions, I need not remind you of. The sublime discoveries Newton taught, with his not less wonderful than fruitful application of the higher mathesis to the movements of the celestial bodies, and to the laws of light, gave almost a religious sanction to the corpuscular system and mechanical theory. It became synonymous with philosophy itself. It was the sole portal at which truth was permitted to enter. The human body itself was treated of as an hydraulic machine, the operations of medicine were solved, and too often directed, partly by gravitation, and the laws of motion, and partly by chemistry which itself, as far as theory was concerned, was but a branch of mechanics, working by imaginary wedges, angles, and spheres. Should you chance to put your hand at any time on *The Principles of Philosophy* by De La Forge, an immediate disciple of Descartes, you may see the phenomena of sleep explained, and the results demonstrated by mathematical

---

[170] *Aids to Reflection*, 313-14.

calculation. In short . . . from the time of Kepler to Newton, and from that to Hartley, not only all things in external nature, but the subtlest mysteries of life and organization, even of the intellect and moral being, were conjured within the range of mathematical formality.[171]

Coleridge did very much less than justice to Hobbes as a thinker. As Miss Kathleen Coburn observes: "Nowhere does Coleridge honour Hobbes with anything like systematic criticism. He . . . usually mentions him to attack him for his materialism, associationism, atheistic tendencies, or his political absolutism."[172]

In a typical passage in *The Friend* Coleridge attacks Hobbes's political philosophy, implying that philosophy is wrong because Hobbes's view of human nature is wrong, the view of man as a machine of passive impressions[173] and savage appetites, whose natural life is "nasty, brutish and short." When Coleridge mentions Hobbes in *Biographia*, it is to ridicule (as we have already seen) "successive particles propagating motion like billiard balls,"[174] to dismiss his system as "exclusively material and mechanical,"[175] and to rob Hobbes of all credit as an originator in the field of association theory, in spite of Hobbes's real originality in linking the associative fancy to the creative power.

Coleridge's attitude to Locke is little more favorable than it was to Hobbes. We find belittling expressions when Locke's name is mentioned in the letter to Poole of 1801; Locke is referred to as the prince of "Little-ists."[176] Coleridge's charge against Locke is similar to that brought against Hobbes, a total

[171] *Philosophical Lectures of S. T. Coleridge*, ed. Coburn, 341-42.

[172] *Ibid.*, 456.

[173] "The human mind consists of nothing but manifold modifications of passive sensation" is Coleridge's representation of Hobbes's psychology, *The Friend* (3 vols.; London, 1818), I, 283-84.

[174] *Biographia*, I, 71.

[175] *Ibid.*, I, 68.

[176] *Letters*, I, 351. For Coleridge's opinion of Locke, see also Mrs. Sanford, *Thomas Poole and his Friends* (2 vols.; London, 1898), II, 31n.

lack of originality. He claims that he has systematically compared Locke, point by point, with Descartes and that all of
Locke is to be found in Descartes in a much more pure and
elegant form.[177]

The real point of Coleridge's vexation with the mechanist
psychology was the passivity of the mind in this system. In a
letter to Poole (March 23, 1801) he wrote:

> The more I understand of Sir Isaac Newton's works, the more
> boldly I dare utter to my own mind, and therefore to *you*, that
> I believe the souls of five hundred Isaac Newtons would go to the
> making up of a Shakespeare or a Milton. . . . Newton was a mere
> materialist. Mind, in his system, is always *passive*—a lazy Looker-
> on on an external world. If the mind be not passive, if it be
> indeed made in God's image, and that, too, in the sublimest sense,
> the *Image of the Creator*, there is ground for suspicion that any
> system built on the passiveness of the mind must be false, as a
> system.[178]

Later the same year (July 22, 1801), after reading Duns
Scotus in the cathedral library at Durham, Coleridge decided
that "Locke, Hume and Hobbes . . . stink worse than feather
or assafoetida." [179]

One of the best loci for Coleridge's hostility to Locke's sen-
sationalism is the letter which Coleridge wrote to Wordsworth
in 1815, explaining with rather tactless insistence why *The
Excursion* failed to measure up to his expectations. Coleridge
wrote the letter from Calne, in Wiltshire, where he was composing *Biographia*, and the letter belongs therefore to that period
in the history of Coleridge's mind when the final definition of
imagination was being arrived at and represents his mature
thought. Coleridge had hoped that Wordsworth would follow

[177] *Letters*, I, 351; *Philosophical Lectures of S. T. Coleridge*, ed. Coburn,
375-76; *Collected Letters*, II, 380-84.
[178] *Letters*, I, 351-52   [179] *Ibid.*, 358.

the *Prelude* with the great philosophical poem of the age. This philosophical poem—Coleridge was still nursing the dream of 1801, that of deriving all the senses from one Sense—was to be the final refutation of Locke and the mechanical school:

> I supposed you first to have meditated the faculties of man in the abstract, in their correspondence with his sphere of action, and, first in the feeling, touch, and taste, then in the eye, and last in the ear—to have laid a solid and immovable foundation for the edifice by removing the sandy sophisms of Locke, and the mechanic dogmatists, and demonstrating that the senses were living growths and developments of the mind and spirit, in a much juster as well as higher sense, than the mind can be said to be formed by the senses.[180]

He hoped, too, that Wordsworth would convince people of

> the necessity of a general revolution in the modes of disciplining the human mind by the substitution of life and intelligence . . . for the philosophy of mechanism, which, in everything that is most worthy of the human intellect, strikes *Death*, and cheats itself by mistaking clear images for distinct conceptions, and which idly demands conceptions where intuitions alone are possible or adequate to the majesty of the Truth.[181]

Coleridge's attitude to Hume was one of respectful disagreement. Miss Coburn assures us that " Coleridge admired Hume as having an acute and logical mind, and often defended him against misunderstanding." [182] The ground of his objection to Hume was the same as the ground of his objection to Locke; Hume made the mind as passive as the bed of a river under the constant flow of impressions and ideas (ideas being defined as fainter impressions). It is doubtful whether Coleridge appreciated the keen edge of Hume's scepticism, for he usually treats Hume as a superficial empiricist, not seeing, apparently, that

---

[180] *Letters*, II, 648.   [181] *Ibid.*, 649.
[182] *Philosophical Lectures of S. T. Coleridge*, ed. Coburn, 414.

the depth of Hume's scepticism took him much further than a superficial empiricism. In any case, the ground of their disagreement was fundamental. As the philosopher A. N. Whitehead has observed, " Hume's flux of impressions and of reactions to impressions, each impression a distinct, self-sufficient existence, was very different from the Platonic soul." [183] Very different, indeed.

It is very noticeable in Coleridge's *Philosophical Lectures* that an auditor who went to them in good faith to learn about philosophy would get a dim view and an entirely inadequate exposition of the ideas of Hobbes, Locke, and Hume, whereas, concerning the philosophers with whom Coleridge was in sympathy, namely Leibniz and Kant, he would receive brief but informative and illuminating expositions of some of their leading ideas.

If Hume did not please Coleridge, the French physiological psychologists pleased him even less. Though he respected Descartes for his innate ideas, Coleridge thought him dangerous in tendency. "Descartes was the first man who made nature utterly lifeless and godless, considered it as the subject of merely mechanical laws." [184] To be sure, there was a foundation for his uneasiness, since the followers of Descartes in France took the physiological half of his dualism (including a theory of association based on nervous traces in the brain) and ignored the rest. Coleridge could hardly be expected to like the mechanical associationism of Condillac, who, like Locke, derived all knowledge from association. Nor would he like the *L'Homme Machine* of de la Mettrie or D'Holbach's *System of Nature* any better. Possibly he did not know these writers any too intimately, but was content to lump them all together in a general condemnation.

[183] *Adventures of Ideas* (New York, 1935), 36.
[184] *Philosophical Lectures of S. T. Coleridge*, ed. Coburn, pp. 376-77.

The pages of *The Friend* are sometimes disfigured by violent prejudice against the French. We have in mind one particular passage about "the teeth of the old serpent planted by the Cadmuses of French Literature under Louis XV" [185] which sprang up in the sanguinary crop of follies of the French Revolution. The godless *philosophes* and Encyclopedists were, according to Coleridge, directly responsible for the mischief.

It was for Hartley, however, rather than for Hobbes, Locke, Hume and the French materialistic psychologists, that Coleridge reserved his major effort at refutation. To many *Biographia* is a wandering and confusing book, loosely organized about Coleridge's exposition of the growth of his theory of imagination. But if it has another subject, of major importance, about which it is unified, it is Coleridge's attack on the materialistic position, with its entrenchment in the senses. It may be wondered why Hartley received the brunt of the attack in Chapters V, VI and VII (of *Biographia*). The reason was that at the time Coleridge was writing, Hartley largely dominated the current and fashionable psychology.

The root of Coleridge's objection to Hartley is that in his system the mind is largely passive, subjected to impressions and the single law of association, operating automatically without intervention of the will. From his system

> results inevitably, that the will, the reason, the judgment, and the understanding, instead of being the determining causes of association, must needs be represented as its *creatures*, and among its mechanical effects. Conceive, for instance, a broad stream, winding through a mountainous country with an indefinite number of currents, varying and running into each other according as the gusts chance to blow from the opening of the mountains. The temporary union of several currents in one, so as to form the

---

[185] *The Friend*, I, 69-70. And see the powerful passage condemning the Encyclopedists, *Statesman's Manual* (London, 1818), Appendix C, xvi. Voltaire, D'Alembert, Diderot are there mentioned by name.

main current of the moment, would present an accurate image of Hartley's theory of the will.

Had this been really the case, the consequence would have been, that our whole life would be divided between the despotism of outward impressions, and that of the senseless and passive memory.[186]

Coleridge having, as we have said again and again, a vitalistic, activist and dynamic conception of the mind, is forever fighting the passivity of will and imagination in Hartley's system. He comments once more

on that subordination of final to efficient causes in the human being, which flows of necessity from the assumption, that the will, and with the will, all acts of thought and attention are parts and products of this blind mechanism, instead of being distinct powers, whose function it is to control, determine, and modify the phantasmal chaos of association.[189]

Coleridge, then, in a parting shot at the mechanists, pours unlimited scorn upon

the proselytes of that compendious philosophy, which talking of mind but thinking of brick and mortar, or other images equally abstracted from body, contrives a theory of spirit by nicknaming matter, and in a few hours can qualify its dullest disciples to explain the *omne scibile* by reducing all things to impressions, ideas, and sensations.[188]

With this last thrust at Hume and Hartley, we leave Coleridge's polemic in *Biographia*. We cannot say that Coleridge rejected Hartley ignorantly. He did so knowingly. He understood Hartley's system. We sense the fact all along that the deepest of Coleridge's objections to the mechanistic philosophy is theological. As R. L. Brett has said: " He abandoned Hartley, not only because associationism tried to turn the human mind

---

[186] *Biographia*, I, 76-77.   [187] *Ibid.*, I, 81.   [188] *Ibid.*, I, 163.

into a machine, but because it was based on a philosophy which tried to turn the whole universe into a machine." [189]

Mechanism has had its day. We no longer share the cocksureness of the mechanists, nor do we share their faith in the unlimited predictability of their mechanical universe. We live in the age of Heisenberg's uncertainty principle. Coleridge's objections to the view of mind as machine passively obedient to mechanical stimuli (a view that now appears somewhat crude) have in the main been sustained. I. A. Richards, for example, remarks: "There can be little doubt, in the light of subsequent developments, that Coleridge as against Associationism of the Hartley-Condillac type was right all along the line." [190] Hume's concepts of the mind, which Coleridge attacked, are under criticism today.[191]

Coleridge, however, took a much higher ground than modern critics are apt to do. We can see what kind of insight he was hoping would supply the place of the mechanistic philosophy in a great passage on the philosophic imagination or spiritual intuition:

> They and they only can acquire the philosophic imagination, the sacred power of self-intuition, who within themselves can interpret and understand the symbol, that the wings of the air-sylph are forming within the skin of the caterpillar; those only, who feel in their own spirits the same instinct, which compels the chrysalis of the horned fly to leave room in its involucrum for antennae yet to come. They know and feel, that the potential works in them, even as the actual works on them! In short, all the organs of sense are framed for a corresponding world of sense; and we have

---

[189] R. L. Brett, "Coleridge's Theory of the Imagination," *loc. cit.*, p. 80.
[190] I. A. Richards, *Coleridge on Imagination*, 67.
[191] See for instance Jean-Paul Sartre's acute criticism of Hume's mental images and faded impressions, *The Psychology of Imagination* (New York, 1948).

it. All the organs of spirit are framed for a correspondent world of spirit: though the latter organs are not developed in all alike.[192]

He implies here that the human eye developed as it grew sensitized to light; it is inconceivable that the human eye would have developed without light or a visual world. Just so, there exist universals and symbols and spiritual realities, and there is a corresponding organ or eye of the mind which can become increasingly sensitized to or aware of them.

The majority of men interested in hog-breeding or the World Series stay well on the near or Cisalpine side of the Alps. Coleridge implies that the materialistic philosophers of his day, though no doubt able men, had the organ of non-materialistic vision or insight very rudimentarily developed. In our own time we can produce the names of men—Paul Valéry, T. S. Eliot, Thomas Mann, Rainer Maria Rilke, W. B. Yeats and some others in whom sensitization and development of the organ of vision has proceeded very far. They are in Coleridge's sense, Transalpine men. Their view is not bounded by the immediate valley in which they were born.

Coleridge believed that the empiricists wore blinkers. To put the matter in his own words: " The eye is not more inappropriate to sound, than the mere understanding to the modes and laws of spiritual existence." [193] The modern mind, he wrote in *The Statesman's Manual*, " has become infected with the contagion of its mechanic philosophy." Comparing the kind of history written by Hume with the living imaginative history recorded in the Bible, he contrasts " the product of an unenlivened generalizing Understanding " with " the living *educts* of the Imagination " in the Scriptures.

This is one of the most inspired of Coleridge's utterances; it is a theory of the symbolic imagination the very reverse of the associative imagination of the eighteenth century.

[192] *Biographia*, I, 167.   [193] *Statesman's Manual*, Appendix C, xi.

The same work contains one of the clearest of Coleridge's statements of the difference between the mechanic and vital philosophies. He objects to the reduction of mental as well as physical phenomena to the collision or sterile clicking of atoms, particles or billiard balls:

> The leading differences between mechanic and vital philosophy may all be drawn from one point: namely, that the former, demanding for every mode and act of existence real or possible *visibility*, knows only of distance and nearness, composition (or rather juxtaposition) and decomposition, in short the relations of unproductive particles to each other; so that in every instance the result is the exact sum of the component quantities, as in arithmetical addition. This is the philosophy of death, and only of a dead nature can it hold good. In life, much more in spirit, and in a living and spiritual philosophy, the two component counterpowers actually interpenetrate each other, and generate a higher third, including both the former, *ita tamen ut sit alia et major*.[194]

Here, Coleridge reveals himself to be, both by temperament and conviction a vitalist of the school of Herder and Abraham Tucker.

He continued sniping at the mechanists in *Aids to Reflection*, the most influential of his writings in the nineteenth century. The point need not be labored any longer. Coleridge was a vitalist and the grounds of his objection to mechanism have been made clear.

A good deal of ink has been wasted in pitying " poor Coleridge " for powers dissipated by opium, and we admit that the picture of Coleridge's life is on the whole neither a tidy nor a pretty one. But the attitude that he was a feckless figure who frittered away his best energies, masochistically destroying his

---

[194] *Ibid.*, Appendix C, xxvii. He means that thesis and antithesis, having had fruitful conjugal relations, merge in a higher synthesis. This type of thinking which penetrates the philosophies of Fichte, Schelling, and Hegel is a favorite with Coleridge.

creative gifts in the unwholesome mines of metaphysics, the sense of unsatisfactoriness that always clings like an unwanted smell to his name, typified in the remark of T. S. Eliot, "the sad ghost of Coleridge beckons to me from the shadows" [195] is an attitude that could well be spared. It is not necessary to be pitying or condescending toward the man who, up to his time, was the greatest critic in English. When we discover the extent and the seriousness of his lifelong crusade against the mechanical philosophy, we find his energies were effectively directed and this concentration of energy lends dignity to his life.

For the campaign was effective. It was not an outpouring of wholly unheeded words. He changed the current of a mind like that of John Stuart Mill, brought up in the mental atmosphere of the utilitarian-associational school. His vital reconciliation between Trinitarian Christianity and Neo-Platonic thought influenced the Broad Church Movement.[196] But chiefly his vitalistic thinking about imagination has had incalculable influence on the theory of the subject since his time.

An element of exaggeration, of parody or caricature, exists in Coleridge's picture of the "mechanistic" psychology. "Mechanistic" is, at best, a rather crude label to apply to any psychology that deals at all adequately with the receptive and creative powers of mind. The "mechanists" were shrewd men; there is much more subtlety and vital quality in their account of the mind than Coleridge allows. Nor was the mind as wholly passive with them as Coleridge implies. There is the great passage on invention in Hobbes's Letter to D'Avenant; neither Hume nor Hartley represent the mind entirely inert and uncreative. But the degree of Coleridge's accuracy is not the point

[195] *The Use of Poetry and the Use of Criticism.* The comment with which Eliot ends the book.

[196] For this see C. R. Sanders, *Coleridge and the Broad Church Movement* (Durham, N. C., 1942).

in the present discussion; the point is that Coleridge had a definite *animus* against the mechanists. Moreover, association of ideas was linked in his mind with the mechanistic psychology that he detested.

We can say at this point that Coleridge was committed, when he came to define imagination; committed, first, to an organic or vitalistic view of it; secondly, to a numinous or inspired view of it, since any definition of it that he would give would be part of a Transcendental world view. How he fitted association of ideas into his definition is a question to be answered in the following chapter.

4

THE POLAR

IMAGINATION

i

Coleridge in 1815

Let us now survey how far Coleridge had come in his thinking about imagination, about the year 1815, on the eve of his writing the culminating definition of the imagination in *Biographia*. He felt he had learned from Wordsworth what manly and genuine poetry was, and had been struck, on first hearing Wordsworth recite his poetry, with " the fine balance of truth in observing, with the imaginative faculty in modifying the objects observed." [1] He had learned to distinguish between imagination and fancy. The operation of fancy was like that of a shunting engine in a freight yard; it could combine flat-cars with oil-tankers, could couple and uncouple; could shunt cars in numerous combinations, but it could not create anything that was not already there, on the rails of memory. Certain cars, too, came automatically coupled, articulated by the coupling links of asso-

[1] *Biographia*, I, 59.

ciation. But imagination was a power that did more than combine; it modified and transformed. The creations of imagination seemed to come from some inward depth of the being, they had a way of growing, rather than being put together, and they had a freshness and a dew upon them.

From Kant he had learned the discipline of exact definition. He had discovered in Kant a masterly psychology in which the mind was active, to replace the associationism of Hartley. From Schelling he had learned that imagination is a unifying power, uniting subject and object in the burning glass of consciousness; probably from Herder, and almost certainly from A. W. Schlegel, he had acquired the concept of a work of art being an organic unity, and the process of its creation an organic process. Quite a complex theory of imagination could be built out of these several pieces which fit well enough together. Yet the deepest sources of Coleridge's theory of imagination are, in the above statement, still missing.

The sources are twofold. The deepest source of a metaphysical kind is the debt to antiquity, particularly to Plotinus. The deepest source of a living kind is the sense of community with nature which he shared with Wordsworth. These two sources are inextricably interwoven, however, and really amount to one. The experience of writing the "Ancient Mariner," "Kubla Khan," and other poems should be added as inseparably part of the deepest source of Coleridge's theory.

ii

The Famous Distinction between
Imagination and Fancy

It was inevitable, then, Coleridge being Coleridge and his mental history being what it was, that when he came to define imagination, he would do so in a certain way, in keeping with certain deeply-held convictions. To IMAGINATION, which he liked to capitalize, he would give perhaps an exaggerated and transcendent importance, a mystic significance, linked with the forces of fertility, the powers of growth, and Godhead itself. To association, a rather sorry and secondary power, consisting in the automatic and mechanical linking of ideas embedded through the inlets of sensation in the passive memory, he would assign a subordinate place.

The famous definition follows:

The IMAGINATION then, I consider either as primary, or secondary. The primary IMAGINATION I hold to be the living Power and prime Agent of all human Perception, and as a repetition in the finite mind of the eternal act of creation in the infinite I AM. The secondary Imagination I consider as an echo of the former, coexisting with the conscious will, yet still as identical with the primary in the *kind* of its agency, and differing only in *degree*, and in the *mode* of its operation. It dissolves, diffuses, dissipates, in order to recreate; or where this process is rendered impossible, yet still at all events it struggles to idealize and to unify. It is essentially *vital*, even as all objects (as objects) are essentially fixed and dead.

FANCY, on the contrary, has no other counters to play with, but fixities and definites. The Fancy is indeed no other than a mode of Memory emancipated from the order of time and space; while it is blended with, and modified by that empirical phenomenon of the will, which we express by the word CHOICE. But equally with the ordinary memory the Fancy must receive all its materials ready made from the law of association.[2]

Here the distinction is made in all its glaring contrast. Imagination is robed with the lightnings and thunders of Sinai; Fancy sits in the tavern and plays checkers—it " has no other counters to play with, but fixities and definites." The point, however,

[2] *Biographia*, I, 202.

of significance for us is that Coleridge did not let go of Hartley's law of association; he found a place for it as assistant to, almost synonymous with, the fancy. With Coleridge's remark that "Fancy is . . . no more than a mode of Memory emancipated from the order of time and space" we should couple his other, somewhat ungracious, characterization of fancy as "always the ape, and too often the adulterator and counterfeiter of our memory."[3]

{Since we have the two powers thus confronted, it is time to ask, What is the essential difference between them? The essential difference is that imagination modifies the things it combines and that it is a process of living growth.} Thus the gummy buds of a chestnut tree that uncurl their tight fists and open up their fairy candles are a modification as imagination modifies. {Fancy, on the other hand, can combine and recombine, as we do with checkers or dominoes, but the objects it plays with are "fixities and definites" and all objects (as objects) are essentially fixed and dead. Fancy can shake up the counters but not transform them.

I. A. Richards has conveniently brought together all Coleridge's chief points concerning the fancy into a table as follows:

Of Fancy, Coleridge says:

(1) That it is 'the faculty of bringing together images dissimilar in the main by some one point or more of likeness distinguished' (Raysor, I, 212).[4]

(2) That these images are 'fixities and definites' (B. L. I, 202),[5] they remain when put together the same as when apart.

(3) That the images 'have no connexion natural or moral, but are yoked together by the poet by means of some accidental coincidence' (Table Talk, June 23, 1834).

---

[3] Ibid., II, 208.
[4] Coleridge's Shakespearean Criticism, ed. Raysor, I, 212.
[5] Biographia, I, 202.

(4) The activity putting them together is that of choice, which is 'an empirical phenomenon of the will'—that is, *not* the will as a principle of the mind's being, striving to realize itself, *but* an exercise of selection among objects already supplied by association, a selection made for purposes which are not then and therein being shaped but have been already fixed.[6]

Not only does Fancy use choice, but the choice is made in a cool and calculating manner. "The commonest characteristic effect of Fancy is the coolness and disengagement with which we are invited to attend to what is taking place."[7]

I. A. Richards represents a typically modern and psychological approach. A confessed psychological materialist, he has no truck with transcendentalism. He says: "There is nothing peculiarly mysterious about imagination. It is no more marvellous than any other of the ways of the mind. Yet it has so often been treated as an arcanum that we naturally approach it with caution. It is desirable at least to avoid part of the fate which befell Coleridge, and our own account will be devoid of theological implication."[8] Clean as a fishbone picked in whispers, clean as a whistle of all theological implication, comes Richards's theory.

With his usual air of somewhat weary condescension to Coleridge's outmoded theology, Richards explains the primary and secondary imaginations as he understands them:

The Primary Imagination is normal perception that produces the usual world of the senses,

> That inanimate cold world allowed
> To the poor loveless ever-anxious crowd

the world of motor-buses, beef-steaks, and acquaintances, the framework of things and events within which we maintain our everyday existence, the world of the routine satisfaction of our minimum exigences. The Secondary Imagination, re-forming this

---

[6] *Coleridge on Imagination*, 77.   [7] *Ibid.*, 82.
[8] *Principles of Literary Criticism* (New York, 1925), 191.

world, gives us not only poetry—in the limited sense in which literary critics concern themselves with it—but every aspect of the routine world in which it is invested with other values than those for our bare continuance as human beings: all objects for which we can feel love, awe, admiration; every quality beyond the account of physics, chemistry, and the physiology of sense-perception, nutrition, reproduction and locomotion; every awareness for which a civilized life is preferred by us to an uncivilized.[9]

Since Richards himself is such a strict reader of texts, and berates others for loose readings, it is amusing to see that his scientific training actually disqualifies him to read Coleridge's meaning here. Coleridge talks in terms of the cloud-capped mountain and the great I AM, while Richards can see in perception nothing but busses and beefsteaks. The impercipience of Richards is the more remarkable since he has himself pointed the way to the right interpretation by insisting that a comprehension of Plotinus is a clue to the understanding of Coleridge.[10] Close attention to Plotinus's theory of perception would clear up much of the darkness surrounding Coleridge's primary imagination.

Let us now take Coleridge's words, "The primary IMAGINATION I hold to be the living Power and prime Agent of all human Perception, and as a repetition in the finite mind of the eternal act of creation in the infinite I AM." Coleridge could not have meant by this the simple act of seeing, by which, for instance, a crowd of tent-like mountains would be assimilated by the eye, the simple drinking-in of the scene. He was always deprecating the despotism of the eye and the tyranny of the senses. Coleridge's theory of perception was undoubtedly influenced by Plotinus's theory that the mind is *active* and *creative* in perception. Kant probably contributed too. According to Kant what is given as sensation or the sense-manifold is synthesized into

[9] *Coleridge on Imagination*, 58-59.   [10] *Ibid.*, 27.

wholes through the activity of perception. And, as D. G. James says, " it is because the imagination in its prehension of the world dissolves the comparative confusion of sense impressions and effects a synthesis [one could almost say a *Gestalt*], that it may be called, at this 'primary' level, creative." [11] But there is much more to it than that. Perception intuitively organizes the whole, the confused corrugation of mountains, into ideal concepts (like Platonic ideas) of mass, majesty, eternity, beauty, infinity and the like. The mind, in other words, intuits the real forms or the ideas behind the sensuous forms and establishes, in this way, direct contact with the divine. Thus the mind of the poet is creative in perception and, in its lesser degree, participates in the creative power which formed the mountains in the first place, as cloudy symbols or concrete objectifications of itself.

Richards evidently did not connect the definition with the preparatory metaphysical discussion; if he had, he could not have failed to see what Coleridge means by "prime agent of all human perception." It is not a case of "the eye it cannot choose but see," of photographic film or passive impression. Nor is it a case of putting together in an instant of perception double-decker red-painted coach on wheels and recognizing "London bus."(The imagination is *active* in perception) and is indeed the means to that "intimate coalition"—the phrase is Coleridge's—between subject and object. Indeed, Richards himself, in his finer moments, understands Coleridge much better. He says that Coleridge's subject-object nexus "is for him only a device for noting, and insisting, that nothing in which we are in any way conscious is *given* to the mind. Into the simplest seeming 'datum' a constructing, forming activity of the mind

[11] *Skepticism and Poetry: An Essay on Poetic Imagination* (London, 1937), 24. According to one, and as it seems to me, correct explanation, the primary imagination is "Coleridge's name for the act of cognition." Millar, "The Inward Eye," 97.

has entered. And the perceiving and the forming are the same. The subject (the self) has gone into what it perceives, and what it perceives is, in this sense, itself. So the object becomes the subject and the subject the object." [12]

Nature is multiform, and some domestication has to take place before it is assimilable by the human mind; thus the object is transformed. But the subject, gazing on a silver birch, and seeing, as Dorothy Wordsworth did once, that it is " a spirit of water," is, in a way, transformed by the object, and assimilates a certain "birchness" into itself, some of the qualities of papery peeling whiteness of the bark, and some of the airy grace, with which, in spring, the green-laced branches give themselves to the wind. It is not, however, in the quiet absorption that the mind is active in perception; it is in seeing the birch as a "spirit of water" that the imagination is engaged. There is a marriage or fecundation of subject and object at the moment of vision.

To illustrate the subject further, we may say that there is more than one way of looking at a mountain. It would be possible to look at it with a military eye and to see only its contours. It would be possible to look at it aesthetically and empathically, in other words, to receive a lift from the rise of the mountain and a pleasure from its outline and disposition of mass, its organization of form. It would be possible also to look at it numinously, as a seat of majesty and terror. The latter two ways come much nearer to Coleridge's active perception.

Coleridge does not talk in terms of busses and beefsteaks, but he talks in terms like these: "The Mystics . . . define beauty as the subjection of matter to spirit so as to be transformed into a symbol, in and through which the spirit reveals itself." [13] Or, again, "The Beautiful arises from the perceived harmony of an object, whether sight or sound, with the inborn and constitu-

[12] *Coleridge on Imagination*, 56-57.
[13] " On the Principles of Genial Criticism," *Biographia*, II, 239.

tive rules of the judgement and imagination: and it is always intuitive. As light to the eye, even such is beauty to the mind, which cannot but have complacency in whatever is perceived as preconfigured to its living faculties. Hence the Greeks called a beautiful object Καλόν quasi Καλοῦν, i. e. *calling on* the soul, which receives instantly, and welcomes it as something connatural." [14]

(Poe, steeped as he was in the romantic tradition,) made no such mistake as that of I. A. Richards. He perfectly understood Coleridge's meaning, saying simply: ("Imagination is, possibly, in man, a lesser degree of the creative power in God." [15])

The passage in *Biographia* likening the creative or imaginative power in man to a miniature in the microcosmos of the creative power in the macrocosmos was no new idea to Coleridge. He had already spoken of imagination as a " dim analogue of creation." [16] The idea is already implicit in " The Aeolian Harp."

Professor W. J. Bate provides what is, perhaps, to date the most illuminating comment of all. He believes that the " primary " imagination, as defined in the famous passage, is directed to universals, perhaps to disengaging universals from the forms of nature. [17] Confirmation of this interpretation is to be had in Coleridge's known concern with universals, as in his statement, the basis of his Wordsworth criticism: " I adopt with full faith the principle of Aristotle, that poetry as poetry is essentially *ideal*, that it avoids and excludes all *accident* . . ." [18] The poet's eye kindles at the fountains of vision. The force that " through

---

[14] *Ibid.*, II, 243. Coleridge's etymology is open to question.

[15] Poe in a review in the *Southern Literary Messenger*, II, 328, as quoted by Margaret Alterton, " Origins of Poe's Critical Theory," *University of Iowa Humanistic Studies*, Vol. II, No. 3 [n. d.], 104.

[16] Coleridge to Richard Sharp, January 15, 1804. *Letters*, II, 450.

[17] W. J. Bate, " Coleridge on the Function of Art," *Perspectives of Criticism*, ed. Harry Levin (Cambridge, Mass., 1950), 146.

[18] *Biographia*, II, 33.

the green fuse drives the flower" is the same force that through
the green fuse of a fired imagination drives the poet through
the poem. The poet is in alliance with the creative principle
at work in the unfolding of nature. Perception, thus creative
in the primary imagination, has the immediacy of insight of
the reason (νοῦς); it goes straight to the inner principles of
things.

What, then, does Coleridge mean by the "secondary" imagination? What does he mean by calling it the "echo" of the
former? Surely that it, too, when drawing on the inspiration of
the "primary" imagination it creates a poem, is part of the same
divinely creative power, echoed or repeated in man. He specifically says that the secondary imagination is "identical with the
primary in the kind of its agency." [19] Coleridge's two definitions
of the primary and secondary imagination are confusing mainly
because he juxtaposes them as though there were no time interval
between them. Actually, there may be a considerable time
interval, time for the process which Henry James describes:
"I dropped it [my idea] for the time into the deep well of
unconscious cerebration: not without the hope, doubtless, that
it might eventually emerge from that reservoir, as one had
already known the buried treasure to come to light, with a firm
iridescent surface and a notable increase of weight." [20] This
is what occupies the interval between the operation of Coleridge's primary imagination and the activity of the secondary.
Coleridge, indeed, assumes such a transmutation at work in his
threefold "dissolves, diffuses, dissipates in order to recreate."
More probably, however, on account of his dynamic theory of
creation, he is not here referring to the "sea change" or permu-
tation that takes place in the marine or unconscious life of the

[19] *Ibid.*, 202.

[20] *The Art of the Novel: Critical Prefaces by Henry James*, with an introduction by R. P. Blackmur (New York, 1937), 23.

mind; he rather refers to a deliberate reshaping of the material for an artistic purpose, or perhaps to the interaction of the two.

He further says that the secondary imagination "struggles to idealize and unify." In other words, imagination, as it works upon a poem, is essentially a *vital* power that fuses divers materials into one; there is nothing mechanical about this; it is contrasted to fancy or mechanical association, which plays with objects that (as objects) are dead, and are simply joined by a single note of likeness, like dominoes of one spot which are placed next to each other. The dominoes undergo no modification. But imagination modifies; its materials are assimilated and transformed and absorbed as part of a living, vital process. Coleridge's vitalistic theory of imagination is the culmination of the vitalistic reaction to rationalism which, as we have seen, was growing powerful in the late eighteenth century. Basil Willey fears:

> that some readers are misled by the oracular sublimity of Coleridge's definition [21] . . . : 'The primary Imagination,' he declares (in oft-quoted words), 'I hold to be the living Power and prime Agent of all human Perception, and as a repetition in the finite mind of the eternal act of creation in the infinite I AM.' This is not to be dismissed as metaphysical babble; a weight of thought, indeed a whole philosophy, lies beneath each phrase. Coleridge is here summarizing the great struggle and victory of his life—his triumph over the old tradition of Locke and Hartley, which had assumed that the mind in perception was wholly passive, 'a lazy looker-on on an external world.' [22]

When Coleridge's lifelong warfare against the mechanist psychologists is remembered, the force of Willey's assertion will be appreciated.

[21] Cf. Hugh Sykes Davies' remark that Coleridge's "declaration concerning the powers and privileges of the imagination . . . approaches megalomania in its imitation of royal proclamations." *Surrealism*, ed. Herbert Read (London, 1936), 132.

[22] *Nineteenth Century Studies* (New York, 1949), 13-14.

(Imagination is a modifying power. The modification which it induces, however, is not always structural; it has "the original gift of spreading the tone, the *atmosphere*, and with it the height and depth of the ideal world, around forms, incidents and situations, of which, for the common view, custom had bedimmed all the lustre, had dried up the sparkle and the dew drops." [23]) Imagination adds "the sudden charm, which accidents of light and shade, which moonlight or sun-set diffused over a known and familiar landscape." [24]) Imagination, as here understood, seems to be in charge of lighting, rather than in any way changing the substance of prose reality. A landscape seen by plain daylight is prose. The landscape mildly steeped in moonlight is the same landscape, only now the milky light has softened all the outlines, the highlights are antique silver, and the shadows are the subterfuges and secret hiding places of mystery.[25] This view of imagination is peculiarly romantic. It was that kind of imagination in which the romantic poets excelled, almost their trade secret.

It could be objected, of course, that this concern with optics, or with optical illusions, with a spiritual meteorology or "inner weather," with moods and atmospheric effects must lead to an exclusionist kind of poetry, by which a great deal in the objective normal world of men is cut out; moreover, this ideal for poetry accounts for the love of the misty and the infinite. To be sure, to compensate for the exclusion, certain special effects are gained which can be gained in no other way. And Wordsworth, with

[23] *Biographia*, I, 59.   [24] *Ibid.*, II, 5.
[25] This haziness or blurring of the outlines was essential to the effect, for by it was gained a suggestiveness, a sense of the illimitable. Coleridge says the soul ought to reserve deep feelings "for objects which their very sublimity renders indefinite no less than their indefiniteness renders them sublime"—C. M. Bowra, *The Romantic Imagination* (Cambridge, Mass., 1949), 190.

his greater grip on the objective world, was there as counter-
balance to Coleridge.

iii

Fancy: a Comparison of Views

We now come to the difference between Wordsworth's and
Coleridge's assignment of place and function to the associative
power. Coleridge reserved to the imagination all that was creative, all that was shaping, all that created incantation, all that
created magic. The associative power, in his view, was part of
the *vis receptiva*, to use the old schoolmen's phrase which Coleridge himself uses, part of the passive powers of the mind. To
this Coleridge adhered firmly. Nothing, then, brings out more
clearly Coleridge's view of the place of the associative power than
the difference of opinion he had on the subject with Wordsworth.

Coleridge had assumed that Wordsworth and himself, having
talked over the subject together frequently, had similar views.
What was his astonishment, therefore, as he was struggling to
finish *Biographia*, to read in Wordsworth's Preface to his poems
of 1815 opinions on fancy and imagination that differed radically
from his own. Coleridge first notices their difference in these
words:

> The explanation which Mr. Wordsworth has himself given will
> be found to differ from mine, chiefly perhaps, as our objects are
> different . . . It was Mr. Wordsworth's purpose to consider the
> influences of fancy and imagination as they are manifested in
> poetry, and from the different effects to conclude their diversity
> in kind; while it was my object to investigate the seminal prin-
> ciple . . . My friend has drawn a masterly sketch of the branches
> with their poetic fruitage. I wish to add the trunk and even the

roots as far as they lift themselves above ground, and are visible to the naked eye of our common consciousness.[26]

We may well wonder what Coleridge means by investigating the "seminal principle" and by wishing to dig down to the trunk and even the roots. He is saying that Wordsworth is simply producing examples of fancy and of imagination—"by their fruits ye shall know them"—, but that he (Coleridge, wishes to dig deeper, to go into the psychological roots for the distinction between fancy and imagination, finding in the mind a separate faculty for each, fancy belonging to the passive *vis receptiva*, and imagination being the active power.) He felt the distinction to be deep and fundamental. Though he is polite about it, he implies a superficiality in Wordsworth's distinction.

After an enormous gap and sundry digressions, Coleridge, at the point where he is about ready to give his definitions says: "I shall now proceed to the nature and genesis of the imagination; but I must first take leave to notice, that after a more accurate perusal of Mr. Wordsworth's remarks on the imagination, in his preface to the new edition of his poems, I find that my conclusions are not so consentient with his as, I confess, I had taken for granted."[27] Wordsworth, Coleridge reports, argued that

"to aggregate and to associate, to evoke and to combine, belong as well to the imagination as to the fancy." I reply, that if, by the power of evoking and combining, Mr. Wordsworth means the same as, and no more than, I meant by the aggregative and associative, I continue to deny, that it belongs at all to the imagination; and I am disposed to conjecture, that he has mistaken the co-presence of fancy with imagination for the operation of the latter singly. A man may work with two very different tools at the same moment; each has its share in the work, but the work effected by each is distinct and different.[28]

---

[26] *Biographia*, I, 64.   [27] *Ibid.*, 193.   [28] *Ibid.*, I, 194.

Coleridge was defending a principle to him vitally important or he would not thus have publicly disagreed with his friend. We believe that the difference between the two poets is due to the strong eighteenth-century cast of Wordsworth's mind. His mind was grounded in Locke in a way that Coleridge's certainly was not; Hartley was a far more deep and lasting influence on Wordsworth than on Coleridge. Wordsworth preserves Hartley's idea of the " three ages of man " in two of his major poems, "Lines above Tintern Abbey" and the "Immortality Ode." Hartley's idea about the importance of early associations for the child is all-important in the first book of *The Prelude*. And Hartley's theory of association remained permanently with Wordsworth as a major part of his poetics, "how we associate ideas in a state of excitement" being one of his chief concerns. Therefore Wordsworth would see no incongruity in attaching the associative power to the imagination; Coleridge, on the other hand, engaged in his lifelong warfare with the mechanist theory of mind, could only admit Hartley's law of association as part of the *vis receptiva* and an aid to the cool and superficial fancy.[29]

The dust of controversy between Coleridge and Wordsworth has long since settled and Coleridge's distinction between fancy and imagination may be stated in this manner. Certain materials are given in experience. Inevitably the materials become clustered about foci of interest; associations are formed. Fancy, an inferior faculty, avails itself of "mechanical" combinations among the sense impressions and the passive materials of the memory. Imagination is a higher faculty, a mediator for the Reason. It can go behind the sense impressions to the Ideas. It is creative in the highest degree, transforming whatever it

---

[29] For an excellent account of this difference of opinion, see C. D. Thorpe, "The Imagination: Coleridge *versus* Wordsworth," *Philological Quarterly*, XVIII (January, 1939), 1-18.

touches. It is holistic and creates organic wholes. The contrast
may be pointed up by the diseased condition of either faculty:
just as uncontrolled association would lead to delirium, a de-
ranged imagination (like that of Lady Macbeth) would end
in mania. Coleridge does not deny the value of the passive
and unconscious as basis and substratum of creation, but he
makes the passive part of the mind (associated with association
and with the fancy) subordinate. One suspects, too, that he
wants to have it both ways. Though in controversy with Wordsworth he specifically allocates association to the fancy, it seems
unlikely that imagination could never invade fancy's domain.
But imagination, when it uses the passive contents of the mind,
does so creatively, organizing them into its own master-design.

iv

The Genesis of a Distinction

Coleridge, in thus sharply distinguishing between fancy and
imagination, was but giving decisive authority to a distinction
that was coming increasingly into use as the eighteenth century
advanced. *Phantasia*, of course, had in classical times been considered the creative power, while *imaginatio* strictly belonged
to the receptive or passive part of the mind, and was nothing
more than reproductive or imitative of an image once received.[30]
It remained so all through the Middle Ages and was still so with
Hobbes. Addison started the semantic shift, for while he often
uses fancy and imagination indiscriminately or interchangeably,
he tended in the main to use imagination for the more weighty
or creative power, especially as a power productive of the sublime
in Milton's *Paradise Lost*. A critical tendency exists, all down

[30] M. W. Bundy, *Theory of Imagination in Classical and Medieval Thought*
(Urbana, 1927), esp. 140-41, 277-78.

the eighteenth century, to use fancy for the facetious, light, trivial, licentious or sportive, while imagination is used for effects that are serious or sublime. Duff states that the imagination is able " to present a creation of its own," [31] but that fancy with the aid of association and memory calls forth ideas " by the suggestion of some distant, perhaps, but corresponding circumstances." [32] Coleridge's distinction is already in being in Duff, for whom fancy is simply an associative power whose proper function is to assemble materials for the more creative imagination. Coleridge's distinction, moreover, is already found, fully realized, in Dugald Stewart. " Fancy," according to the latter, is essentially " a power of associating ideas according to relations of resemblance and analogy "; [33] and when most properly functioning " the office of this power is to collect materials for the Imagination; and therefore the latter power presupposes the former, while the former does not necessarily suppose the latter. A man whose habits of association present to him, a number of resembling or analogous ideas, we call a man of fancy; but for an effort of imagination, various other powers are necessary . . .[34]

v

Reconciliation of Opposites

(Coleridge's whole theory of imagination, then, rests on a sharp distinction between active and passive powers) The two features of Coleridge's theory which are its distinguishing marks (and herein lies its originality) are organic unity and reconciliation

[31] *Essay on Original Genius*, 6-7.   [32] *Ibid.*, 48-49.

[33] *Elements of the Philosophy of the Human Mind* (Edinburgh, 1792), 305.

[34] *Ibid.*, 284-85. The whole subject has been ably and comprehensively treated by John M. Bullitt and Walter J. Bate and by Wilma L. Kennedy. See above, p. 55, n. 38 and p. 23, n. 45.

of opposites. Imagination is a power that unifies, that cooperating with living powers of growth, produces organic unity. It is also a power that reconciles opposites. The two are not unconnected. It is by and through reconciling opposites that the esemplastic or fusing power creates unity.

The reconciliation of opposites was one of Coleridge's dearest and most fundamental principles. It runs through all his thinking. The usual supposition concerning it is that he derived it from Fichte and Schelling. To be sure, thesis, antithesis, synthesis is a principle that runs throughout German post-Kantian philosophy and triads (thesis, antithesis, resultant synthesis) are found everywhere in Hegel; the interaction between subject and object was, we know, the central point that Coleridge took from Schelling's philosophy. But it has not been sufficiently noticed, even in the distinguished monograph by Alice D. Snyder,[35] that the true origin of this principle in Coleridge's critical thinking is Neo-Platonic. For that matter, Coleridge knew that the principle of the synthesis of opposites goes further back than that, to Heracleitus.[36]

The paradox of the One and the Many is central in the philosophy of Plotinus. All discords are ultimately resolved in the universal harmony. In the ninth century John Scotus Erigena says: "God is the totality of all things . . . He is the similarity of the similar, the dissimilarity of the dissimilar, the opposition of opposites, and the contrariety of contraries."[37] Again we find the thought in Nicholas of Cusa; the central tenet of his philosophy is the coincidence of contraries. They coincide in God, in whom all opposites are reconciled.

A deep and basic polarity running through all existence was

[35] *The Critical Principle of the Reconciliation of Opposites, as Employed by Coleridge.* (Doctoral Dissertation, University of Michigan, 1918).

[36] *The Friend* (London, 1818), I, 155.

[37] W. R. Inge, *Christian Mysticism* (New York, 1899), 134.

an idea that appealed to Coleridge, possibly because it is a profound *aperçu* into the nature of life in the universe, possibly because, when the negative and positive polarity flows in a circuit, the power generated, whether electrical, sexual, or creative, is frequently potent. He observes that Schelling and himself "had both equal obligations to the polar logic and the dynamic philosophy of Giordano Bruno." [38] The philosopher of Nola believed in the coincidence of contraries; his system was circular, death or decay being necessary to generation. Bruno was one of those poetic and imaginative philosophers in whom Coleridge delighted. That which in Bruno principally attracted him was the principle of the synthesis of opposites. [39]

Polarity lay at the heart of the thinking of another man whose influence on Coleridge we know to have been great: Jakob Boehme. Boehme was an earlier and German incarnation of Blake. One of the deepest of this shoemaker's intuitive principles was that "without contrasts there is neither life nor manifestation. Without contrast, without another, there is only internal immobility, stillness and repose, in which nothing can be distinguished . . ." [40] In *Ja* and *Nein* all things consist. In his thought, polarity or opposition is the very principle of life itself: "if there were not this contrariety, there would be no life, and there would be no good, also no evil . . . for if there were no violence there would be no motion." [41] This is the root idea of Blake's *Marriage of Heaven and Hell*. One of Blake's proverbs in that work reads, "Without contraries there is no progression." The same doctrine has great bearing on Goethe's theory of good and evil in *Faust*; it also affected the ethical thinking of Thomas Mann.

[38] *Biographia*, I, 103.

[39] Alice D. Snyder, " Coleridge on Giordano Bruno," *Modern Language Notes*, XLII (Nov., 1927), 435.

[40] Hans L. Martensen, *Jacob Boehme* (New York, 1949), 28.

[41] Quoted by Karl Viëtor, *Goethe the Poet* (Cambridge, Mass., 1949), 299.

Martensen, who is perhaps the best explicator of Boehme's thinking, says: "Boehme is never weary of enforcing the necessity of contrasts in order to have life and manifestation. All things not merely earthly and diabolic, but also heavenly and Divine, consist of *Yes* and *No* (*Ja und Nein*). The Eternal Will of Unity is the eternal *Yes*; but this Yes cannot be manifested without the eternal No, which provides a contradiction to the Unity, and posits multiplicity and variety."[42]

Boehme was a blunt and powerful thinker; he did not attempt to sugar over the existence of evil or to explain it away. The opposition between good and evil is very real for him, because evil is regarded by him, not as a negative (the absence of good), but a positive force:

> Le mal n'est pas simplement négation, limitation, absence du bien. Boehme n'accepte pas l'identification trompeuse, commune à la philosophie chrétienne et à la philosophie antique, du mal avec la négation et la néant. La lumière et les ténèbres, si on reprend cette comparaison classique, s'opposent, mais ne s'opposent nullement comme l'être et le non-être de la lumière, car les ténèbres *sont* aussi bien que la lumière. L'obscurité réelle est quelque chose de positif, une qualité perçue. La lutte entre le Bien et le Mal est un combat entre puissances contraires, réelles toutes deux.[43]

He once said "All things are created out of imagination."[44] Newton P. Stallknecht comments: "For Boehme, Nature is God's imagination. God creates the world in his image and his image and his creative power enters not only the forms of Nature but the spirit of man, who is capable of participation in such creation. The analogy of the Eolian harp appears in Boehme, as well as the notion of a dynamic intercourse between mind and

---

[42] Hans L. Martensen, *Jacob Boehme*, 45.
[43] Alexandre Koyré, *La Philosophie de Jacob Boehme*, 73.
[44] *The Signature of All Things* (Everyman Edition; London, 1912), 207.

its object . . ." [45] The kinship of these ideas to Coleridge's Plotinian doctrine of imagination needs no underlining. Boehme, moreover, would be congenial to Coleridge because he had a Platonic insistence upon *essence*.

The importance of Boehme as a bridge between classical theory on reconciliation of opposites and theory on that subject by German philosophers of the post-Kantian era is considerable. Hegel devoted a whole chapter to him in his history of philosophy, and the reason Boehme figures so prominently there is precisely that he so clearly perceived the principle of contradiction and the reconciliation of contraries. Boehme, too, influenced Schelling.

In Schelling's philosophy the reconciliation of contraries is definitely present, for in his philosophy subject and object coalesce in cognition, consciousness and unconsciousness coalesce in creation. Thus, the thought became central to the philosophy of Coleridge; "extremes meet," as has often been pointed out, was his favorite proverb. "Indeed," as Willey has excellently said, "he saw in the interpenetration of opposites the very meaning and inmost process of existence. Life itself . . . consists in the tension between polar opposites, the One becoming the Many, and the Many resolved into the One." [46] It might be added that nowadays tension is a favorite critical term.

The importance and centrality of this principle to Coleridge can be demonstrated by a citation from *The Friend*: "Every power in nature and in spirit must evolve an opposite, as the sole means and condition of its manifestation: and all opposition is a tendency to re-union. . . . The identity of thesis and antithesis is the substance of all being." [47]

[45] *Strange Seas of Thought*. See also Alice D. Snyder, "Coleridge on Böhme," *PMLA* (June, 1930), 616-18.

[46] *Nineteenth Century Studies*, 20.

[47] *The Friend*, in *Works*, ed. Shedd, II, 91n. On the same subject, see *ibid.*, 434.

Since the tension between polar opposites is the central mystery of life itself, it can hardly fail to be the central mystery of imagination also. " That synthetic and magical power," wrote Coleridge in the most elaborate account he ever gave of the poetic act: " reveals itself in the balance or reconciliation of opposite or discordant qualities: of . . . idea with the image; the individual with the representative; . . . a more than usual state of emotion, with more than usual order; judgement ever awake and steady self-possession, with enthusiasm and feeling profound or vehement . . ." [48] All these reconciliations are accomplished in the supreme act of poetic creation, but the essential reconciliation is that between the active and passive powers of the mind.

Coleridge says that the poet " brings the whole soul of man into activity, with the subordination of its faculties to each other." [49] The poet will chiefly call on his imagination, but that does not mean that he will not, at the same time, call on his associative power (fancy) too. " Imagination must have fancy, in fact the higher intellectual powers can only act through a corresponding energy of the lower." [50] The creative act calls for the energy of the whole mind, the whole man.

Coleridge's account of the creative act invites comparison with Wordsworth's: " I have said that poetry is the spontaneous overflow of powerful feelings: it takes its origin from emotion recollected in Tranquillity: the emotion is contemplated till, by a species of reaction, the tranquillity gradually disappears, and an emotion, kindred to that which was before the subject of contemplation, is gradually produced, and does itself actually

[48] *Biographia*, II, 12. The fusion of the idea in the image is the theory of the image put forward by Pound and Eliot. Fusion of the individual with the representative is that principle of the concrete-universal which derives from Aristotle's dictum that poetry is more philosophical than history because it deals with universals.

[49] *Ibid.*   [50] *Table Talk*, April 20, 1833.

exist in the mind."[51] Wordsworth's account of the creative experience is simpler than Coleridge's and no metaphysics is involved in it. But it, too, essentially has a balance or reconciliation of emotion and tranquillity. The original emotion was too tumultuous for artistic control; recollected in tranquillity, it is too cool. Part of the original emotion is revived.

The creative act, then, to return to Coleridge, calls "the whole soul of man" into activity—the higher intuitive reason, the intellect, the imagination, the associative fancy, judgment or common sense, powers conscious and unconscious: the poet calls on everything he has.

In the act of composing poetry two powers, active and passive, are at work and this is only possible through the reconciling faculty of imagination. "Now let a man," says Coleridge, "watch his mind while he is composing," and he illustrates the process as follows:

> Most of my readers will have observed a small water-insect on the surface of rivulets, which throws a cinque-spotted shadow fringed with prismatic colors on the sunny bottom of the brook; and will have noticed, how the little animal *wins i*ts way up against the stream, by alternate pulses of active and passive motion, now resisting the current, and now yielding to it in order to gather strength and a momentary fulcrum for a further propulsion. This is no unapt emblem of the mind's self-experience in the act of thinking. There are evidently two powers at work, which relatively to each other are active and passive. (In philosophical language, we must denominate this intermediate faculty in all its degrees and determinations, the IMAGINATION . . .)[52]

To interpret this figure of the water-insect: Coleridge means that in the act of composing poetry there are both passive and active powers involved; the *vis receptiva*, with the images stored in the mind or unconsciously associated there is passive; the

---

[51] Preface to *Lyrical Ballads*, 1800.   [52] *Biographia*, I, 85-86.

active spurts of progress are made by the originating imagination, instigated by the conscious intellect and will. These active powers of mind, though all-important in creation, would be helpless without the passive reservoir or content of images to draw from, just as the insect must have water to swim in. The imagination does more than originate; it is the *liaison* or link between active and passive powers. It helps them to function together as one.

Nowhere has Coleridge more powerfully stated the tension and the reconciliation effected between opposing powers than in his critique of *Venus and Adonis* and his analysis of the early promise of genius in Shakespeare. It is like the biblical account of Jacob wrestling with the angel. "No man was ever yet a great poet, without being at the same time a profound philosopher . . . In Shakespeare's *poems* the creative power and the intellectual energy wrestle as in a war embrace. Each in its excess of strength seems to threaten the extinction of the other. At length in the DRAMA they were reconciled." [53] It is hardly necessary to say that this is one of the profoundest of Coleridge's perceptions.

Imagination, then, for Coleridge, as traditionally in classic psychology, as in Addison, as in Kant, is the intermediate and reconciling faculty. Coleridge defines taste (whose psychological organ is the imagination) as follows: "Taste is the intermediate faculty which connects the active with the passive powers of our nature, the intellect with the senses; and its appropriate function is to elevate the images of the latter, while it realizes the ideas of the former. We must therefore have learned what is peculiar to each, before we can understand that 'third something,' which is formed by a harmony of both." [54]

<hr />

[53] *Biographia*, II, 19.

[54] "On the Principles of Sound Criticism Concerning the Fine Arts," *Miscellanies Aesthetic and Literary*, ed. T. Ashe (London, 1892), 14; the same passage will be found in *Biographia*, II, 225.

Coleridge's formulation of the theory of the balance of opposites receives from I. A. Richards the highest praise: "The original formulation was Coleridge's greatest contribution to critical theory, and except in the way of interpretation, it is hard to add anything to what he has said . . ." [55] And, in a footnote, Richards says, "Coleridge's debt here to Schelling has been overestimated. Such borrowings as he made were more hampering to him than helpful." We are inclined to agree that Coleridge did better when he drew straight from his own experience. The passages of greatest insight in *Biographia* are not those which he borrowed from anybody. Schelling's theory of reconciliation of subject-object was epistemological; he could, and, indeed, did, extend the principle of reconciliation (of the conscious with the unconscious) to the creative act. But Schelling dealt technically with philosophical concepts; his knowledge of creation was theoretic. He had written neither an "Ancient Mariner" nor a "Kubla Khan." Coleridge on the act of creation speaks with more authority.

vi

Organic Unity

Coleridge's theory of imagination is distinctly an organic theory. This means that the process of creation as it takes place in the poet's mind is likened to a process of nature, like the ripening of an ear of corn. The original idea for a poem or a tragedy might be small indeed, a seed or germ like the famous mustard seed of the parable. The development of the poem, the evolution of the plot, and the symbolism imbedded in the play, grow and gradually mature in the poet's mind, as he draws upon

[55] *Principles of Literary Criticism*, 242-43.

deeper and deeper layers of experience. And the play or poem thus produced, itself, inevitably, as a result of this process of organic growth, possesses organic unity. A play like *Hamlet* possesses it.

Coleridge named the imagination an *esemplastic* power.[56] By that he meant a plastic or shaping power that formed into *one* or formed into organic unity. He was evidently dissatisfied by the term imagination as used by Hume and other eighteenth-century writers. He needed something better than the compounding power of Addison. He therefore invented the term "esemplastic."

We do not wish to convey the impression that Coleridge was without a sense of the necessity of a design; his only stipulation was that it must be a living design. In designing a work of art, the artist should keep in mind an over-all view of the whole, or that which Coleridge described as the "sur-view"[57] which "enables a man to foresee the whole of what he is to convey, appertaining at any one point; and by this means to subordinate and arrange the different parts according to their relative importance, as to convey it at once, and as an organized whole."[58]

Gordon McKenzie, in his able study of organic unity in Coleridge,[59] is interested in organic unity as a principle of Coleridge's criticism; he makes no mention of origins. Some notion of organic unity in a work of art is to be found in criticism from Plato onward. Plato certainly recognized the principle of organic unity: "Every discourse ought to be constructed like a living creature, having a body of its own as well as a head

[56] P. L. Carver, "The Evolution of the Term Esemplastic," *MLR*, XXIV (1929), 329.

[57] *Biographia*, II, 44.

[58] *Ibid.* A precisely similar passage will be found in *The Friend*, *Works*, ed. Shedd, II, 408-09.

[59] *Organic Unity in Coleridge* (Berkeley, California, 1939).

and feet, and with a middle and extremities also in perfect keeping with one another and the whole." [60] Aristotle has a more logical and structural definition: "The truth is that, just as in the other imitative arts one imitation is always of one thing, so in poetry the story, as an imitation of action, must represent one action, a complete whole, with its several incidents so closely connected that the transposal or withdrawal of any one of them will disjoin or dislocate the whole. For that which makes no perceptible difference by its presence or absence is no real part of the whole." [61] The concept of unity, such as that of a body and its members, belongs to the classical tradition, rather than to any one writer. Longinus, true to the tradition, says, "We shall find one source of the sublime in the systematic selection of the most important elements, and the power of forming, by their mutual combination, what may be called one body." [62] And so the metaphor of the human body continues to be echoed; we find it in Horace, who had it of Aristotle who had it of Plato's *Phaedrus*.

Perhaps if we search for the root of the concept of organic unity in Coleridge's thinking, we may trace it to the Plotinian unity of the One which embraces the many. Coleridge found a symbol of it in the surge of wind through a forest of fir and pine in Germany (the sound was multitudinous and yet one):

> Now again is nothing but firs and pines above, below, around us! How awful is the deep unison of their undividable murmur; what a one thing it is—it is a sound that impresses the dim notion of the Omnipresent.[63]

We do not as yet, however, find the distinction, so important

[60] *Phaedrus*, 246c.
[61] *Aristotle On the Art of Poetry*, in *The Works of Aristotle*, ed. W. D. Ross (Oxford, 1946), XI, 1451a.
[62] *On the Sublime*, tr. W. Rhys Roberts (Cambridge, 1899), 69.
[63] *Biographia Epistolaris*, ed. A. Turnbull (2 vols.; London, 1911), I, 171.

for Coleridge, between a mechanical unity and an organic. The distinction between a man-made object such as a watch or a plough and a living organism with the (divine) principle of growth within it is very clearly made by the Neo-Platonist, Henry More: " in every *particular* World, such as Man is especially, his own Soul is the peculiar and most perfective architect thereof, as the Soul of the World is of it. For this *vital* Fabrication is not as in artificial Architecture, when an external person acts upon Matter; but implies a more particular and near union with that Matter it thus intrinsically shapes out and organizes." [64]

This idea of organizing from within ought to be connected with the Aristotelian concept of the soul or Form as organizing principle, the Aristotelian entelechy, *i. e.*, that the acorn has *in potentia* the oak that it will become, the Aristotelian " doctrine of teleology; namely the notion that things carry within them a proliferating germ of completeness which leads them finally to assume the shape and nature latent within them. Thus, the seed or root of an oak becomes an oak-tree and not a willow; a caterpillar, a butterfly or moth, and not a lady-bird or stag-beetle." [65]

Leibniz, too, formulated a distinction between an organic body and a machine made by the skill of man which was often echoed in German aesthetics.[66]

Actually, Coleridge could have derived so pervasive an idea from many sources. C. D. Thorpe suggests that " from intima-

[64] " The Immortality of the Soul," *Philosophical Writings of Henry More*, ed. Flora Isabel MacKinnon (New York and London, 1925), 147.

[65] Derek Stanford, *Christopher Fry: An Appreciation* (London, 1951), 107.

[66] On this and related topics, cf. James Benziger, " Organic Unity: Leibniz to Coleridge," PMLA, LXVI (1951), 24-48. German theory of unconscious genius and organic growth, together with the aesthetics of organism developed by A. W. Schlegel and by Coleridge, is treated with great ability by Meyer H. Abrams in *The Mirror and the Lamp*, 184-225.

tions in Johnson, Warton, and Hurd he went on to his theory of organic form." [67] Another plausible suggestion is that he might have obtained a hint from Tucker's *Light of Nature Pursued*; indeed, such a theory as that of organic unity was almost certain to arise (as we have seen) from the vitalistic conceptions of the late eighteenth century. For instance, Edward Young in his *Conjectures* distinguishes between organic and mechanic form: "An original may be said to be of a vegetable nature; it rises spontaneously from the vital root of genius; it grows, it is not made. Imitations are often a sort of manufacture wrought up by those mechanics, art and labour, out of pre-existent materials not their own." [68]

Herder, as already remarked, is another very probable source for such a theory. The youthful Herder in his *Von Deutscher Art und Kunst* (1773) found that Shakespeare out of more complex manifold aspects of nature and of human life than were fused together into one by the Greek tragedians did nevertheless produce plays, such as the tragedy of *King Lear*, equally unified. The greater complexity made the achievement of unity more hazardous, but more gratifying. The welding of complexity into unity, the combining of *Vielheit* and *Einheit*, the achievement of organic unity was for Herder a criterion of tragedy. [69]

Herder, in turn, exerted considerable influence upon Schlegel:

The idea of drama as having an inherent, living unity, grounded in nature, its form shaped by the imaginative insight of genius into the heart of great struggle, while it owed something to Lessing, contributed more to Schlegel and to Coleridge and became the foundation of our later theory of drama. Schlegel, in his

---

[67] "Coleridge as Aesthetician and Critic," *Journal of the History of Ideas*, V (October, 1944), 390.

[68] "Conjectures on Original Composition" (1759), in Schorer, *Criticism: The Foundations of Modern Literary Judgment*, 13.

[69] Margaret Sherwood, *Undercurrents of Influence in English Romantic Poetry*, 122-23.

Dramatic Art, through patient study of the drama of various lands, in tracing the development from early times, among different peoples, in interpreting the indigenous nature of drama, in emphasizing the inner vital unity of a great tragedy and the power of the shaping imagination of genius to body this forth, was but carrying out exhaustively, with painstaking application, the principles of Herder.[70]

The concept of organic unity is unquestionably present in Schlegel. For instance, in his notable chapter on Shakespeare he says:

> It was, generally speaking, the prevailing tendency of the time which preceded our own (and which has showed itself particularly in physical science) to consider everything having life as a mere accumulation of dead parts, to separate what exists only in connexion and cannot otherwise be conceived, instead of penetrating to the central point and viewing all the parts as so many irradiations from it. Hence nothing is so rare as a critic who can elevate himself to the comprehensive contemplation of a work of art. Shakespeare's compositions, from the very depth of purpose displayed in them, have been especially liable to the misfortune of being misunderstood.[71]

Miss A. A. Helmholtz, in her monograph on the indebtedness of Coleridge to Schlegel, notes that the distinction between organic and mechanical form occurs in Schlegel; Schlegel's *Über dramatische Kunst und Literatur* is one of several German sources for Coleridge's critical theory.[72] The classic passage from Schlegel's work is the following: " The form is mechanical

---

[70] *Ibid.*, 135-36.

[71] August Wilhelm von Schlegel, *Lectures on Dramatic Art and Literature*, tr. John Black, 2nd ed., rev. by A. J. W. Morrison (London, 1914), 360.

[72] For the whole subject of Coleridge's indebtedness to Schlegel, Raysor's scholarly introduction and notes to his *Coleridge's Shakespearean Criticism* are valuable and important. Raysor thinks that Coleridge's indebtedness to Schlegel for his aesthetic theory is heavy, but that his specific insights, *e. g.*, into the character of Hamlet, are his own.

when through outside influence it is imparted to a material merely as an accidental addition, without relation to its nature (as e. g. when we give an arbitrary shape to a soft mass so that it may retain it after hardening). Organic form, on the other hand, is innate; it unfolds itself from within and acquires its definiteness simultaneously with the total development of the germ." [73] This is the distinction (as we shall presently see) echoed by Coleridge.

Of course, a work of art is not the same thing as a biological organism with living cells, yet the metaphor is illuminating. A plant is not conscious of the fact that it grows. An oak-tree is not self-conscious. "There is," Coleridge learned from Schelling, though he must have known it himself, for he had only to dip into his consciousness with deep introspection to find it, "in genius itself an unconscious activity; nay, that is the genius of the man of genius." [74] The unconscious activity is the organic principle at work.

Coleridge has several statements of the principle of organic unity; his best, which closely parallels Schlegel, is the following:

> The true ground of the mistake [of those who condemn Shakespeare, according to the rules of unities, as a lawless genius] lies in the confounding mechanical regularity with organic form. The form is mechanic, when on any given material we impress a predetermined form, not necessarily arising out of the properties of the material;—as when to a mass of wet clay we give whatever shape we wish it to retain when hardened. The organic form, on the other hand, is innate; it shapes, as it developes, itself from within, and the fulness of its development is one and the same with the perfection of its outward form. Such as the life is, such is the form. Nature, the prime genial artist, inexhaustible in diverse powers, is equally inexhaustible in forms;—each exterior

---

[73] Tr. René Wellek in *A History of Modern Criticism: 1750-1950* (New Haven, 1955), II, 48.

[74] "On Poesy or Art" (1818), *Biographia*, II, 258.

is the physiognomy of the being within . . . ;—and even such is the appropriate excellence of her chosen poet, of our own Shakespeare—himself a nature humanized, a genial understanding directing self-consciously a power and an implicit wisdom deeper even than our consciousness.[75]

We notice here the balance of opposites, the coöperation, according to Coleridge's theory of organic unity, of conscious and unconscious powers in Shakespeare.

Schlegel, while admitting that the activity of such a genius as Shakespeare is "in a certain sense unconscious," added, "To me (Shakespeare) is a profound artist, not a blind and wildly-coursing genius. What has been babbled on this subject, I hold, in general, to be a mere fable . . ." [76] Coleridge, in like manner, never fell into the trap of supposing that the unconscious power, "the genius in the man of genius," could be counted upon to do all the work of organizing a poem or play. He agreed with Schelling and with Schlegel that the work of genius is a collaboration between conscious and unconscious powers, and he was never tired of insisting that Shakespeare's judgment was equal to his genius.

> In all the successive courses of lectures delivered by me, since my first attempt at the Royal Institution, it has been, and it still remains, my object, to prove that in all points from the most important to the most minute, the judgment of Shakespeare is commensurate with his genius, nay, that his genius reveals itself in his judgment, as in its most exalted form.[77]

[75] Shakespeare Lectures (1818), *Coleridge's Shakespearean Criticism*, ed. Raysor, I, 223-24. "The intent of this passage is excellent, and the result of Coleridge's insistence upon the principle has been wholly good for criticism" —Craig La Drière, "Organic Form," *Dictionary of World Literature*, ed. Joseph Shipley (New York, The Philosophical Library, 1943). For comment and criticism of Coleridge's distinction, the same article may be consulted.

[76] *Dramatic Lectures* (1808) in *Sämtliche Werke* (Leipzig, 1846), VI, 157, 182, tr. Meyer H. Abrams, *The Mirror and the Lamp*, 213.

[77] "Shakespeare's Judgment Equal to His Genius," in *Criticism: The Major Texts*, ed. W. J. Bate (New York, 1952), 391.

Coleridge, then, was always combatting the idea that Shakespeare was a "wild" genius, a sport, as the neo-classic critics would have it. His genius was orderly, but the form it imposed was not mechanical, but organic. "No work of genius dares to want its appropriate form." [78] "What then shall we say? even this; that Shakespeare, no mere child of nature; no automaton of genius,[79] no passive vehicle of inspiration possessed by the spirit, not possessing it; first studied patiently, meditated deeply, understood minutely, till knowledge, become habitual and intuitive, wedded itself to his habitual feelings, and at length gave birth to that stupendous power, by which he stands alone, with no equal or second in his class." [80] Dry judgment would not by itself have created Shakespeare's plays; neither would giving a free rein to unconscious associative powers. Nor would dictation by the Holy Ghost account for them. It was the combination of intellectual and passive and absorptive faculties, the steady possession and exercise of intuitive vision, that produced them.

Beaumont and Fletcher did not work from within, like Shakespeare, but from without, copying superficial resemblances:

> What had grammatical and logical consistency for the ear, what could be put together and represented to the eye, these poets [Beaumont and Fletcher] took from the ear and the eye, unchecked by any intuition of an inward impossibility, just as a man might fit together a quarter of an orange, a quarter of an apple, and the like of a lemon, and a pomegranate, and make it look like one round diverse coloured fruit. But nature, who works from within by evolution and assimilation according to a law, cannot do it. Nor could Shakespeare, for he too worked in the

---

[78] *Coleridge's Shakespearean Criticism*, ed. Raysor, I, 223. The denial that Shakespeare is a wild, untutored genius is found in Schlegel.

[79] Could this be a thrust at Gerard's notion of genius—a genius based on mechanical precision of the associative power?

[80] *Biographia*, II, 19-20.

spirit of nature, by evolving the germ within by the imaginative power according to an idea . . .[81]

The above is another good statement of Coleridge's theory of organic unity. It happens, incidentally, to be an excellent account of the germination and growth of the *Rime of the Ancient Mariner*. It is to be noted, too, that there is no contradiction here between this concept of evolving the germ from within and the definition of Imagination as emanating from the great I AM. For the great I AM is the force that works in and through nature; the artist, like Shakespeare, in evolving *Hamlet*, works in the spirit of nature, in ways like those of the growing plant, from within also. The artist simply coöperates with *natura naturans*. For, to continue the line of Coleridge's thought: "The *rules* of the IMAGINATION are themselves the very powers of growth and production. The *words*, to which they are reducible, present only the outlines and external appearance of the fruit. A deceptive counterfeit of the superficial form and colors may be elaborated; but the marble peach feels cold and heavy, and children only put it to their mouths."[82] The artificial peach or *trompe l'oeil* is produced by fancy; but the fruit of imagination has the fuzz on it and the juice inside.

Between the acorn and the oak there is an appreciable difference in size; the acorn never, however, threatens to grow into a rose. The oakness of the acorn keeps it growing into an oak. Between the germinal idea of the *Rime of the Ancient Mariner* (Cruickshank's dream, Lieutenant Hatley shooting the albatross) and the finished ballad there has been a great expansion and development, but it took place around an organizing and unifying principle, the theme of a crime and its punishment, and the architectonic scheme furnished by what Lowes calls the great curve or arc of the voyage. The poem has what Coleridge

[81] *Miscellaneous Criticism*, ed. Raysor 42-3.   [82] *Biographia*, II, 65.

calls "keeping" and I. A. Richards unity of tone. Amid the thousand images that fused into its composition, the oakness, the essential wizardry of the supernatural ballad and the sturdiness of the mariner's yarn, has been preserved.

Just so, from rude and primitive beginnings the legend of a king and ungrateful daughters grew into a tragedy. For "still mounting the intellectual ladder, he [Shakespeare] had as unequivocally proved the indwelling in his mind of imagination, or the power by which one image or feeling is made to modify many others, and by a sort of fusion to force many into one;— that which afterwards showed itself in such might and energy in Lear, where the deep anguish of a father spreads the feeling of ingratitude and cruelty over the very elements of heaven." [83] Fascinating as the subject is, however, Coleridge's application of the principle of organic unity to his criticism of Shakespeare's plays cannot be entered into here.

In developing his theory of organic unity Coleridge uses an interesting figure:

> The BEAUTIFUL, contemplated in its essentials, . . . is that in which the *many*, still seen as many, becomes one. Take a familiar instance, one of a thousand. The frost on a window-pane has by accident crystallized into a striking resemblance of a tree or seaweed. With what pleasure we trace the parts, and their relations to each other, and to the whole! Here is the stalk or trunk, and here the branches or sprays—sometimes even the buds or flowers. Nor will our pleasure be less, should the caprice of the crystallization represent some object disagreeable to us, provided only we can see or fancy the component parts each in relation to each, and all forming a whole. [84]

Coleridge believed, as we know, that a single principle of being underlies all the multiplicity of natural forms. He saw

[83] " Shakespeare as a Poet Generally," in Bate *Criticism: The Major Texts*, 388-89.
[84] " On the Principles of Genial Criticism," *Biographia*, II, 232.

no break between organic and inorganic—all nature is *one*. Here his thought is in agreement with the theory of the chain of being, and to illustrate this imperceptible shading of organic into inorganic, he again uses the figure of which he is fond: " The arborescent forms on a frosty morning, to be seen on the window and pavement, must have *some* relation to the more perfect forms developed in the vegetable world." [85]

Another figure which also serves the turn is that of the V-formation of migrating ducks, geese, or swans. These often fly with something approaching the precision of military planes in formation. The figure is all the more apt because the flight of migrating birds is on the wing; a moving rather than a static unity is preserved.

He employs still another figure for this living and moving unity, one that develops the theme of unity in multeity, as did the figure of the wind through the firs and the pines: " Oh, said I, as I looked at the blue, yellow-green and purple-green sea, with all its hollows and swells, and cut-glass surfaces—oh, what an *ocean* of lovely forms! And I was vexed, teased that the sentence sounded like a play of words! *That* it was not— The mind within me was struggling to express the marvellous distinctness and unconfounded personality of each of the million millions of forms, and yet the individual unity in which they subsisted." [86]

In one of the supreme passages on imagination which Coleridge has given us, he really repeats an old distinction in a new form, for the distinction between fancy and imagination is the same as that between talent and genius:

' The man that hath not music in his soul can never be a genuine poet.' Imagery (even taken from nature, much more when trans-

---

[85] " The Theory of Life," in *Miscellanies Aesthetic and Literary*, ed. T. Ashe, 383n. See the definition of life and of living unity, *ibid.*, 384-85.

[86] *Anima Poetae*, 100.

planted from books, as travels, voyages, and works of natural history); affecting incidents; just thoughts; interesting personal or domestic feelings; and with these the art of their combination or intertexture in the form of a poem; may all [like the color on the marble peach] by incessant effort be acquired as a trade, by a man of talents and much reading, who as I once before observed, has mistaken an intense desire of poetic reputation for a natural poetic genius; [87] the love of the arbitrary end for the possession of the peculiar means. / But the sense of musical delight, with the power of producing it, is a gift of imagination; and this together with the power of reducing multitude into unity of effect, and modifying a series of thoughts by some one predominant thought or feeling, may be cultivated and improved, but can never be learned. It is in these that *poeta nascitur non fit.*[88]

I. A. Richards comments: "to point out that 'the sense of musical delight is a gift of the imagination' was one of Coleridge's most brilliant feats. It is in such a resolution of a welter of disconnected impulses into a single ordered response that in all arts imagination is most shown." [89] The sense of musical delight arises when all an artist's faculties, conscious and unconscious, are in harmonious play.

Walter Pater offers the chief criticism of Coleridge's theory of organic unity. According to Coleridge organic form is innate, shaping as it develops itself from within. Pater objected that the theory did not give enough credit to the conscious and laborious shaping of the work of art.[90] As T. S. Eliot has wisely said, "There is a great deal in the writing of poetry, which must be conscious and deliberate." [91] Though the poet may be lucky to have Valéry's "*une ligne donnée,*" or perhaps, as with A. E.

---

[87] Could Coleridge have had Southey in mind?

[88] *Biographia,* II, 14.

[89] *Principles of Literary Criticism,* 245.

[90] Walter Pater, *Appreciations* (London, 1889), 80-81.

[91] "Tradition and the Individual Talent," *Selected Essays* (New York, 1932), 10.

Housman, as much as a stanza, the rest of the poem has to be sweated out. But when it is recollected how firmly Coleridge insisted upon " judgment ever awake and steady self-possession " [92] Pater's criticism loses a good deal of its force.

Few poets have done more in the twentieth century to provide other poets, "makers," practicing craftsmen, with a workable poetic than T. S. Eliot. On this subject of the balance between conscious and unconscious powers he has said, so far as at any stage of thought it is possible to do so, the last word:

The poet's progress is dual. There is the gradual accumulation of experience, like a tantalus jar: it may be only once in five or ten years that experience accumulates to form a new whole and finds its appropriate expression. But if a poet were content to attempt nothing less than always his best, if he insisted on waiting for these unpredictable crystallizations, he would not be ready for them when they came. The development of experience is largely unconscious, subterranean, so that we cannot gauge its progress except once in every five or ten years; but in the meantime the poet must be working; he must be experimenting and trying his technique so that it will be ready like a well-oiled fire-engine, when the moment comes to strain it to its utmost.[93]

The poet never knows when those subterranean rumblings will occur, and if he is to rise to the occasion, his technique must be in readiness, for

. . . a poet's work may proceed along two lines on an imaginary graph; one of the lines being his conscious and continuous effort in technical excellence, that is, in continually developing his medium for the moment when he really has something to say. The other line is just his normal human course of development, his accumulation and digestion of experience (experience is not sought for, it is merely accepted in consequence of doing what

[92] *Biographia*, II, 12.
[93] Introduction to *Ezra Pound: Selected Poems* (1928), xviii. Quoted by George Williamson, *A Reader's Guide to T. S. Eliot* (New York, 1953), 39.

we really want to do), and by experience I mean the results of reading and reflection, varied interests of all sorts, contacts and acquaintances, as well as passion and adventure. Now and then the two lines may converge at a high peak, so that we get a masterpiece. That is to say, an accumulation of experience has crystallized to form material of art, and years of work in technique have prepared an adequate medium; and something results in which medium and material, form and content, are indistinguishable.[94]

The emphasis, then, should be placed on the word "balance." In the reconciliation of opposites achieved by imagination in the creative act, there is a balance of active and passive, or conscious and unconscious powers. Undue emphasis upon conscious and deliberate control leads to imbalance; undue emphasis upon the unconscious, or the deep well, the free or unconscious association of ideas and images, does the same. It is Coleridge's signal achievement that he established a balanced theory.

An organic theory of creative imagination, then, carries within it a certain implication. While it is a metaphor merely, and does not assume that a work of art takes shape altogether as painlessly and naturally as an ear of corn, while the creator thereof is asleep, or, to use Joyce's phrase, "paring his fingernails"—while it assumes that the artist takes thought and exercises, indeed, relentless vigilance—nevertheless, it is paradoxical, for it implies, too, that the artist, if he is wise, is in league with all the forces of secret growth and germination, and that these forces do, in fact, work for him while he is asleep or dreaming, or maybe, has dropped off, like Coleridge at Porlock, under the influence of opium. For, whatever else it implies, an organic theory of imagination supposes that the silent forces of growth— the unnoticed coalescence of images in the unconscious mind— are an integral part of the process.

[94] *Ibid.*

5

CREATION AND

THE UNCONSCIOUS

Coleridge, we know, had an active-dynamic theory of mind; he strongly objected to the mind regarded as passive, a "lazy looker-on" at external nature. Nature itself, the passive landscape, had qualities read into it by the active observing mind of the poet:

> O Lady! we receive but what we give,
> And in our life alone does Nature live.[1]

In this respect, he shared the view of William Blake who asserted flatly, "Imagination has nothing to do with memory."

Every student of Coleridge knows how he exalted the Imagination, making it the eye of reason, the νοῦς or noblest part of the mind, "distinguishing between the Fancy, which is merely 'a mode of Memory emancipated from the order of time and space' and which, like Memory, receives its materials from the laws of association, and the Imagination, which transcends sensational material and brings the mind into direct connection with

---

[1] "Dejection: An Ode," Poems, 365.

the ultimate and supersensuous reality." [2] In spite of this exaltation of the Imagination, however, Coleridge was sufficiently a realist (in the modern sense) to admit the *vis receptiva* as one half of his polar theory of imagination, the passive powers of the mind being necessary to the active.

Chapter I of the present study has amply demonstrated Coleridge's familiarity with Hartley and the law of association. He found a place (as we have seen) for association among the passive powers of the mind. Was this a single isolated acknowledgment in a formal definition? To what degree was Coleridge aware—steadily and consistently aware—of association among the semi-conscious or unconscious powers of the mind? Was he aware of a continuous stream or flow of consciousness? Was he aware of the unconscious as aiding creation, not merely as a matter of theory but as a matter of experience?

i

The Stream of Mind

One of Coleridge's chief claims to interest at the present day is that he was a pioneer psychologist with unequalled gifts of introspection. Not only was he aware that association is rather an emotional than an intellectual matter—as he wrote Southey, " I almost think that ideas never recall ideas, as far as they are ideas, any more than leaves in a forest create each other's motion—the breeze it is that runs through them—it is the soul, the state of feeling " [3]—but almost a hundred years before William James and James Joyce, he was aware of the

[2] Samuel C. Chew in *A Literary History of England*, ed. Albert C. Baugh (New York, 1948), 1157.

[3] *Letters*, II, 428. Coleridge believed that contemporaneity was the condition of all association. Cf. *Biographia*, I, 86.

stream of consciousness, and expressed it, too, in the sovereign phrase: " the streamy nature of association which thinking curbs and rudders." [4] Here is brilliant recognition of the collaboration of active and passive powers.

Coleridge, too, was aware of a mental phenomenon of which many people are aware, the phenomenon that, because of some similarity of the exciting cause, a similarity occurs in a person's nervous response to the reaction he had on the previous occasion, thus giving rise to " recall." In a letter to Southey, when he has just used a far-fetched metaphor, he continues: " while I wrote that last sentence I had a vivid recollection, indeed an ocular spectrum, of our room in College Street, a curious instance of association. You remember how incessantly in that room I used to be compounding these half-verbal half-visual metaphors." [5]

Lowes pounced on the phrase, " the hooks-and-eyes of the memory," which occurs quite early in *The Friend*; [6] Coleridge himself, however, made very little use of it, introducing it quite casually in a passage on the debilitating effects of much light novel reading. The use Lowes makes of it is more interesting; he likens " hooks-and-eyes of the memory to the hooked atoms of Epicurus; " [7] and he uses " hooks-and-eyes " as a rough and ready metaphor for the numerous subtle links of association which he demonstrates to have been the passive half of the creation of the " Rime of the Ancient Mariner " and " Kubla Khan."

Coleridge himself was not unaware of foci of association, nuclei, or image-clusters; he uses his favorite images of crystallization when (in a letter of April 8, 1820) he speaks of " the confluence of our recollections," and of how " We establish a centre, as it were, a sort of nucleus in the reservoir of the soul;

[4] *Anima Poetae*, 46.
[5] *Letters*, I, 427.
[6] (London, 1818), I, 25-26.
[7] *The Road to Xanadu*, 62.

and towards this needle shoots after needle, cluster points on cluster points, from all parts of contained fluid, and in all directions." [8]

Dreams always fascinated him; indeed, in the limbo of books which he was to have written but which remained embryonic was a treatise on the subject:

> I have long wished to devote an entire work to the subject of Dreams, Visions, Ghosts, Witchcraft, &c., in which I might first give, and then endeavor to explain the most interesting and best-attested fact of each, which has come within my knowledge, either from books or from personal testimony. I might then explain in a more satisfactory way the mode in which our thoughts in states of morbid slumber, become at times perfectly *dramatic* (for in certain sorts of dreams the dullest Wight becomes a Shakespeare) and by what law the Form of the vision appears to talk to us in its own thoughts in a voice as audible as the shape is visible; and this too oftentimes in connected trains.[9]

The latter phrase suggests association at work in dreams; indeed, the whole passage suggests, what has since become a commonplace of modern criticism, that the dream-work or *Traum-arbeit*, to use the Freudian term, is often the matrix of artistic creation. The dullest oaf, as Coleridge says, in dreams becomes a Shakespeare.

From Coleridge's interpretation of the character of Hamlet we might suspect that Coleridge himself, sublime somnambulist, had intense mental or interior activity going on all the time— " My Dreams become the Substances of my Life," as he once wrote to his friend Poole.[10] In his case he was singularly fortunate in his dreams, for though they did not always materialize,

[8] *Biographia Epistolaris*, ed. Turnbull, 182.

[9] *The Friend* (London, 1818), I, 246-47. Coleridge was probably acquainted with a very interesting treatise *On Dreams* by Synesius of Cyrene, a Neo-Platonist.

[10] Letter to Thomas Poole, Oct. 3, 1803, *Unpublished Letters*, I, 286.

they were sometimes the stuff of which great poetry is made. He pitied Hazlitt for his poverty of dreaming:

> Coleridge used to laugh at me for my want of the faculty of dreaming; and once, on my saying that I did not like the preternatural stories in the *Arabian Nights* (for the comic parts I love dearly), he said, "That must be because you never dream. There is a class of poetry built on this foundation, which is surely no inconsiderable part of our nature, since we are asleep and building up imaginations of this sort half our time." [11]

Coleridge realized that the timelessness of the dream becomes the timelessness of the poem. At what exact latitude or longitude did the Ancient Mariner shoot the albatross? Or on what date?

> You will take especial note of the marvellous independence and true imaginative absence of all particular space or time in the Faery Queene. It is in the domains neither of history nor of geography; it is ignorant of all artificial boundary, all material obstacles; it is truly in (and of) Faery, that is, of mental space. The poet has placed you in a dream, a charmed sleep, and you neither wish, nor have the power, to inquire where you are, or how you got there. [12]

Furthermore, he anticipated Freud in finding significance in dreams; "Dreams have nothing in them absurd or nonsensical." [13] And again: "You will perceive that even in dreams nothing is fancied without an antecedent *quasi* cause." [14] Not only that, but he realized that "the reproductive imagination, unsophisticated by the will, and undirected by intrusions from the sense" [15] might perhaps, through that very freedom, be prophetic—especi-

---

[11] William Hazlitt, "On Dreams," in *The World of Dreams*, ed. Ralph L. Woods (New York, 1947), 858.

[12] *Miscellaneous Criticism*, ed. Raysor, 36.

[13] *Table Talk*, May 1, 1832.   [14] *Ibid.*, June 1, 1830.

[15] *Appendix to Statesman's Manual, Works*, ed. Shedd, I, 466.

ally significant and pregnant in its imaginings. One is reminded
of Polonius's comment on Hamlet, " How pregnant sometimes
his replies are! a happiness that often madness hits on, which
reason and sanity could not so prosperously be delivered of." [16]

It is probable that Coleridge's imaginings, his mental images,
as he was reading, or in the act of composing, or in his dreams
were, if not visually sharp, emotionally intensely powerful and
vivid. He says so himself in several places, for instance: In
the act of metrical composition (he wrote Sir Humphrey Davy)
" voluntary ideas were every minute passing, more or less transformed into vivid spectra." [17] In fact, Coleridge, has presented
us with a perfect parallel, in describing Luther in the castle of
the Wartburg, poring over the Septuagint and falling asleep,
with himself, in a farmhouse near Porlock, Somerset, poring over
Purchas, and falling asleep (the circumstances of the composition of " Kubla Khan "): " he sinks, without perceiving it, into
a trance of slumber: during which his brain retains its waking
energies, excepting that what would have been mere *thoughts*
before, now (the action and counterweight of his senses and
of their impressions being withdrawn) shape and condense themselves into things, into realities! " [18] The images in his mind's
eye are intensely real.

In the celebrated note in which he explained the composition
of " Kubla Khan," a key piece of evidence in our present discussion, he testifies to the vividness of the spontaneous imagery:
" The Author continued for about three hours in a profound
sleep, at least of the external senses, during which time he has
the most vivid confidence, that he could not have composed less
than from two to three hundred lines; if that indeed can be

[16] *Hamlet*, II. ii. 205-08.
[17] *Letters*, I, 341. Lowes has collected other instances of Coleridge's vivid
spectra, *Road to Xanadu*, 66.
[18] *The Friend* (London, 1818), I, 240.

called composition *in which all the images rose up before him as things,*[19] with a parallel production of the correspondent expressions, without any sensation or consciousness of effort." [20]

He was aware, too, that the mind when it idles or in dreams is characteristically in a streamy state. In fact, he once characterized the state of dreaming as " the shifting current in the chaos of the fancy in which the *streaming* continuum of passive association is broken into *zig-zag* by sensations from within or from without." [21] His phrase " streaming continuum of passive association " leaves his insight beyond all doubt.

He had, too, an almost uncanny anticipation of what in modern psychological terms is called a *Gestalt.* Aristotle had showed in his treatise *De somniis* that the course of a dream is sometimes ruddered or interrupted by some external sensation such as of coldness or heat, feeling the foot of the bed, or the like. In a discussion of nightmares Coleridge explains how a limb deadened by some interruption of the circulation " transmits double touch as single touch, to which the imagination, the true inward creatrix, instantly out of the chaos of elements or shattered fragments of memory, puts together some form to fit it." [22] We shall see in a moment how this works.

Some years later Coleridge was still holding forth on his theory of dreams to an uncomprehending Keats. Let Keats himself tell the story:

> Last Sunday I took a walk towards Highgate and in the lane that winds by the side of Lord Mansfield's park I met Mr. Green

---

[19] Italics ours.

[20] Coleridge's note to the original edition of 1816, reprinted in *The Complete Poetical Works,* ed. James Dykes Campbell (London, 1925), 592.

[21] In a manuscript note to Tenneman's *Geschichte der Philosophie,* quoted in *Biographia,* I, 225.

[22] *Anima Poetae,* 206. Lowes has brilliantly seen in this description an account of how imagination, the true inward creatrix, worked in the composition of " Kubla Khan." He says, " That comment bares, as it happens, the secret springs of *Kubla Khan* "—*The Road to Xanadu,* 56.

our Demonstrator at Guy's in conversation with Coleridge—I joined
them after enquiring by a look whether it would be agreeable—
I walked with him at his alderman-after-dinner pace for near two
miles I suppose. In those two Miles he broached a thousand
things . . . Different genera and species of Dreams—Nightmare—
a dream accompanied with a sense of touch—single and double
touch—" [23]

How exterior sensation or touch, in the confused state of dreaming when the mind has not yet surfaced to consciousness, may
be mingled or fused with the dream itself is illustrated by the
following curious dream of Coleridge's:

> Dozing, dreamt of Hartley as at his christening—how, as he was
> asked who redeemed him, and was to say ' God the Son,' he went
> on humming and hawing in one hum and haw . . . so as to
> irritate me greatly. Awakening gradually, I was able completely
> to detect that it was the ticking of my watch which lay in the
> pen-place in my desk, on the round table close by my ear, and
> which . . . had fretted on my ears. I caught the fact while Hartley's
> face and moving lips were yet before my eyes, and his hum and
> haw and the ticking of the watch were each the other." [24]

The interest of all this is Coleridge's awareness of the interplay
between the conscious and the unconscious. Conscious sensation or the conscious mind will present the unconscious with a
shaping hint and instantly the pieces fall together in a *Gestalt*.
" He related as a sort of disease of imagination, what occurred
to himself. He had been watching intently the motions of a
kite among the mountains of Westmoreland, when on a sudden
he saw two kites in an opposite direction. This delusion lasted
some time. At last he discovered that the two kites were the
fluttering branches of a tree beyond a wall." [25]   Some kinetic

[23] Keats to George and Georgiana Keats. Keats's walk with Coleridge
was on the 15th of April, 1819. *The Letters of John Keats*, ed. Forman, 324.
[24] *Anima Poetae*, 33-34.
[25] Crabb Robinson, *Diary*, November 15, 1810. *Blake, Coleridge, Words-*

resemblance in the movement probably touched off the illusion. The same principle of the *Gestalt* is at work in Coleridge's brilliant accounting for the illusion of Martin Luther when, in the castle of the Wartburg, seeing a stain on the wall, his imagination likened the stain to a figure of the devil, at whom he threw the ink-pot.[26]

Coleridge was not only aware of the usually rudderless stream of mind, but aware, too, in a very modern way, of the indivisibility of the stream. " How opposite," he had written " to nature and the fact to talk of the ' one moment' of Hume, and of our whole being an aggregate of successive single sensations! Who ever felt a single sensation? . . . And what is a moment? Succession with interspace? Absurdity! It is evidently the *licht-punct* of the indivisible undivided duration! "[27]

And in the same vein, Coleridge was saying, " Again, what is a thought: What are its circumscriptions, what the interspaces between it and another: When does it begin: Where end?—Far more readily could one apply these questions to an ocean billow or the drops of water which we may imagine as the component integers of the ocean." [28]

Even the drop within the stream is a microcosm in itself. "What a swarm of thoughts and feelings, endlessly minute fragments, and, as it were, representations of all preceding and embryos of all future thought, lie compact in any one moment.

worth, Lamb: Reminiscences of Henry Crabb Robinson, ed. Edith S. Morley (Manchester, 1922), 31-32.

[26] *The Friend* (London, 1818), I, 240ff.

[27] *Anima Poetae*, 86-87.

[28] Quoted by Richards, *Coleridge on Imagination*, 68. When Coleridge starts to ask " Is Logic the *Essence* of Thinking? In other words, Is Thinking impossible without arbitrary signs?" (*Unpublished Letters*, I, 156), or, as in the above quotation, "What is a thought? " he is raising fundamental questions. Actually he foreshadows Husserlian phenomenology. I am indebted for this suggestion to Dr. Maurice Natanson.

So in a single drop of water the microscope discovers " [29] swarms of animalcules.

Coleridge's conception of the continuous stream of mind is supported by William James, who likewise controverts " the Humian doctrine that our thought is composed of separate independent parts and is not a sensibly continuous stream. That the doctrine entirely misrepresents the natural appearances is what I next shall try to show." [30] James asserts that " within each personal consciousness, thought is sensibly continuous " and he can only define continuous as " that which is without breach, crack, or division." [31]

Coleridge had constantly combatted the theory of the materialists that the mind is a sort of container or warehouse of hard clear images. Again he is supported by William James, who scorns

> the ridiculous theory of Hume and Berkeley that we can have no images but of perfectly definite things. . . . What must be admitted is that the definite images of traditional psychology form but the very smallest part of our minds as they actually live. The traditional psychology talks like one who should say a river consists of nothing but pailsful, spoonsful, quartpotsful, barrelsful, and other moulded forms of water. Even were the pails and the pots all actually standing in the stream, still between them the free water would continue to flow. It is just this free water of consciousness that psychologists resolutely overlook. Every definite image in the mind is steeped and dyed in the free water that flows round it. With it goes the sense of the relations, near and remote, the dying echo of whence it came to us, the dawning sense of whither it is to lead. The significance, the value, of the image is all in this halo or penumbra that surrounds or escorts it—or rather that is fused into one with it. . . ." [32]

In these poetical words, extremely poetical words to come from

[29] *Anima Poetae*, 208.
[30] *Principles of Psychology* (2 vols.; New York, 1890), I, 237.
[31] *Ibid.*   [32] *Ibid.*, I, 254-55.

a professional psychologist, Coleridge's conception of the fluidity of the stream of mind and the subtlety of its tonal associations is roundly vindicated.

It is of some significance, in view of the fact that we are here attempting to gather evidence of Coleridge's awareness of association, that William James quotes Coleridge's statement of the general law of association as though he were an authority on the subject.[33]

Coleridge shows himself aware, in a very modern way, that a great deal of the activity of the mind takes place below the level of consciousness. In a passage which recalls the Aristotelian *reminiscentia*, he tells his experience with the recall of a name:

> I feel that there is a mystery in the sudden by-act-of-will-unaided, nay, more than that, frustrated recollection of a Name. I was trying to recollect the name of a Bristol Friend, who had attended me in my Illness at Mr. Wade's. I began with the letters of the Alphabet—A B C etc.—and I know not why, felt convinced that it began with H. I ran thro' all the vowels, aeiouy, and with all the consonants to each—Hab, Heb, Hib, Hob, Hub and so on—in vain. I then began other Letters—all in vain. Three minutes afterwards, having completely given it up, the name, Daniel, at once started up, perfectly insulated, without any the dimmest antecedent connection, as far as my consciousness extended. There is no explanation . . . of this fact, but by a full sharp distinction of Mind from Consciousness—the Consciousness being the narrow *Neck* of the Bottle.[34]

All those who have had the maddening experience of being unable to recall a name when wanted will sympathize with Coleridge in his predicament. It might be remarked in this connection that it is of no use to browbeat the mind if a name is urgently needed. Panic, fear, or disturbing emotion blot out memory; but when, after some time, the cloudy sediment has

[33] *Ibid.*, I, 572. (He quotes *Biographia*, I, 72).
[34] *Inquiring Spirit*, ed. Coburn, 30-31.

settled, then, all at once, in the clear and in tranquillity, the name will be recollected.

But what is of most interest here is Coleridge's recognition that the conscious level of the mind is only the surface, the narrow neck of the bottle, and that vastly more than is on the surface lies below the threshold of consciousness. Coleridge's figure of bottleneck and bottle antedates by a century the one that has become fashionable in modern times, namely, that of the iceberg, the part of the iceberg above the waterline representing consciousness, and the much greater part of the iceberg, submerged and invisible, representing the unconscious.

ii

Unconscious Association in Shakespeare

Our next inquiry will be directed to the question whether Coleridge found association at work in the genius of Shakespeare. The associationist criticism of Shakespeare (and it is very considerable in bulk, to be found in the critical essays of Hume, Kames, Gerard, William Richardson, Priestley, Beattie and Alison) was in the main following up a blind alley. The criticism was applied to Shakespeare's depiction of passion; it was concerned, to use the language of Wordsworth's preface, certainly derived from this school, with "the manner in which we associate ideas in a state of excitement." [35] As though Shakespeare founded his insight into human nature on a few laws of association! Coleridge, "library cormorant" and voracious reader that he was, could hardly fail to be aware that such a school of Shakespeare criticism existed.

[35] Preface to Second Edition of *Lyrical Ballads*, 1800, in Bate, *Criticism: The Major Texts*, 336.

For the new associationist criticism of Shakespeare, with its psychological interest, succeeds often in being just as stupid as neo-classic criticism, only it is stupid in a new way. A good example of this is the Shakespearean criticism of Alexander Gerard. Instead of the neo-classic unities, a new set of rules is applied to Shakespeare which is equally iron-clad. If Shakespeare fails to observe the laws of associationist human nature, he is mistaken! The vast superiority of Coleridge over the literalist criticism of critics like Gerard lies in his realization of the necessity for dramatic illusion; the highly improbable is successful in the theatre provided it *goes*; the successful bringing off of dramatic illusion is a cloak that covers a thousand sins against literal verisimilitude. For the audience there is a "willing suspension of disbelief."

A much more profitable direction of inquiry was taken by Walter Whiter, who investigated association in the creative process of Shakespeare. He had the wit to perceive that a number of subtle connections probably occurred in Shakespeare's mind below the threshold of consciousness. He stated his conclusion thus: "I define therefore the power of this association over the genius of the poet to consist in supplying him with words and ideas which have been suggested to the mind by a principle of union unperceived by himself." [36] Did Coleridge follow up this clue?

Coleridge was not ignorant—whether or not he knew of the work of Whiter—that associated thoughts or images are part of the creative process of a poet like Shakespeare. In his valuable critique of Shakespeare's *Venus and Adonis* he believes that a strong passion or interest could suck a throng of associated thoughts or images into its vortex. Coleridge found that images in and for themselves are of little value; they "become proofs of

[36] Walter Whiter, *A Specimen of a Commentary on Shakespeare* (London, 1794), 68. See below, pp. 229-30.

original genius only as far as they are modified by a predominant passion; or by associated thoughts or images awakened by that passion." [37] This remark looks as though Coleridge grasped the image-clusters found in Shakespeare, the dominant imagery found by Spurgeon, and the symbolic structure of a play like *Lear*. The images are of value insofar as they contribute to a design.

He noted that Shakespeare commonly wrote his best dramatic verse in a fluent stream, one image frequently suggesting another by some subtle connection. In fact, he used this seamless robe or continuous texture as a test of genuineness, doubting the authenticity of lines that seemed to be added as carpenter's work or joinery. For example, he doubted whether the last two lines of Antony's speech in *Julius Caesar* (III. i. 207-08) were genuine:

> O world! thou wast not forest to this hart,
> And this, indeed, O world! the heart of thee

" because they interrupt not only the sense and connection, but likewise the flow both of the passion and . . . the Shakespearean link of association." [38] While this recognition by Coleridge is in itself interesting evidence, the fact remains that Coleridge did nothing with the hint. He did nothing to illumine the numerous associations which were (doubtless often unconsciously) at work in Shakespeare's creative process.

As far as the evidence now before us permits, we may say that Coleridge was aware of a continuous stream or flow of consciousness. He was steadily and consistently aware of association among the semi-conscious or unconscious powers of the mind, particularly in dreams. He was perfectly well aware that association is a valuable aid to creation. He says as much,

[37] *Biographia*, II, 16.
[38] *Shakespearean Criticism*, ed. Raysor, I, 17.

although he depresses the observation down into a footnote. Commenting on Dryden's famous line

Great wit to madness sure is near allied

Coleridge says, "Now as far as the profound sensibility, which is doubtless *one* of the components of genius, were alone considered, single and unbalanced, it might be fairly described as exposing the individual to a greater chance of mental derangement; but then a more than usual rapidity of association, a more than usual power of passing from thought to thought, and image to image, is a component equally essential; and in the due modification of each by the other GENIUS consists." [39] When Coleridge writes here about the "more than usual rapidity of association" in connection with genius, we seem almost to be listening to Gerard, but it is Gerard harnessed to greater insight, for Coleridge here is asserting once more the balance of active and passive powers which he consistently maintained.

iii

The Unconscious Element in Poetry

Coleridge, then, was aware of association as part of the passive powers of the mind assisting creation. But to what degree was he aware of the unconscious playing a part in the act of composing poetry? To be sure, the distinction may seen artificial, for associations and unconscious activity may often be, and usually are, one and the same thing. But many theorists were aware of association who had no distinct concept of the unconscious.

"The unconscious" is a fashionable term and it has been said that "the looseness with which the word 'unconscious' is at

[39] *Biographia*, I, 30-31n.

present used is a psychological scandal of the first magnitude." [40] To avoid making the present study scandalous, I define the unconscious as the content of the mind so submerged that it cannot be called up to consciousness through an act of reflection. It is important, too, to insist at the outset that the mind is not being divided into two parts: conscious and unconscious, but rather what we have under consideration is *one mind* in its conscious and unconscious, its waking and sleeping (or dreaming), aspects. We have, then, to do with a paradox, almost *the* paradox to end all paradoxes, and certainly one to stimulate Mr. Cleanth Brooks; namely, that we can know nothing directly about the unconscious, that unexplored territory, *terra incognita*, or last home of mystery, because, if we did, it would by definition, *ipso facto*, cease to be " the unconscious " by the very fact of our being conscious of it. Researches, therefore, into the nature of the unconscious proceed always by indirection, " by indirection find directions out," [41] through the partial recollection by the conscious mind of what passed in sleep, through the analysis of dreams, and the like.

Freud was too well read in literature and philosophy to claim a Columbus-like rôle as the discoverer of the unconscious. When, on the occasion of his seventieth birthday, he was credited with that distinction, he corrected the speaker. " The poets and philosophers before me discovered the unconscious," he said. " What I discovered was the scientific method by which the unconscious can be studied."

Many philosophers have been poetical, and many poets have been philosophical; insights respecting an unconscious activity

C. D. Broad, " Various Meanings of the Term Unconscious," *Aristotelian Society Proceedings*, April 9th, 1923. Quoted by John M. Thornburn, *Art and the Unconscious* (London, 1925), 6.

[41] Lionel Trilling, " Freud and Literature,' in *The Liberal Imagination* (New York, 1953), 44.

of mind have been written by philosopher-poets or poet-philosophers in which the term "the unconscious" is not used, but in which it is nevertheless implied. Plato, for instance, in the *Ion*, is playfully ironic on the subject, making the poet admit that he does not always know what he is doing. Even in the age of reason, when the imagination was supposed to be strictly controlled by judgment, Dryden speaks of his play, *The Rival Ladies* "before it was a play; when it was only a confused mass of thoughts, tumbling over one another in the dark; when the fancy was yet in its first work, moving the sleeping images of things towards the light," [42] thereby indicating depths in the mind from which images proceeded.

Coleridge's sympathy with the Cambridge Platonists has already been noticed. Not only did Cudworth in his *True Intellectual System* believe in a "plastic nature," but he was aware also, like Saint Augustine, of sleeping depths in the mind, a sunken treasure:

> It is certain our human souls themselves are not always conscious of whatever they have in them; for even the sleeping geometrician hath, at that time, all his geometrical theorems and knowledges some way in him; as also the sleeping musician, all his musical skills and songs: and therefore, may it not be possible for the soul to have likewise some actual energy in it, which it is not expressly conscious of? We have all experience of our doing many animal actions nonattendingly, which we reflect upon afterwards; as also that we often continue a long series of bodily motions, by a mere virtual intention of our minds, and as it were by half a cogitation. [43]

Here is a clear and early statement that there are activities in the mind which are not conscious.

All Coleridge's references to Leibniz are respectful and show

[42] "Epistle Dedicatory of *The Rival Ladies*," *Essays of John Dryden*, ed. W. P. Ker (2 vols.; Oxford, 1926), I, 1.

[43] Ralph Cudworth, *The True Intellectual System of the Universe* (3 vols.; London, 1845), I, 247.

that to him, of all the modern philosophers from Bacon to Kant, Leibniz (with the possible exception of Berkeley) was the most congenial. Spinoza, with his propositions in an adamant chain like those of Euclidian geometry, a method somewhat rigid for the study of a subject so fluid as consciousness, had no conception of an unconscious. To Leibniz, then, belongs the honor of being among the first of modern philosophers, indeed, one of the first in the history of European psychology, to have a distinct conception of an unconscious.

Leibniz's *New Essays Concerning the Human Understanding* are a direct answer to Locke, and Leibniz could not conceive of a condition of the mind in which it was an absolute vacuum. Something is going on, even if we are not conscious of it:

> I do not know whether it will be so easy to harmonize him (Locke) with us and the Cartesians, when he maintains that the mind does not always think, and particularly that it is without perception when we sleep without dreaming; and he objects that since bodies can exist without motion, souls can also exist without thought. But here I make a somewhat different reply than is customary, for I hold that naturally a substance cannot exist without action, and that there is indeed never a body without movement. Experience already favours me, and you have only to consult the book of the distinguished Mr. Boyle against absolute rest. . . .

> Moreover, there are a thousand indications which make us think that there are at every moment an infinite number of *perceptions* in us, but without apperception and reflection, i. e. changes in the soul itself of which we are not conscious, because the impressions are either too slight and too great in number, or too even, so that they have nothing sufficiently distinguishing them from each other; but joined to others they do not fail to produce their effect and to make themselves felt at least confusedly in the mass.

> And to judge still better of the minute perceptions which we cannot distinguish in the crowd, I am wont to make use of the example of the roar or noise of the sea which strikes one when on its shore. To understand this noise as it is made, it would be

necessary to hear the parts which compose the whole, i. e. the noise of each wave, although each of these little noises makes itself known only in the confused collection of all the others, i. e. in the roar itself, and would not be noticed if the wave which makes it were alone. For it must be that we are affected a little by the motion of the wave, and that we have some perception of each one of these noises, small as they are; otherwise we would not have that of a hundred thousand waves, since a hundred thousand nothings cannot make something. One never sleeps so soundly as not to have some feeble and confused sensation. . . .[44]

Leibniz's contribution to psychology, his theory of "*petites perceptions*," has not gone unrecognized. A. G. Langley, his editor and translator, says that his "doctrine of minute perceptions" or, in the philosophical language of today, "unconscious mental states," is of the greatest significance in psychology and epistemology, and never more so than at the present time.[45] Bertrand Russell draws attention to "a very important advance which Leibniz made in Psychology. Locke thought there could be nothing in the mind of which the mind was not conscious. Leibniz pointed out the absolute necessity of unconscious mental states. He distinguished between perception, which consists merely in being conscious of something, and apperception, which consists in self-consciousness, i. e. in being aware of perception." [46] And a recent historian of modern philosophy concedes that "Leibniz was one of the first to call attention to the fact that much goes on in our minds of which we are only confusedly aware; in some ways he is the forerunner of contemporary doctrines of the subconscious and unconscious nature of many mental processes." [47]

[44] Leibniz, *New Essays Concerning Human Understanding*, tr. A. G. Langley (New York, 1896), 47-48.
[45] *Ibid.*, 727.
[46] Bertrand Russell, *A Critical Exposition of the Philosophy of Leibniz* (London, 1937), 156.
[47] W. K. Wright, *A History of Modern Philosophy* (New York, 1941), 122-23.

It was Leibniz who said, "The insensible perceptions are as important in pneumatology (i. e. psychology) as corpuscles are in physics," who saw no distinct boundary between conscious and unconscious mental states,[48] and who referred to "these unconscious acts of mind called obscure ideas, insensible perceptions." [49] This line of thinking, whose inception we trace to Leibniz, was continued in German philosophy. For instance, George Henry Lewes says, "Kant admits that unconscious sensations and obscure perceptions form the larger proportion of our mental states." [50] And Schelling, whose influence on Coleridge, Coleridge himself freely acknowledged, says with approval, "Leibniz, in *Als denkbar*, was the first to assert the existence of unconscious perceptions as ideas." [51]

The word consciousness or *Bewusstsein* came into use in Germany in the eighteenth-century as an all-inclusive term:

> ... the word *Bewusstsein* (a translation of *conscientia*) first *appears* ... in the works of Christian Wolff. Very gradually it comes into usage as a composite idea for all feeling, thinking, sensation, and volition. But with Kant and his followers consciousness (*Bewusstsein*) is still not only the sum of conscious experiences, but also includes the inner structure of the mind, the "potentialities," and the essentially unconscious "categories." [52]

Though Kant acknowledged the existence of unconscious mental states, it is probably true that for him "'nature' had been something hostile, the overcoming of which was one of

[48] Richard Müller-Freienfels says, "With Leibniz the line of demarcation between consciousness and unconsciousness is again obliterated, since his 'perceptions' could be both conscious and unconscious." *The Evolution of Modern Psychology* (New Haven, 1935), 37.

[49] Leibniz, *Nouveaux Essais*, vol. II, chap. i, as quoted by Alfred T. Schofield, *The Unconscious Mind* (New York, 1898), 84.

[50] G. H. Lewes, *Study of Psychology*, 17 as quoted by Schofield, *ibid.*, 87.

[51] Schelling, *Psychology*, 108-15, as quoted by Schofield, *ibid.*, 84.

[52] Müller-Freienfels, *The Evolution of Modern Psychology*, 37.

the tasks of ethics. Along with his English predecessors and most of his contemporaries, he harbored a rationalistic mistrust of the unconscious, the subconscious, the impulsive." [53]

It was on ethical grounds, and especially on the part of the emotions in the ethical life, that Coleridge's thinking diverges most sharply from Kant's, yet Coleridge was probably of all Englishmen of his period best equipped to understand Kant's thought. One point, says Professor René Wellek, " of Coleridge's interpretation of Kant, which shows considerable insight, is his insistence on the unconsciousness of the synthesizing processes. He rightly insists that the " synthetic unity or the unity of apperception is presupposed in, and in order to, all consciousness. It is its condition (*conditio sine qua non*) or that which constitutes the possibility of consciousness *a priori*." [54]

Herder has more than a suggestion of the unconscious mind in the following passage:

> We are accustomed to attribute to the soul a group of underpowers (*Unterkräfte*) such as imagination and foresight, the gift of poetic composition and memory. . . . We will never unearth the roots of these powers, if we consider them only from above as ideas, which are located in the soul, or if we separate them one from another as special departmentalized activities and conceive of them as independent particular entities. In imaginative recall, in memory, and in foresight must the *one* God-like power of our soul present itself . . .[55]

The term " underpowers " may simply mean subordinate powers, however, not unconscious powers, and the passage may be only a powerful plea for regarding the mind as an organic unity.

Novalis was fascinated by the night-side or under-side of the

[53] Alfred Einstein, *Music in the Romantic Era* (New York, 1947), 22.

[54] *Immanuel Kant in England*, 123. Wellek quotes Coleridge's manuscript Logic (1822-27), II, 56.

[55] J. G. Herder, *Works*, VIII, 195, quoted by Newton P. Stallknecht, *Strange Seas of Thought*, 180.

mind. Perhaps no phrase of Novalis's is more frequently quoted than "*Die Welt wird Traum, der Traum wird Welt*"; and it is this somnambulistic confusion of actual world and dream world, the no man's land between the two, which is peculiarly Coleridge's territory. Novalis was convinced that dreams reveal a profounder stratum of universal experience.[56] He also declared "that the art of revealing the interior life of dream demanded something higher than our common logic, which is the art of deliberate thinking. He conceived, too, of a prose literature which would not be logically joined together but where the connection would be through the association of ideas, as in dreams." [57]

For Goethe, the work of a genius is "related to the daemonic, which does with him whatever it pleases, overwhelmingly, and to which he unconsciously surrenders, while believing he is acting on his own initiative." [58] But Goethe, as was to be expected of a man of his wisdom and insight, believed in a balance or reconciliation of powers. "Two kinds of *dilettanti*," says Goethe, "there are in poetry, he who neglects the indispensable mechanical part, and thinks he has done enough if he shows spirituality and feeling; and he who seeks to arrive at poetry merely by mechanism, in which he can acquire an artisan's readiness, and is without soul and matter." [59]

Schiller, too, was aware of a fountain of freely rising ideas from the deep reservoir of the unconscious. A very real possibility exists that too sharp a development of critical or analytical powers, too tight a control by the intellect, may upset the balance

[56] Katherine E. Gilbert and Helmut Kuhn, *A History of Esthetics* (New York, 1939), 376.

[57] Mary M. Colum, *From These Roots* (New York, 1937), 332.

[58] Eckermann, *Gespräche mit Goethe*, ed. A. Bartels (2 vols.; Jena, 1908), II, 380.

[59] Matthew Arnold interpreting Goethe, Preface to *Poems* of 1853, in Bate *Criticism: The Major Texts*, 451.

of active and passive, may lead to a drying-up of creative power, as indeed, happened in Matthew Arnold when the critic smothered the poet. Freud quotes Schiller replying in the following words to a friend who complained of his lack of creative power:

> The reason for your complaint lies, it seems to me, in the constraint which your intellect imposes upon your imagination. Here I will make an observation, and illustrate it by an allegory. Apparently it is not good—and indeed it hinders the creative work of the mind—if the intellect examines too closely the ideas already pouring in, as it were, at the gates. . . . In the case of a creative mind, it seems to me, the intellect has withdrawn its watchers from the gates, and the ideas rush in pell-mell, and only then does it review and inspect the multitude. You worthy critics, or whatever you may call yourselves, are ashamed or afraid of the momentary and passing madness which is found in all real creators, the longer or shorter duration of which distinguishes the thinking artist from the dreamer. Hence your complaints of unfruitfulness, for you reject too soon and discriminate too severely.[60]

It makes a difference whether the visitants be from the gate of ivory or the gate of horn, but to reject the bold simply because it is bold would be to travel the road to sterility.

Coleridge, then, could hardly escape becoming aware of the unconscious activity in poetry. As has been suggested above, it is to be suspected that a mind as introspective and self-aware as his, would sense it in himself. His experience with " Kubla Khan " surely convinced him that unconscious powers aid the conscious. And in any case, his stay in Germany in 1798-99 and his study of German literature would put him in touch with the thought of Leibniz and Herder, of Novalis and Schelling upon this subject, if not while he was in Germany, then when

---

[60] Letter of December 1, 1788. Quoted by Sigmund Freud in *The Interpretation of Dreams, Basic Writings of Sigmund Freud*, ed. A. A. Brill (New York, 1938), 193.

in Keswick in the years from 1800 onwards he had leisure to assimilate the German experience.

It is no surprise, then—whether from his own introspection or from his knowledge of German literature—to find him very much aware of what he calls "the twilight realms of consciousness." Such realms were particularly congenial to him, because in them one was cut loose from the contingencies of time and space, and the necessities of decision, will, foresight and action which they impose. The phrase occurs in his defence of Wordsworth's "Immortality Ode": "The ode was intended for such readers only as had been accustomed to watch the flux and reflux of their utmost nature, to venture at times into the twilight realms of consciousness, and to feel a deep interest in modes of being, to which they know that the attributes of time and space are inapplicable and alien, but which yet cannot be conveyed save in symbols of time and space." [61] Coleridge is aware, as Eliot is, of the intersection of time with the timeless.

A study of *Anima Poetae* and of such extracts from Coleridge's notebooks as are now available in print convinces us that Coleridge was a man "accustomed to watch the flux and reflux" of his own mind. That being so, it would be pleasant to record that a definite awareness of the unconscious playing a part in creation noted by Coleridge antedates his acquaintance with Schelling. Pending the publication of Miss Kathleen Coburn's complete edition of Coleridge's notebooks, any statement on this topic must be provisional, but so far as we at present know Coleridge's statements on the unconscious post-date rather than antedate acquaintance with Schelling. The celebrated note on "Kubla Khan" dates from 1816. To be intuitively aware that one has unconscious powers and to state in written or printed form that "the unconscious" aids the poet are two different

[61] *Biographia*, II, 120.

things and it is very possible to possess the first without having achieved the second. Our tentative conclusion, then, is that the presence of an idea of the unconscious in German literature and philosophy—particularly in Schelling—helped Coleridge to know his own mind better, or rather, let us say, to put into words that of which he was already intuitively aware. For aware he must have been, in some fashion, as early as 1797 or 1798, when he wrote "Kubla Khan."

Coleridge's two descriptions of the creative act, the central passage on the reconciliation of opposites [62] and the "water insect" passage,[63] both assume the collaboration of conscious and unconscious powers. This was the central assumption in Schelling's theory of art and of creative imagination.[64] In his important early work, his *Ideas for a Philosophy of Nature* (1797), Schelling assumes that nature is not wholly objective, but has a subjective side, is indeed semi-conscious, not fully awake, but struggling towards consciousness.[65] The artist, too, has an unconscious substratum in his mind, struggling towards consciousness. It is above all in the aesthetic act, the act of creation of a work of art, that the unconscious objective world,

[62] "The balance or reconciliation of opposite or discordant qualities." *Biographia*, II, 12.

[63] *Ibid.*, I, 85-86.

[64] Cf. Schelling, *Transcendental Idealism*, Part VI, and his lecture " On the Relation of the Formative Arts to Nature." Coleridge's statement on the reconciliation of opposites and the water-insect passage, both in *Biographia* of 1816, were made well subsequent to acquaintance with Schelling.

[65] Shawcross points out (*Biographia*, I, 272n.) that the same idea is found in Schelling's *Transcendental Idealism*: " *Die objective Welt ist nur die ursprüngliche, noch bewusstlose Poesie des Geistes*"—the objective world is the primitive half-conscious poetry of the spirit. *Sämmtliche Werke* (Stuttgart, 1858), III, 349. The opening words of Schelling's Introduction to his *Entwurf eines Systems der Naturphilosophie* (1799) read: " Intelligence is productive in twofold wise, either blindly and unconsciously, or with freedom and consciousness; unconsciously productive in the perception of the universe, consciously in the creation of an ideal world."

that gets into the artist's mind *via* the passive *vis receptiva*, and the highly conscious articulate world of the artist, are fused. For this reason, because the aesthetic act is a fusion of conscious and unconscious, the philosophy of art is the keystone of Schelling's whole philosophic structure.[66]

Coleridge expresses the same thought in his lecture "On Poesy or Art," in words taken more or less verbatim from Schelling: "In every work of art there is a reconcilement of the external with the internal; the conscious is so impressed on the unconscious as to appear in it. . . . He who combines the two is the man of genius; and for that reason he must partake of both. Hence there is in genius itself an unconscious activity; nay, that is the genius in the man of genius." [67]

Coleridge uses Shakespeare as the prime example of the poetic genius who combines these two powers, "Shakespeare . . . directing self-consciously a power and an implicit wisdom deeper than consciousness." [68] Elsewhere he refers to the "region of unconscious thoughts, oftentimes the more working the more indistinct they are." [69] He speaks of the Greek conception of the "mysterious Pan, as representing the intelligence blended with a darker power, deeper, mightier, and more universal than the conscious intellect of man." [70] No, we are not dreaming;

[66] This statement is fully borne out by the *System des Transcendentalen Idealismus.*

[67] *Biographia,* II, 258. The lecture " On Poesy or Art " was Lecture XIII of Coleridge's course in 1818. The close resemblance of many parts of this essay to Schelling's Oration *On the Relation of the Formative Arts to Nature* has been fully pointed out by Sara Coleridge, in the Appendix to her edition of the *Notes and Lectures* (1819), and illustrated by a translation of the most striking passages. The parallel passage in Schelling to the passage from Coleridge quoted above is Schelling's Oration, in *Werke,* II, 300. Cf. Shawcross, *Biographia,* II, 317-18. See, too, *Miscellaneous Criticism,* ed. Raysor, 209-10.

[68] *Shakespearean Criticism,* ed. Raysor, I, 224.

[69] *Biographia,* II, 250.   [70] *Ibid.,* 93.

this is not David Herbert Lawrence but Samuel Taylor Coleridge. He links the poet Daniel with Wordsworth, saying that his sentiments are "drawn up from depths which few in any age have courage or inclination to descend." [71] Coleridge himself did not often have that courage.

It is probable that Coleridge had more of that courage in his poems than in his theoretical writings in prose. Read as parables of the creative act, his three poems, "The Ancient Mariner," "Kubla Khan," and "The Ode to Dejection" are documents of supreme importance for his theory of imagination, and are valuable for his, perhaps, unconscious revelations of the hidden depths from which his poems proceeded.

Examined from this point of view, and, of course, this is only one way in which the poem may be read, "The Rime of Ancient Mariner" is very revealing. The mariner's crime of shooting the albatross is a crime against the seamless robe of God's love, the unity of all nature and all creatures, a wanton act, a gratuitous act, to use Gide's term; underlying the concept of violation is the Plotinian doctrine of the One and the Many. The secondary theme of the poem, as Robert Penn Warren has pointed out, is the imagination, and the mariner's crime is a crime against the imagination, for surely, as in Baudelaire's poem, the albatross is an imagination symbol. By the same token the mariner's redemption is first effected through the imagination; his imagination is touched by the beauty of the watersnakes

> Blue, glossy green, and velvet black

and he blesses them unawares. Imagination, or imaginative sympathy, induces love.

Just as Dante's *Divine Comedy* can be read at more than one level of meaning, so "The Ancient Mariner." Read in one way, it is a ballad story of action, involving crime and punishment.

[71] *Ibid.*, 120.

Read in another way (it is not certain how far Coleridge himself was aware of this consciously) it is a parable of the creative
imagination.

> The very deep did rot: O Christ!
> That ever this should be!
> Yea, slimy things did crawl with legs
> Upon the slimy sea

expresses stagnation of the creative power accompanied by feelings of slimy insufficiency and guilt. Maud Bodkin in her
Jungian study of archetypal myths in poetry regards this becalm-
ment and the subsequent freshening of the breeze as a pattern
of death and rebirth, but also as symbolizing Coleridge's states
of mental depression followed by a rising spate of creativity.[72]
Moreover the thirst

> Water, water, every where
> Nor any drop to drink

relates itself to the desiccation and spiritual dearth of Eliot's
Waste Land. But when the nightmare of stagnation and *acedia*
is broken, it is impossible not to feel the energy of

> The fair breeze blew, the white foam flew,
> The furrow followed free;
> We were the first that ever burst
> Into that silent sea

or, once more, after the blessing of the snakes, the sense of
release, the "silly buckets" filled with water, the grateful rain,
the "roaring wind" as a recovery of creative power. In Coleridge's divinely-impregnated universe, the wind that makes the
sails sigh like sedge is the wind that quickens the poet's spirit.
A creative force in nature *is* the creative force of the poet.

Another document of scarcely less importance for Coleridge's

[72] Maud Bodkin, *Archetypal Patterns in Poetry* (Oxford, 1934), 40-48.

theory of creative imagination is " Kubla Khan." It is difficult
not to feel the symbolic force of:

> deep romantic chasm which slanted
> Down the green hill athwart a cedarn cover:
> A savage place! as holy and enchanted
> As e'er beneath a waning moon was haunted
> By woman wailing for her demon-lover!
> And from this chasm, with ceaseless turmoil seething,
> As if this earth in fast thick pants were breathing,
> A mighty fountain momently was forced:
> Amid whose swift half-intermitted burst
> Huge fragments vaulted like rebounding hail
> Or chaffy grain beneath the thresher's flail. . . .

Here is a symbol for unbounded energy of creative power,
welling up, a subterranean fountain, from some profounder
source than the underground ocean of Burnet's *Theoria Sacra*.[73]
Attention, too, is invited to the conclusion of the poem; the
poet there assumes an aggressive, demonic character. He is like
Moses descending with the tables of the law, eyes ready to
kill with a look. Or he is like the ancient mariner, who has
been into such forbidden territory that the very sight of him
causes the pilot's boy to go insane. The wish-fulfilment theory
of dreams is common property now, and possibly Coleridge's
unconscious, here coming up to the surface, is describing the
poet as he would like to be:

> A damsel with a dulcimer
> In a vision once I saw:
> It was an Abyssinian maid,
> And on her dulcimer she played,
> Singing of Mount Abora.
> Could I revive within me
> Her symphony and song,
> To such a deep delight 'twould win me,

---

[73] Cf. *ibid.*, 107ff.

That with music loud and long,
I would build that dome in air,
That sunny dome! those caves of ice!
And all that heard should see them there,
And all should cry, Beware! Beware!
His flashing eyes, his floating hair!

Everyone has at some time or other experienced that sensation immediately upon waking from a dream of something irrecoverable but infinitely precious, irretrievable, irredeemable, yet which, could it once be found, would be the key to all felicity. Coleridge himself thought the poem merely " a psychological curiosity "[74] and Eliot, speaking of its " exaggerated repute " complains that

> the imagery of that fragment, certainly, whatever its origin in Coleridge's reading, sank to the depths of Coleridge's feeling, was saturated, transformed there—' those are pearls that were his eyes '— and brought up into daylight again. But it is not *used*: the poem has not been written. . . . Organization is necessary as well as ' inspiration.'[75]

Actually, however, although the poem may not measure up to Eliot's standards, there is more organization to it, albeit the organization of a dream or the logic of the imagination, than a cursory examination would suggest.

" The sunny dome " that the poet would create is the heaven of art, Keats's rounded urn, Eliot's Chinese jar that moves continually in its stillness, or Yeats's holy city of Byzantium. The sunny dome has caves of ice inside; just so, Keats's urn is a " cold pastoral," for the significant moment of art is eternally frozen. The view of the poet's power here expressed is at the

[74] His opinion is quoted by Richards, *Principles of Literary Criticism*, 227n.
[75] *The Use of Poetry and the Use of Criticism*, 146. Kenneth Burke has called " Kubla Khan " the first surrealist poem. For a discussion of whether the poem was as magical as Coleridge claimed and of the part that opium may have played in its composition, see Elisabeth Schneider, " The ' Dream ' of *Kubla Khan*," *PMLA*, LX (September, 1945). Lowes discusses its sources.

opposite pole to the mechanistic view. The poet is in touch with secret magic and demonic powers (the Platonic divine madness, the modern unconscious), but at the same time what he creates is by divine fiat. His power is not to be explained by a simple bag of tricks, the superficial fancy, or Hartley's law of association.

Coleridge resented the declining prestige of the writer and the poet. A strong tendency existed among many scientific minds in the eighteenth century to see poety, myth, imagination as belonging to the primitive state of the race (the Viconian theory) or essentially childish—the child's rattle as Peacock provocatively put it. This was the tendency of minds like Hartley's and Erasmus Darwin's. Once you explained away poetic creation as the association of brain traces, you took away the mystery and the magic, the nimbus of the awe-inspiring and the un-known. What became of the poet who has so shattering an experience that you had to beware of his flashing eyes and weave a circle round him thrice? His prestige evaporated.

The same theory of imagination, though here in its negative aspect, is found in the "Dejection Ode," which dates from April, 1802. Nature was a decodable cryptogram and symbol-language of the divine, yet a disenchanted Coleridge could sometimes look languidly at the forks of Borrowdale, turning a muddy and jaundiced eye upon the tented mountains around him:

> But oh! each visitation
> Suspends what nature gave me at my birth
> My shaping spirit of Imagination!

Coleridge felt the well-known spiritual state of *acedia* and what irked him was the spiritlessness of his condition:

> A grief without a pang, void, dark, and drear,
> A stifled, drowsy, unimpassioned grief,
> Which finds no natural outlet, no relief,
>   In word, or sigh, or tear.

He was going through a state of spiritual privation, and he perhaps less than Wordsworth was equipped to deal with Cistercian bareness, lacking the gift to turn spiritual or emotional spareness, deprivation and Franciscan poverty to account. This perhaps revealed a weakness in his theory of imagination; he felt that without exaltation there was nothing at all.

Deflation and inflation were the systole and diastole of the pumping romantic heart. He felt the flatness and the reaction from the over-stimulated imagination into listlessness and apathy. As he once wrote in one of these moods: "My imagination is tied down, flat and powerless, and I languish after home for hours together in vacancy, my feelings almost wholly unqualified by *thoughts*. I have at times experienced such an extinction of *light* in my mind, as if the *organs* of life had been dried up; as if only simply Being remained, blind and stagnant." [76] By far the best account of stagnation, however, is the passage about "the very deep did rot," upon which we have already dwelt. The miserable tragedy of his private life increased the creeping paralysis of his will.

"Dejection" reveals the same theory of imagination as the other poems do. It is Coleridge's salute or farewell to his imagination. Joy is the lubricant which causes all the faculties to work together. When the poet is cut off from the springs of his imagination—when the strings of his Æolian lyre no longer vibrate to the Plotinian breeze—then he must say farewell to his plastic power. For some reason of general frustration in his being, the subterranean fountain was frozen over.

It is a pity that Coleridge allowed himself to be temporarily swamped by German metaphysics during the period when his intellect was reaching its prime. The unhappy affair with Sara Hutchinson and the guilty feelings connected with opium drove

[76] Quoted by A. E. Powell, *The Romantic Theory of Poetry* (London, 1926), 79.

him deeper and deeper into metaphysics as into a womb of refuge.[77]

> And haply by abstruse research to steal
> From my own nature all the natural man.

He knew in doing so he was playing false to his own creative power. Yet we cannot say that his creative power was entirely idle or that he " toiled out " nothing for himself. He was unable to deaden his poetic nerve and this is what makes his speculations in the interesting province where poetry and psychology march together so valuable. The mere effort of assimilation, so that the ideas of Kant and Schelling were not a deluge which drowned all his own mental landmarks, but were canalized to the irrigation of his own thought, and domesticated to his own Plotinian climate of opinion, must have been considerable.

Coleridge's awareness of what has nowadays come to be referred to as " the deep well " of the unconscious is not, then, in any doubt. He must have been intuitively aware of unconscious or semi-conscious processes in the composition of poetry from his own experience with the " Mariner," " Kubla Khan," and " Christabel," which antedated the reading of Schelling. " Kubla Khan " particularly, whose images were given, presented with all the freshness of rainwashed April, seems to have welled up like a cold spring from inward depths. " The mighty fountain," with " ceaseless turmoil seething " and forcing itself from the earth in " fast thick pants " is an image, surely, of creative potency coming in continuous pulses.[78] He did not, however, define his awareness till after he had made contact with the ever-present idea of an unconscious in German philos-

---

[77] Earl Leslie Griggs points out that 1802 seems early for guilt feelings concerning the opium habit.

[78] Cf. " alternate pulses of active and passive motion " in Coleridge's description of the creative act, *Biographia*, I, 86. The parallel to the sexual act is apparent.

ophy and literature. It seems likely, then, he was made more consciously or overtly aware of it through his reading of Leibniz and Schelling, particularly the latter. We have no intention of magnifying or minimizing Coleridge's debt to Schelling with regard to the imagination; in the main that debt is not significant (Coleridge's theory of imagination would have been substantially the same as we now have it, if he had never read a line of Schelling); but for the explicit concept of an unconscious Coleridge's debt to Schelling cannot be denied.

The question of priority as between Coleridge and Schelling is of minor importance, however, the important fact being that Coleridge recognized the unconscious as a source of poetry. Professor J. L. Lowes, who handles the term " unconscious" very gingerly and with unnecessary apology,[79] says:

> The term . . . as I shall employ it, assumes the existence of what Coleridge called ' the twilight realms of consciousness';[80] it assumes that ' in that shadowy half-being' (as he once put it), ' that state of nascent existence in the twilight of imagination and just on the vestibule of consciousness,'[81] ideas and images exist; it assumes (and again I am quoting Coleridge) a ' confluence of our recollections,' through which ' we establish a centre, as it were a sort of nucleus in [this] reservoir of the soul.'[82]

Coleridge with his awareness of a polarity of the imagination anticipates a favorite mode of analysis practiced by critics today, namely, the examination of the structure of a poem in terms of image clusters organized by acts of unconscious association.[83]

---

[79] " I am not a trained psychologist, and I am fully aware that in using, as I sometimes have to use it, the term 'unconscious,' I am playing with fire "—*The Road to Xanadu*, 55.

[80] *Biographia*, II, 120.   [81] *Letters*, I, 377.

[82] J. L. Lowes, *The Road to Xanadu*, 55. He refers to *Biographia Epistolaris*, II, 182.

[83] An example of this procedure is Lowes's study of " The Rime of the Ancient Mariner " and " Kubla Khan " in the *Road to Xanadu*; also Kenneth Burke's examination of Coleridge's " Aeolian Harp " and " The Rime of the

Such an analysis, though it undoubtedly does bring a certain insight and illumination to the poem under scrutiny, is of far less value than a study which sees a tragedy as an organization of agony, and proceeds to study the imagery and symbolism as contributory to the meaning of the dramatic *agon* or struggle. The best and most sensitive modern criticism does precisely that: an example would be Robert Bechtold Heilman's *The Great Stage: Image and Structure in King Lear*.[84]

Coleridge's awareness of the unconscious was one that he shared with the romantic poets in general. Other poets were aware of the "caverns measureless to man." If Coleridge had a sunny dome with "caves of ice"—which to Professor George Wilson Knight "hint cool cavernous depths in the unconscious mind"[85]—Wordsworth, too, knew about caves. Speaking in *The Prelude* of how he has traced the growth of a poet's mind, he says:

> we have traced the stream
> From darkness, and the very place of birth
> In its blind cavern, whence is faintly heard
> The sound of waters; followed it to light
> And open day . . .[86]

Shelley, too, is full of streams, sometimes subterranean streams, and caves, which are symbols of the unconscious:

> . . . O stream!
> Whose source is inaccessibly profound,
> Whither do thy mysterious waters tend?
> Thou imagest my life. Thy darksome stillness
> Thy dazzling waves, thy loud and hollow gulfs,
> Thy searchless fountain and invisible course . . .[87]

Ancient Mariner " in his book, *The Philosophy of Literary Form* (Baton Rouge, 1941). For more detailed discussion of this topic, see chapter VI.

[84] Baton Rouge, 1948.

[85] *The Starlit Dome* (New York, 1941), 94.

[86] *The Prelude* (1805), ed. Ernest de Selincourt, Book XIII, ll. 172-76.

Lines from "Alastor," as quoted by Carl Grabo, *The Magic Plant*
177.

These lines remind us of " Kubla Khan," especially since Shelley, in the continuation of them, talks about a " measureless ocean " and an " oozy cavern."

Freud made the unconscious mind a commonplace of contemporary criticism. But many writers of the romantic movement were aware of the depths from which they drew and the term " unconscious " was coming into use in English criticism, introduced by Coleridge in 1818, almost a hundred years before Freud published his findings.

It will not be necessary to multiply examples, but a few will be given to show how widespread the idea had become. " The definition of genius," says Hazlitt, " is that it acts unconsciously; and those who have produced immortal works, have done so without knowing how or why; the greatest power operates unseen." [88] The deeper mind, according to Emerson, " flows into the intellect and makes what we call genius." [89] Emerson, like Coleridge on Hamlet, wanted a balance maintained between the interior dream-life and the life of action: " Inaction is cowardice, but there can be no scholar without the heroic mind. The preamble of thought, the transition through which it passes from the unconscious to the conscious, is action." [90] Hawthorne, too, recognized the existence of unexplored regions of the mind; in his story, " Rappacini's Daughter," we are told that, when Giovanni was walking with Beatrice in the exotic garden, " there came thoughts, too, from a deep source, and fantasies of a gem-like brilliancy, as if diamonds and rubies sparkled upward among the bubbles of the fountain "; [91] and in the same story he speaks

[88] Quoted by Ernest Bernbaum, *Guide through the Romantic Movement* (New York, 1949), 327.

[89] Quoted by F. M. Prescott, *The Poetic Mind* (New York, 1926), 91.

[90] " The American Scholar," *The Complete Works of Ralph Waldo Emerson*, ed. Edward Waldo Emerson (12 vols.; Cambridge, Mass., 1903-04), I, 94-95.

[91] *The Complete Works of Nathaniel Hawthorne* (13 vols.; Boston and New York, 1909), II, 131.

of "those shapeless half ideas which throng the dim region beyond the daylight of our perfect consciousness." [92] Carlyle's expression is to the same effect. "Of our thinking, we might say, it is but the mere upper surface that we shape into articulate thoughts." [93] Great significance for the modern tradition is attached to Baudelaire's injunction, "*plonger au fond du gouffre*," the gulf being taken to be the unconscious, and the phrase becoming a sacred text of the surrealist movement.[94]

Thomas Mann has insisted that the real fountain-source of the modern awareness of the unconscious is to be found in Schopenhauer's exposition of the world as Will and Idea:

> Schopenhauer, as psychologist of the will, is the father of all modern psychology. From him the line runs, by way of the psychological radicalism of Nietzsche, straight to Freud and the men who built up his psychology of the unconscious and applied it to the mental sciences. Nietzsche's antisocratism and hostility to mind are nothing but the philosophic affirmation and glorification of Schopenhauer's discovery of the primacy of the will, his pessimistic insight into the secondary and subservient relation of mind to will.[95]

Thomas Mann, though, is probably at fault in seeing a direct line between Schopenhauer-Nietzsche-Freud. It is always tempting to assume such direct lines of influence, but often in the history of thought we find similar ideas arising in separated minds at about the same time; we find a general climate favorable to certain ideas. The concept of the unconscious should really be regarded as the psychological discovery of the romantic movement, rather than the exclusive patented property of Goethe or Schiller, Schelling or Coleridge, Schopenhauer or Nietzsche.

[92] *Ibid.*, 133.

[93] Quoted by Prescott, *The Poetic Mind*, 94-95.

[94] Anna Balakian, *Literary Origins of Surrealism* (New York, 1947), 7.

[95] *The Living Thoughts of Schopenhauer*, ed. Thomas Mann (Philadelphia, 1939), 28.

As Lionel Trilling temperately and wisely says: " when we think of the men who so closely anticipated many of Freud's own ideas—Schopenhauer and Nietzsche, for example—and then learn that he did not read their works until after he had formulated his own theories, we must see that particular influences cannot be in question here but that what we must deal with is nothing less than a whole *Zeitgeist*, a direction of thought." [96]

Schopenhauer tended to show that the conscious intelligence was rather like the rider of a surfboard, doing his best to control the surface of the life-situation in which he found himself, but with profound life-forces or groundswell beneath, which mere logic was powerless to control. The blind will to reproduce, for instance, for no other reason than that life wills to continue itself, whether in a simple organism like the amoeba or a com- plicated organism like man, can be successfully evaded (without the more drastic resort to suicide) through the contemplative activity of the Nirvana of art. The extraordinary valuation which Schopenhauer, in common with all the romantics, placed on music—for, in their aesthetic theory, all of the arts, as Walter Pater said, aspire to the condition of music—is perhaps to be attributed to the fact that music organizes experience deliciously, or in Keats's phrase, causes all disagreeables to evaporate; like the weeds in the stream which the current causes to go all one way, or the reeds that bend together in the wind, it lays our jangled nerves soothingly together in one master direction, while, though the composer cunningly weaves his sonata-form with theme and counter-theme, in a conscious and highly-articulated design, it, through the immediate enchantment of rhythm and melody, stirs the deeper layers of memory. Schopenhauer openly says so: " The composition of melody, the disclosure in it of all the deepest sources of human willing and feeling, is the work of genius, whose action, which is more apparent here than

[96] Trilling, " Freud and Literature," *loc. cit.*, 44.

anywhere else, lies far from all reflection and conscious intention, and may be called an inspiration." [97]

More than this, and much more interesting, is the fact that Schopenhauer attributes a metaphysical, almost, one might say, a phenomenological, value to music, as a means of direct introspection into the nature of consciousness itself, i. e. consciousness in its pure givenness. His theory of the value of music is, in part, Platonic, for it acknowledges the existence of ideas, but un-Platonic in that in his aesthetic music is no copy or imitation of anything at all—it simply sidetracks the ideas and the whole of their phenomenal manifestation—to go straight to the center of being:

> . . . Music also, since it passes over the ideas, is entirely independent of the phenomenal world, ignores it altogether, could to a certain extent exist if there was no world at all, which cannot be said of the other arts. Music is as *direct* an objectification and copy of the whole *will* as the world itself, nay, even as the Ideas, whose multiplied manifestation constitutes the world of individual things. Music is thus by no means like the other arts, the copy of the Ideas, but *the copy of the will itself,* whose objectivity the Ideas are. This is why the effect of music is so much more powerful and penetrating than that of the other arts, for they speak only of shadows, but it speaks of the thing itself.[98]

Coleridge, one feels, would have readily agreed. One who sensitively recorded his pleasure in the music of Cimarosa [99] and who was affected by a sudden burst of landscape—by the visual experience of aesthetic depth or distance, by the instant organization of multeity (Coleridge's word) into unity—as by music, would likely have accepted this metaphysic of music, without necessarily accepting all the rest of Schopenhauer's philosophy.

[97] *The Living Thoughts of Schopenhauer*, ed. Mann, 118.
[98] *Ibid.*, 117.   [99] Italian composer, 1749-1801.

For Coleridge had a feeling about music very similar indeed, except that for him it carried transcendental assurances of a future state:

> Music is the most entirely human of the fine arts, and has the fewest analoga in nature. Its first delightfulness is simple accordance with the ear; but it is an associated thing, and recalls the deep emotions of the past with an intellectual sense of proportion. Every human feeling is greater and larger than the exciting cause,— a proof, I think, that man is designed for a higher state of existence; and this is deeply implied in music, in which there is always something more and beyond the immediate expression.[100]

Eduard von Hartmann, disciple of Schopenhauer, in his *Philosophy of the Unconscious*, emphasized the unconscious as the underlying ground from which all conscious phenomena arise. For example, it was Hartmann who first realized that the inspiration of the muses, the "divine frenzy" of Plato in *Phaedrus* and *Ion*, and the tradition stemming therefrom all down the centuries, from Cicero's *furor poeticus* to Shaftesbury's enthusiasm, was nothing more than a poetical tribute to the unconscious.[101]

Coleridge, as we have said, had a theory of imagination which called for the coalition of active and passive powers. Conciliation of active and passive is the core of his theory. Essentially, conciliation of active and passive means conciliation of conscious and unconscious. Coleridge, as usual, acted as the fruitful transplanter of German ideas into English criticism, and to Coleridge, as far as English criticism is concerned, with his full recognition of unconscious powers at work in poetry, belongs the chief credit for the rapid spread of the idea.

---

[100] "On Poesy or Art," *Biographia*, II, 261.

[101] Eduard von Hartmann, *Philosophy of the Unconscious*, tr. Coupland (2 vols.; New York, 1884), I, 276.

iv

Imagery and Symbol

A strictly Aristotelian theory of poetry would probably not countenance an exclusive attention to imagery and symbol, for the structure of a tragedy is found in the relation of part to part, and the insight into the agony of existence, and whatever resolution of that agony is possible though heroic acceptance or stoic fortitude, comes to the perceiver through imaginative identification with the crucial action and the suffering of the crucified or transfigured one. Nevertheless, a full understanding of the Aeschylean, Sophoclean, or Shakespearean tragedy would not be obtained without an understanding of the functional imagery, for the images and symbols are piers and pillars, that it, supporters of essential meaning, not merely gargoyles, to grin and carry off water; they are more than impish or devilish spouts and gutters.

We agree at the onset with Muirhead's comment: "Coleridge had reflected profoundly on the process by which poetic images are generated in the mind. No psychologist had ever had a better opportunity of first-hand observation of it in his own mind, and there is no reason to believe that he here owed anything at all to German philosophy." [102]

Coleridge's opinion coincided with that of Addison, Gray and Johnson in *Rasselas* that it was the duty of the poet to augment his reservoir, to be continually storing his mind with images. He was not averse at all to storing his mind with new images from fields not heretofore available to poetry, for instance, from new discoveries in science; he wanted to attend Sir Humphrey Davy's lectures in order to increase his store of images. Two of his notebook entries indicate this desire: " Sadly do I need

[102] Muirhead, *Coleridge as Philosopher*, 199.

to have my Imagination enriched with appropriate Images and Shapes. Read Architecture and Ichthyology"; "To read most carefully for the purpose of poetry Sir W. H.'s account of the earthquakes &c in the New Annual Register, 1783—or Phil. Trans. 73rd Vol." [103] The entires, the first dated 26th October, 1803, and the second probably written in December 1809, illustrate what a naturally studious person Coleridge was .all his life. To find the author of *The Rime of the Ancient Mariner*, a man whose cormorant-capacity for reading was so enormous, whose wealth of imagery was so Croesus-like by ordinary standards, confessing a sense of poverty and a need to increase his stock is a little startling. But even he felt the need for enlargement.

Mere industry, however, would soon acquire a large capital of images, and Coleridge felt that industry without the imagination to use the imagery poetically was not enough.[104] Images by themselves do not make a poet, just as a few circling swallows round the barn do not make a summer. They "become proofs of original genius only as far as they are modified by a predominant passion." [105] Imagery becomes effective when it is functional to the poem as a whole. It is more than imagery which makes the difference between the man of talent and the genuine poet. It is "the sense of musical delight"; [106] it is the power of fusion of multitude into unity; it is the power of conciliating the conscious and the unconscious; as light permeates the figure in plastic or glass, it is the power of making image or symbol the instrument of the poet's vision.

[103] The transcription of these notebook entries is from R. C. Bald, "Coleridge and the Ancient Mariner," *Nineteenth Century Studies*, ed. Herbert Davis, *et al.* (Ithaca, 1940), 15-16.

[104] Possibly he had in mind the diligence of a Southey or an Erasmus Darwin.

[105] *Biographia*, II, 16.   [106] *Ibid.*, 14.

Though there was a radical difference of opinion between Coleridge and Wordsworth on the subjects of poetic diction and meter and though their respective theories of poetry were at variance,[107] yet on one point there was perfect agreement between them, namely, that powerful feeling or passion, not necessarily that of the poet himself personally, but that of his characters, was the justification of image or figure of speech. Both concurred in a dislike of cold rhetorical figures, typical of the eighteenth century, which were illustrative, or ornamental, or artificial. As far as Wordsworth " has evinced the truth of passion, and the *dramatic* propriety of those figures and metaphors in the original poets, which, stripped of their justifying reasons and converted into mere artifices of connection or ornament, constitute the characteristic falsity in the poetic style of the moderns," and as far as he has distinguished the latter from " the natural language of empassioned feeling," he " deserves all praise, both for the attempt and for the execution." [108]

Coleridge is psychological and genetic in his discussion of imagery; he inquires into the origin of the figure in the creative process of the mind. Objects " faithfully copied from nature " are products of the fancy and essentially dead, whereas living images are those to which " a human and intellectual life is transferred . . . from the poet's own spirit,

'Which shoots its being through earth, sea, and air.' " [109]
In this power of giving " dignity and a passion to the objects which he presents," Shakespeare " surpasses all other poets." Coleridge disliked " pseudo-poesy " or " the startling hysteria of weakness overexerting itself " as in the eighteenth-century personification

" INOCULATION, heavenly maid! descend! " [110]

---

[107] See Coleridge's critique of Wordsworth's Preface of 1800, *Biographia*, chapters **XVII** and **XVIII.**
[108] *Biographia*, II, 28.   [109] *Ibid.*, 16.   [110] *Ibid.*, 65-66.

But he admired empathy or *einfühlung* or projection of human feeling into natural form, citing as his example of real imagination at work two lines from Shakespeare's sonnet

> " Full many a glorious morning have I seen
> *Flatter* the mountain tops with sovereign eye." [111]

Vital image, symbol, simile, or metaphor are formed under considerable imaginative pressure. Coleridge is very good on the subject of low-pressure similes, such as are to be found in a minor poet like Bowles or Wordsworth in his prosier moments, rather than Wordsworth in his hours of real inspiration:

> Nature has her proper interest, and he will know what it is who believes and feels that everything has a life of its own, and that we are all One Life. A poet's heart and intellect should be *combined*, intimately combined and unified with the great appearances of nature, and not merely held in solution and loose mixture with them, in the shape of formal similes. I do not mean to exclude these formal similes; there are moods of mind, and such as a poet will often have, and sometimes express; but they are not his highest and most appropriate moods. They are " sermoni propriora," which I once translated " properer for a sermon." The truth is, Bowles has the *sensibility*, of a poet, but he has not the passion of a great poet.[112]

When a poet finds himself writing things in a poem that are " properer for a sermon," he is not writing poetry; it is a sign, perhaps, that he is tired. Faded metaphor and rhetorical image are like immortelles or artificial flowers, never to be mistaken for crowsfeet, dogroses, buttercups, or daisies, nor confounded with fresh insights expressed in a startling figure.

Images are not pillars supporting vacancy, but caryatids sustaining weight; they are not empty casks, but barrels containing

[111] *Ibid.*, 17.

[112] Coleridge to W. Sotheby. Greta Hall, Keswick. September 10, 1802, *Letters*, I, 403-04.

meaning. Eliot has praised the imagery of Dante for this quality of being the reverse of empty:

> We have to consider the type of mind which by nature and *practice* tended to express itself in allegory: and for a competent poet, allegory means *clear visual images*. And clear visual images are given much more intensity by having a meaning. . . . Dante's is a visual imagination . . . it is visual in the sense that he lived in an age when men still saw visions. It was a psychological habit, the trick of which we have forgotten . . . We have nothing but dreams . . . It is the allegory which makes it possible for the reader who is not even a good Italian scholar to enjoy Dante. Speech varies, but our eyes are all the same.[113]

Coleridge praises the imagery of Dante for the same reason: " The Images in Dante are not only taken from obvious nature, and are all intelligible to all, but are ever conjoined with the universal feeling received from nature, and therefore affect the general feelings of all men." [114]

Similarly he says that in *Venus and Adonis* through the use of images Shakespeare was trying to " provide a substitute for that visual language, that constant intervention and running comment by tone, look and gesture, which in his dramatic works he was entitled to expect from the players." [115] If Elizabethan London had possessed the contemporary attractions of cinemascope and cinerama, Shakespeare perhaps would not have exerted his extraordinary powers of visual imagery to convey to every eye the story of Ophelia's death:

> There is a willow grows aslant a brook,
> That shows his hoar leaves in the glassy stream.
> There with fantastic garlands did she come
> Of crow-flowers, nettles, daisies and long purples . . .
> There, on the pendent boughs her coronet weeds

[113] *Selected Essays*, 204.
[114] *Miscellaneous Criticism*, ed. Raysor, 152.
[115] *Biographia*, II, 15.

Clambering to hang, an envious sliver broke;
When down her weedy trophies and herself
Fell in the weeping brook. Her clothes spread wide;
And mermaid-like awhile they bore her up:
Which time she chanted snatches of old tunes,
As one incapable of her own distress,
Or like a creature native and indued
Unto that element: but long it could not be
Till that her garments, heavy with their drink,
Pulled the poor wretch from her melodious lay
To muddy death.[116]

Everyone can picture Ophelia temporarily buoyed up by the air in her dress, and everyone with experience of the weight of garments when wet can see her dragged down. The visual accuracy of the opening two lines, even to the silvered undersides of the willow leaves, is unsurpassed, combined as it is with the sense of " musical delight," and the appropriateness of liquid syllables to a watery death.

Coleridge's own images have the quality of recent immersion, as though, while perfectly adapted to the purpose of the poem, they are still freshly wet and iridescent with the dream-life of the mind, and not quite sure what they are doing at the surface level. His very much admired images, such as the red sun in the copper sky, the painted ship upon the painted ocean, the red shadow of the ship, or

About, about in reel and rout
The death-fires danced at night;
The water like a witch's oils
Burnt green and blue and white

and the glossy watersnakes, have a phosphorescent or atmospheric quality about them—their reason for being is the tonal feeling, whether of guilt or terror, or mystery or forgiveness, which they

[116] *Hamlet*, IV. vii. 182-99.

convey, and therein lies their power. They are symbolic of universal states (who has not at some time known the terror of aloneness?) and have an infinite suggestiveness, which was what he asked of them. For Coleridge was no imagist poet, demanding that images be hard, clear, and distinct; to attempt to reconcile Coleridge's view of the image with that of a reactor to romanticism like T. E. Hulme would be a waste of time—it cannot be done. Indeed, Coleridge so valued the quality of suggestion of infinite and unexplored depths that he thought: " the grandest effects of poetry are where the imagination is called forth, not to produce a distinct form, but a strong working of the mind . . . ; the result being what the poet wishes to impress, namely, the substitution of a sublime feeling of the unimaginable for a mere image." [117] And he was repelled by " a skeleton, the dryest and hardest image that it is possible to discover." [118]

He did not have the type of mind that submits itself readily to positivist, scientific, or mathematical disciplines. This may be its weakness, but, on the other hand, in certain other directions, may be its strength. Just as he was skeptical whether *all* value is to be contained in clear and distinct ideas,[119] so was he doubtful whether all value is to be packaged in clear and distinct images. He once jotted this thought in a notebook: *Quaere*, whether or no too great definiteness of terms in any language may not consume too much of the vital and idea-creating force in distinct, clear, full-made images, and so prevent originality. For original might be distinguished from positive thought.[120] The profoundest intuitions of the mind cannot be expressed in a neat formula, and much wisdom is found, with

[117] In a criticism of *Romeo and Juliet*, *The Best of Coleridge*, ed. E. L. Griggs (New York, 1934), 288-89.

[118] *Ibid.*, 289.

[119] He deplored the " misuse" of the word idea by Descartes and Locke, since their usage differed from that of Plato.

[120] *Anima Poetae*, 19.

hints of more to be known, in fitful flashes of partial illumination, and that which is only half-grasped is not necessarily non-existent. We do not expect the diver after one dive to chart the whole floor of the ocean.

He once observed that " an whole essay might be written on the danger of thinking without images." Such a remark, without explanation, is cryptic. Of what danger could he have been thinking? Probably he had in mind increasing degrees of abstraction, by which, as on an interplanetary rocket voyage the anchorage of referents would be left behind and the earth seen (if seen at all) as a diminishing planet. Ideas, abstract ones, have an extraordinary ease of manipulation, and it is possible for a theorist like Godwin to construct a perfected system of social justice, though the stubborn prejudices of a human community are not so readily uprooted. Then, too, Coleridge could have had in mind the sensuously-concrete manner of thinking which is characteristic of poets, in contrast to the cleansed and conceptual manner which is characteristic of philosophers.

As Coleridge's thought matured, he grew less and less disturbed by the danger of thinking without images, more and more concerned with the opposite danger, namely, that which he connected with the mechanists, of conceiving the mind as stored with impressions derived from the senses and with clear distinct images, the mind so conceived only having power of classification or re-arrangement. He wished to raise the mind above the " despotism of the eye " and the " tyranny of the senses " into the region of reason and Platonic ideas. He complained that " according to the creed of our modern philosophers, nothing is deemed a clear conception, but what is representable by a distinct image. Thus the *conceivable* is reduced within the bounds of the *picturable*." [121]

[121] *Biographia*, I, 189. For similar complaints, see his *Philosophical Lectures*, ed. Coburn, 343 and 352.

Coleridge says little about metaphor directly, but by implication makes illuminating comment. Familiar from his reading of German philosophy with the formula thesis-antithesis-synthesis, he once stated his favorite principle of the reconciliation of opposites in such a way as to show he favored imaginative and creative unions: "The mechanic system . . . knows only of distance and nearness . . . in short, the relations of unproductive particles to each other; so that in every instance the result is the exact sum of the component quantities, as in arithmetical addition . . . In Life . . . the two component counterpowers actually interpenetrate each other, and generate a higher third including both the former, ' *ita tamen ut sit alia et major.*' " [122] This interpenetration by two different qualities to form a " higher third " could be used to explain the potency of the interaction of tenor and vehicle in a good metaphor, for instance the compasses and the lovers in Donne's celebrated " Valediction forbidding Mourning," [123] the cat and the fog in Eliot's " Prufrock," or the giantess and the mountain in Baudelaire's " *La Geante.*"

The term symbol which is so central to philosophies like those of Ernst Cassirer and Suzanne Langer, which see man's prodigious mental development as made possible by the control of experience which the symbol gives him, is in need of careful definition, for the symbol as used in algebra or in symbolic logic or in philosophy is to be distinguished (in spite of a basic resemblance which all symbols have in virtue of being symbols) from the use of image or symbol that is made by the poet. The essential difference is this: in symbolic logic unisignificance rather than plurisignificance is desirable, whereas for a poet the

[122] MS. note printed by A. D. Snyder, " Coleridge's ' Theory of Life,' " *Modern Language Notes,* XLVII (1932), 301.

[123] Coleridge: " Nothing was ever more admirably made out than the figure of the compass."—*Coleridge on the Seventeenth Century,* ed. Roberta F. Brinkley (Durham, N. C., 1955), 523.

greater the density that an image or symbol comes charged with the better.

A symbol may be defined as the equivalent in words of an iconic sign in plastic art: it is, indeed, like the catholic definition of a sacrament, the outward and visible sign of an inward invisible meaning. To it, further, inheres a weight and profundity of meaning in excess of that which adheres to a single metaphor or image.[124]

Coleridge's imagination is symbolic. For instance, he says: " The Mystics . . . define beauty as the subjection of matter to spirit so as to be transformed into a symbol, in and through which the spirit reveals itself." [125]

Bate complains that Coleridge has surprisingly few definitions of the imagination.[126] But how many does he want? Actually, a reading of *Biographia Literaria,* Coleridge's *Shakespearean Criticism, The Statesman's Manual, The Friend, Anima Poetae* and his *Letters* reveals that Coleridge has " god's plenty " in the way of definitions, and that his definitions, whenever he is not chiefly concerned with " reconciliation of opposites " or " organic unity " imply that imagination is symbolic.[127] How could it be otherwise, if the imagination (the eye of the reason) is to be the chief organ of transcendental insight, and the interpreter of those symbols which " the Divine imagination " creates " in virtue of its omniformity? " [128]

Coleridge does not necessarily derive his conception of the

[124] For discussion and definition of " Image, Metaphor, Symbol, Myth," see René Wellek and Austin Warren, *Theory of Literature* (New York, 1949), 190-218.

[125] " On the Principles of Genial Criticism," *Biographia,* II, 239.

[126] Bate, " Coleridge on the Function of Art," *loc. cit.,* 144.

[127] Coleridge explicitly says " Imagination, or idealising Power, of symbols mediating between the Reason and Understanding "—*Miscellaneous Criticism,* ed. Raysor, 286.

[128] *The Friend,* Section II, Essay 11.

symbol from contemporary German aesthetic thought, for as early as " Religious Musings " (1794) he possessed the prevalent romantic idea of nature as a veil (a veil of finely-woven and translucent texture, at times penetrated by the light behind it to the point of revelation) through which nature's essence or Divine Being shone or manifested itself. Yet he undoubtedly shared the view of nature as a symbol-language found in Schelling and the Schlegels. He was certainly in agreement with Schelling's opinion that " the artist must imitate that which is within the thing, that which is active through form and figure, and discourses to us by symbols—the *Natur-geist*, or spirit of nature." [129]

One of the earliest, as it is also one of the clearest and most beautiful of his statements of the symbolic imagination occurs in " The Destiny of Nations." The poet's duty is to seek out the One behind appearances:

> him First, him Last, to view
> Through meaner powers and secondary things
> Effulgent, as through clouds that veil his blaze.
> For all that meets the bodily sight I deem
> Symbolical, one mighty alphabet
> For infant minds; and we in this low world
> Placed with our backs to bright Reality,
> That we may learn with young unwounded ken
> The substance from its shadow.[130]

The thought here is to be connected with the still earlier " Aeolian Harp." The phrase " placed with our backs to bright Reality " seems an undoubted reference to Plato's allegory of the cave and implies a commitment to a metaphysical view of supra-empirical existence or realm of value. The notion of the translucent veil is (as already remarked) common to transcend-

[129] " On Poesy or Art," *Biographia*, II, 259.
[130] " The Destiny of Nations," ll. 13-23, *Poems*, 132.

entalism; the belief that every object is a double, is but an imperfect type or shadow of a real idea in the supra-empirical realm, is Platonic and Plotinian, with numerous echoes in the thought of mystics, with parallels, too, in the thought of Sweden-borg and the Baudelairean theory of symbols.

Again in 1805 Coleridge set down these reflections in his notebook:

> In looking at objects of Nature while I am thinking, as at yonder moon dim-glimmering through the dewy window pane, I seem rather to be seeking, as it were *asking* for, a symbolic language for something within me that always and for ever exists, than observing anything new. Even when that latter is the case, yet still I have always an obscure feeling as if that new phenomenon were the dim awaking of a forgotten or hidden truth of my inner nature. It is still interesting as a word—a symbol.[131]

Here we witness an introspection that is not the introverted turning of the neurotic into the neural entrails of his personal dilemma, nor Narcissus gazing at his own reflection, but an inward that finds the outward a manifestation of the extra-temporal or eternal.

Coleridge once gave a homely definition of the symbol as " that which means what it says and something more beside." [132] He elsewhere said that "an idea, in the *highest* sense of that word cannot be conveyed but by a *symbol*; and, except in geometry, all symbols of necessity involve an apparent contra-diction." [133] In other words, the only manner in which a divine or Platonic idea can be conveyed is through a symbol. And the paradoxical mode of the conveyance would win the approval of Mr. Cleanth Brooks.

[131] *Anima Poetae*, 136.
[132] Quoted by Richard Harter Fogle, " The Dejection of Coleridge's Ode," *ELH: A Journal of English Literary History*, XVII (March, 1950), 73.
[133] *Biographia*, I, 100.

Coleridge's distinction between allegory and symbol parallels his distinctions between talent and genius, fancy and imagination, understanding and reason. He says:

> Allegory is nothing but a translation of abstract notions into a picture-language which is itself nothing but an abstraction from objects of the senses; the principal being more worthless even than its phantom proxy, both alike unsubstantial and the former shapeless to boot. On the other hand a symbol . . . is characterized by a translucence of the special in the individual, or of the general in the special, or of the universal in the general; above all by the translucence of the eternal through and in the temporal. It always partakes of the reality which it renders intelligible; and while it enunciates the whole, abides itself as a living part in that unity, of which it is the representative. The other [i. e. the representations of allegory] are but empty echoes which the fancy arbitrarily associates with apparitions of matter, less beautiful but not less shadowy than the sloping orchard or hillside pasturefield seen in the transparent lake below.[134]

Perhaps the key to this somewhat involved passage is the phrase "translucence of the eternal through and in the temporal." Yeats had the same preference for symbol over allegory: " I find that though I love symbolism, which is often the only fitting speech for some mystery of disembodied life, I am for the most part bored by allegory, which is made, as Blake says, by the ' daughters of memory,' and coldly, with no wizard frenzy." [135]

Coleridge makes a similar distinction when he says that " the symbolical . . . is always itself a part of that, of the whole of which it is the representative . . . the latter (the allegory) cannot be otherwise than spoken consciously; whereas in the former

[134] *Statesman's Manual,* in *Works,* ed. Shedd, I, 437. Dante's use of allegory is symbolic, however; see Eliot's excellent discussion of Dante's allegory in *Selected Essays,* 204-05.

[135] *Essays* (London, 1924), 474. James Russell Lowell, who was also bored by allegory, particularly the Spenserian, once said that it reminded him of grit in strawberries and cream!

(the symbol) it is very possible that the general truth may be working unconsciously in the writer's mind." [136] His recognition that the symbol has unconscious sources is one of his best insights.

In the course of comparing scriptural history with history as written by Hume or Robertson, Coleridge defines the symbolic imagination. He says:

> The histories and political economy of the present and preceding century partake in the general contagion of its mechanic philosophy, and are the product of an unenlivened generalizing Understanding. In the Scriptures they are the living educts of the Imagination; of that reconciling and mediatory power, which incorporating the Reason in Images of the Sense, and organizing (as it were) the flux of the Senses by the permanence and self-circling energies of the Reason, gives birth to a system of symbols, harmonious in themselves, and consubstantial with the truths of which they are the *conductors*. These are the Wheels which Ezekiel beheld, when the hand of the Lord was upon him, and he saw visions of God as he sat among the captives by the river of Chebar . . . Whithersoever the Spirit was to go, the wheels went, and thither was their spirit to go:—for the spirit of the living creature was in the wheels also. [137]

Here, surely, is one of Coleridge's greatest definitions of the imagination to set beside the one, quoted to death, of the primary and secondary imagination. The imagination is still defined as " that reconciling and mediatory power," *i. e.*, the reconciliation of opposites is still an essential part of it. Here, however, Coleridge is more explicit in defining the symbol, which is, like the Host in the Eucharist, transubstantiated into the Body and Blood. In other words, a symbol is not like a shoe which can be put on and off; it is livingly a part of that which it symbolizes.

For Coleridge imagination is the binder, the general recon-

---

[136] *Miscellaneous Criticism*, ed. Raysor, 99.
[137] *Statesman's Manual* (London, 1816), 34-35.

ciler of all the faculties. The forms or abstractions of the understanding are analogous to "clearness without depth" and com-
prise "a knowledge of superficies without substance . . . The
completing power which unites clearness with depth, the plenitude of the sense with the comprehensibility of the understanding,
is the imagination, impregnated with which the understanding
itself becomes intuitive, and a living power." [138] Without the
infiltration of this intuitive power "science itself is but an
elaborate game of shadows." This might be another way of
saying that only in higher theoretic reaches of science or in
the mind of an Einstein do the sciences march upon the borders
of philosophy.

Coleridge's thought will not be easy to follow for those who
have been trained in scientific disciplines or in logical positivism
or pragmatism. When he, at the end of the *Statesman's Manual*
drew up a list or glossary of philosophic terms, he thus defined
an idea:

> That which is neither a sensation nor a perception, that which is
> neither individual (that is a sensible intuition) nor general (that
> is a conception), which neither refers to outward facts, nor yet
> is abstracted from the forms of perception contained in the under-
> standing; but which is *an educt of the imagination actuated by
> the pure reason,*[139] to which there neither is nor can be an adequate
> correspondent in the world of the senses;—this and this alone is—
> an Idea. Whether ideas are regulative only, according to Aristotle
> and Kant; or likewise constitutive, and one with the power and
> life of nature, according to Plato and Plotinus . . . is the highest
> problem of philosophy, and not part of its nomenclature.[140]

Do not suppose that Coleridge was sitting on the fence. He had
chosen to believe that ideas are constitutive or creative, with
Plato and Plotinus. The only mode of conveying an idea, thus
defined, is a symbol.

[138] *Ibid.*, Appendix B.   [139] Italics mine.
[140] *Statesman's Manual*, Appendix E, in *Works*, ed. Shedd, I, 484.

Coleridge values the symbol, the living "educt" of the imagination, more than he does the metaphor, simile, or allegory, products of the fancy, probably because the latter are limited, while the former has an unlimited power of suggestion. He values the symbol for its "translucence," as a kind of fenestration or window into infinity, by which the eternal shines through or in the temporal; in this he is not alone, for other romantics, Emerson and Carlyle, value the symbol for the same reason.

In reading Emerson one finds oneself in a similar intellectual climate as one does in reading Coleridge, for Emerson quotes the Neo-Platonists, Iamblichus and Proclus, and is, like Coleridge, convinced of unity of being behind appearances. Perhaps the best *locus* for Emerson's theory of symbols is his essay on "The Poet": "Nature offers all her creatures to him as a picture-language. . . . 'Things more excellent than every image,' says Jamblichus, 'are expressed through images.' Things admit of being used as symbols because nature is a symbol, in the whole, and in every part." [141] Just as for Novalis "the world is a universal trope of the spirit," for Emerson "the Universe is the externalization of the Soul." Further, "since everything in nature answers to a moral power, if any phenomenon remains brute and dark, it is because the corresponding faculty in the observer is not yet active." He speaks of "the universality of the symbolic language" and declares that "the world is a temple whose walls are covered with emblems, pictures and commandments of the Deity." We are reminded at this point of the passage from Coleridge already quoted:

> All that meets the bodily sense I deem
> Symbolical, one mighty alphabet
> For infant minds.

It is the function and privilege of the poet, according to Emerson,

[141] *The Essays of Ralph Waldo Emerson* (New York, 1944), 223-24.

to read this alphabet, to articulate the emblems, and to translate the otherwise-dark hieroglyphs upon the temple wall into luminous poems. "Work and tools . . . birth and death, all are emblems," and it is the poet's gift to put "eyes and a tongue into every dumb and inanimate object."

Carlyle, in an excellent chapter in *Sartor Resartus*, says: "In the Symbol proper, what we can call a Symbol, there is ever, more or less distinctly and directly, some embodiment and revelation of the Infinite; the Infinite is made to blend itself with the Finite, to stand visible, and as it were, attainable there." Moreover, the symbol reveals "Eternity looking through Time" and affords "some dimmer or clearer revelation of the Godlike." His special contribution is to point out that a symbol's power comes from its dual character: "In a symbol," he says, "there is concealment and yet revelation: hence, therefore, by Silence and by Speech acting together, comes a double significance." Coleridge, too, we recall, had said that "all symbols . . . involve an apparent contradiction."

Coleridge's theory of imagination would suffer desiccation and dehydration were it not that it is a symbolic theory. It is this which gives his theory its ever-contemporary quality and its validity.

His theory and his practice are in accord; if one looks for symbols in action, one finds them in his poetry. The shooting of the albatross with a crossbow is an highly symbolic action, a fact which literal-minded critics, who find the poem a tract on "the prevention of cruelty to albatrosses," have ludicrously missed. It is a Dostoievskian poem of crime and punishment, of outrage and redemption. Robert Penn Warren, who has given us what is probably to date the best all-around reading of *The Rime of the Ancient Mariner* [142] (by "all-round" we mean that

[142] *The Rime of the Ancient Mariner* by Samuel Taylor Coleridge, Edited and with an essay by Robert Penn Warren (New York, 1946).

his reading is at once sane and imaginative) has found symbols in the wind (as Maud Bodkin [143] has found symbols in the calm), in the sun, and in the moon. The all-seeing eye of the sun, a father-image, beating down from the copper sky, presides, with pitiless vision over the crime. The moon, a softer and more maternal symbol, to be equated, indeed, with the imagination itself, sheds a mild and beneficent influence, presiding over redemption. Professor G. Wilson Knight has found a symbolic significance (phallic) in the watersnakes.[144] The entire voyage-poem is a myth whose symbols have universal relevance.

The critic last-mentioned has found symbolism in the sur-realist dream-poem, " Kubla-Khan." The fountains, rills and teeming forests enfolding sunny spots of greenery symbolize nature. The " caverns measureless to man " and the " sunless sea " symbolize perhaps, unconscious mental states even reaching back to pre-natal states, or forward to the condition of complete unconsciousness, namely death. The sacred river running through nature towards death is a symbol of life. The pleasure dome which is sunny and radiant, yet within its concave interior contains caves of ice symbolizes the constructs of art which outlast time. It is to be compared to Keats's Grecian urn or Yeats's Byzantium; it has the circular form and the cold stillness of art, beside the turmoil of the river of life.

It is the symbolic power in his poetry that gives Coleridge his standing with poets like Dante, Blake, Eliot, and Yeats. Yeats has written:

> O chestnut tree, great rooted blossomer,
> Are you the leaf, the blossom or the bole?
> O body swayed to music, O brightening glance
> How can we know the dancer from the dance? [145]

---

[143] *Archetypal Patterns of Poetry*, chap. 2, *passim*.
[144] *The Starlit Dome*, 86-87.
[145] " Among School Children," stanza VIII and last.

This is true, in a very deep way, of the symbol as Coleridge understood it: how can we tell apart the body of the symbol and its inward invisible meaning?

Yeats has expressed the same idea in prose: " It is not possible," he writes, " to separate an emotion or a spiritual state from the image that calls it up and gives it expression." [146] Ezra Pound defined the nature of an image in such a way as to stress the union of sense and thought, the presence of the idea *in* the image. " An ' Image ' is that which presents an intellectual and emotional complex in an instant of time." [147] Surely this kind of thinking was founded on Coleridge, who credited the imagination, among its fusions, with that of " the idea, with the image." [148]

The modern symbol, used by poets and symbolic novelists, is nondiscursive; it carries what ordinary discourse could not convey, namely, the poet's otherwise inexpressible intuitions concerning the state of man in the modern world, or concerning religion or art. Examples of such potent and weight-carrying symbols would be the mountain, in Mann's *The Magic Mountain*; the waste land in Eliot's poem of that name; the mist-shrouded castle, symbol of the inscrutability and absurdity of existence in Kafka's *The Castle*; Byzantium, in Yeats's " Sailing to Byzantium," to mention only a few. The symbol is super-charged with meaning, but the modern symbol differs from the romantic in this way: the romantic was vertical, if we assume the old scheme of the chain of being; something " below," on the physical plane, was the analogy of something " above " on the plane of ideas or spiritual realities. In modern symbolism, " above " and " below " have been abolished, and modern sym-

[146] Quoted by Graham Hough, *The Last Romantics* (London, 1949), 228.
[147] Quoted by F. O. Matthiessen, *The Achievement of T. S. Eliot* (New York, 1947), 61.
[148] *Biographia*, II, 12.

bolism is horizontal, the symbol chosen being a means of conveying the author's manifold experience of life as we know it. Consider the very expert use made by T. S. Eliot of the abortive gesture to suggest futility.[149] Though Eliot's symbols, the rose, the garden, the pool, the Chinese jar that moves perpetually in its stillness, are not exactly romantic, they suggest spiritual states won through discipline. The privileged moment is the moment of the intersection of time with the timeless.

Were there no bin or container, corn would be scattered. Were there no myth or symbol, human insight and vision, preciously distilled from experience, would be dispersed or dissipated. The symbol draws on the unconscious; its potency lies here, that it draws on or taps a stored experience and a vestigial wisdom. If, as I believe, myth and symbol are the most valuable modes of insight into the meaning of existence, Coleridge deserves honor as the first philosophic thinker in English to have an adequate account of imagination as symbolic or mythopoeic power.

[149] *Vide* Paul Fussell, Jr. "The Gestic Symbolism of T. S. Eliot," *ELH: A Journal of English Literary History*, XXII (September, 1955), 194-211.

~~~~~~

6

COLERIDGE'S THEORY:

AN APPRAISAL

i

The Transcendental Basis

Coleridge's theory of the imagination would be greatly weakened if it did not have a philosophical basis.[1] No great theory of the imagination has been without it. ⁍A theory of imagination, if it has any claim to greatness, fits into a general view of human nature and a conception of life as a whole.⁍ Plato's theory of imagination could not be other than it was, holding as he did his copy-of-a-copy theory, and distrusting as he did the excitation of emotion. Only a controlled symbolic imagination, mediating Divine Ideas, and inventive of parables like that of the shadows on the cave wall, was admissible in his Republic. Plotinus'

---

[1] I. A. Richards, little sympathetic though he is to transcendentalism, insists that Coleridge's theory is not to be understood without the philosophic background. He says that a spirit of sympathy, almost a willing suspension of disbelief, is needed as we " try to read the more transcendental parts of Coleridge . . . However repugnant to our opinions they may seem, they are, I think, an indispensable *introduction* (from which we may disengage ourselves later) to his theory of criticism." *Coleridge on Imagination*, 18.

theory of imagination is consonant with the world-view of Plotinus. The Cartesian view of imagination—when certain reservations are made, a distrusted faculty—is consonant with the Cartesian view of the importance of the mathematical reason. And, to come to modern times, Jean-Paul Sartre's theory of imagination, as a shadow-world of distortion, unreality and illusion, shattered by the first contact with the absurdity and the horror of real existence, is in keeping with his existential philosophy. Coleridge's transcendental theory of the imagination is only one more example of this rule: it is consonant with a transcendental world-view.

Professor T. M. Raysor concludes that "as an aesthetician, Coleridge . . . was unfortunately derivative, mediocre, and, in a subject which requires system, fragmentary"[2] Derivative he certainly was, as who is not? It is the wise thinker who makes an eclectic and original compound of the best thinking that has gone before him. But Coleridge's theory of imagination is by no means as fragmentary as might at first be supposed. When all his definitions of imagination are collected, not only the single one about the primary and secondary imagination in *Biographia*, but also those in the *Statesman's Manual* and elsewhere, it will be found that Coleridge has a considerable body of aesthetic theory and especially a coherent theory of imagination.

Care has been taken, in the present study, to edit Coleridge to the extent of collecting some of his scattered sayings, under the headings of the primary and secondary imagination, reconciliation of opposites, organic unity, the unconscious in Coleridge's theory of imagination and the degree to which he uses association of ideas. Under all these topics we have found a solid body of thought, and all these solid bodies cohere into one consistent system—as consistent, that is, as most human systems are.

[2] *Coleridge's Shakespearean Criticism*, I, xlviii.

We have seen that Coleridge's transcendental theory of imagination is best understood embedded in his transcendental philosophy. It is equally true that his theory of imagination is best understood as it fits into his total psychology. A few remarks on his psychology, therefore, may now be in order.

ii

The Poet as Psychologist

Shelley credited Coleridge with being a "subtle-souled psychologist,"[3] and, second only to his fame as poet, today it is on being a man of psychological insight that his reputation rests. For example, a contemporary critic writes, "One cannot read his letter to Henry Crabb Robinson written in March, 1811, or the letter to the Reverend John Dawes written in 1822, in which he analyzed the tragically complex personality of his beloved Hartley, without realizing that Coleridge probed deeper into the psychological mystery of the emotions than perhaps any writer before Freud and Havelock Ellis."[4] Yet it remains true that "no detailed study of Coleridge as psychologist has ever been made."[5]

Coleridge himself knew that psychology was a young science with almost everything about the mind still to be found out. "Psychologically, Consciousness is the problem, the solution of which cannot too variously be re-worked, too manifoldly be illustrated. . . . Almost all is yet to be achieved."[6]

We have his own word for it that from the first psychology

[3] Shelley, "Peter Bell the Third."
[4] Roy P. Basler, *Sex, Symbolism and Psychology in Literature* (New Brunswick, 1948), 49-50.
[5] *Inquiring Spirit*, ed. Coburn, 27.
[6] Notebook 51, *Inquiring Spirit*, 25.

as a subject had fascinated him and he had tried to build a solid foundation of knowledge in it. "Facts of mind," as he wrote to Thelwall (Nov. 19, 1796), interested him most. And, referring to his last years at school, his early years at Cambridge, he wrote: "Actuated, too, by my former passion for metaphysical investigations; I labored at a solid foundation, on which permanently to ground my opinions, in the component faculties of the human mind itself, and their comparative dignity and importance. According to the faculty or source, from which the pleasure given by any poem or passage was derived, I estimated the merit of such poem or passage." [7] In other words, he grounded his criticism in psychology.

This is not the time or place to give a full account of Coleridge's psychology, but enough of his view of the mind may be indicated so that it may be seen how the imagination fits into his system. The fact is that Coleridge's psychology is full of paradox, for, on the one hand he was a man, steeped as few men have been, in the traditional psychology, which involved hierarchies of the mind; on the other hand, his view of the mind was beginning to be truly modern, seeing it as an organic unity, or unified function of the nervous system.

According to Coleridge's hierarchical psychology, the mind is seen as organized on three main levels. "Our inward experiences [are] arranged in three separate classes, the passive sense, or what the school-men call the merely receptive quality of the mind; the voluntary; and the spontaneous, which holds the middle place between both." [8]

To fill in the threefold pattern a little: at the bottom is the purely passive part of the mind, the sponge-like absorption of sensuous experience, what the old school men referred to as *vis receptiva*. At the top is the speculative reason or *νοῦς*, the *vis theoretica et scientifica*,[9] whose privilege it is to contemplate

---

[7] *Biographia*, I, 14.   [8] *Ibid.*, I, 66.   [9] *Ibid.*, 193.

the constitutive ideas, laws, or principles *a priori.* This is the active and originative part of the mind that is conscious in the highest degree. Between the two is the imagination " or shaping and modifying power," midway in the stream of the mind, neither active nor passive, but spontaneous, constantly paddling its canoe from one bank to the other. Coleridge, uncertain on the road between Wem and Shrewsbury which side of the way to take, may have typified vacillation, but he was, all unconsciously, emblematic of imagination.

Perhaps Coleridge, as Thorpe has suggested, was essentially a believer in the one mind, using the old terminology to indicate modes of the mind, as a convenience. Certainly in his best moments of insight Coleridge sees the mind working as one. The poet " brings the whole soul of man into activity." [10] The higher powers of the mind cannot work without the lower.[11] Seeing that the mind functions as a unity is one of Coleridge's chief claims to psychological penetration.[12]

Increasingly, during the nineteenth century, the Hartleian, that is, the physiological or biological approach to problems of mind gained ground, and the old psychology of faculties came more and more to be discredited. George Henry Lewes, for example, insisted that " the mind is not made of separable parts . . . Each piece has significance only in its relation to others . . . Nor can experience be likened to any complex of parts put together; it is a living, developing, manifold unity." [13] Coleridge, with his very traditional cast of mind, remained old-fashioned in his attempt to retain separate and sharply-defined

[10] *Biographia,* II, 12.

[11] " Imagination must have fancy, in fact the higher intellectual powers can only act through a corresponding energy of the lower "—*Table Talk,* April 20, 1833.

[12] In his notebooks he speaks of " that deep intuition of our oneness," *Inquiring Spirit,* 32.

[13] C. Spearman, *Psychology Down the Ages* (2 vols.; London, 1937), I, 96.

faculties: reason, judgment, fancy, imagination; yet this view of the mind as an organic unity is so Coleridgean that we believe he would have welcomed, as indeed he partly initiated it.

iii

Strength and Weakness of the Theory

(Be that as it may, the strong point of Coleridge's theory, his coalition of active and passive powers in the act of creation, is unassailable, because in the experience of many poets, as they have testified, this is the way poetic creation works. The recognition of the coalition of active and passive powers is the chief virtue of Coleridge's theory of imagination.) Earlier theories of the imagination in England, those of Dryden and Hobbes, the series of papers on the imagination by Addison in *The Spectator*, had been rudimentary sketches, not without value; no theory of imagination in England approached Coleridge's for subtlety, acuity of psychological insight into the creative process, and completeness.

Since, then, the main point of Coleridge's theory is unassailable, what weakness does his theory have, if any? The weakness of Coleridge's theory is using "fancy" as a name for the associative power and assuming that the associative power is "mechanical." While Coleridge was right to place association among the passive powers of the mind, association is better known as association, and no critic or psychologist, so far as I know, has followed him, except in the exposition of his own theory, in naming association fancy. The use was sanctioned by the eighteenth century, but it has not stuck.

To confound fancy and association can only lead to a critical snarl of the worst kind. Indeed, it has already led to a Goodwin sands of bottomless confusion on which many a critical freight ship has been wrecked. Once the term fancy had been pried away from its older usage as a name for *phantasia* or creative power, then fancy began to be appropriated as the name for that activity of mind which created what is commonly called "the fanciful." In some of her moods Emily Dickinson is a very fanciful poet, as when she wrote, "My heart grows light so fast that I could mount a grasshopper and gallop around the world, and not fatigue him any." [14] Such a *jeu d'esprit* does not come about from any linkings in the unconscious or subconscious; it is obviously a play of very conscious wit—we might even say it is a trifle self-conscious.

What examples does Coleridge give of the typical product of fancy? He says that Cowley—noted for his metaphysical conceits, which are conscious wit—had "a very fanciful mind" [15] (Milton, on the other hand, is imaginative). As an example of fancy he gives Otway's

> Lutes, lobsters, seas of milk and ships of amber,

while of imagination he gives Shakespeare's

> What, have his daughters brought him to this pass? [16]

He gives another example of fancy involving lobsters:

> And like a lobster boyl'd the Morn
> From black to red began to turn—

the example comes from Samuel Butler's *Hudibras.*[17] Obviously, this is simply one more instance of highly conscious metaphysical wit. Butler saw that what the morning and the lobster had in

[14] Quoted by James Granville Southworth, *Some Modern American Poets* (Oxford, 1950), 22-23. An extended example of fancy occurs in Rostand's play *Cyrano de Bergerac.* Cyrano suggests to his dull-witted insulter a large number of wittier ways in which he could have referred to his nose, when it bleeds it is the Red Sea, and so on.

[15] *Biographia*, I, 62.   [16] *Ibid.*   [17] *Table Talk*, June 23, 1834.

common was *turning red.* It would merely be ridiculous to say that Butler, somewhere deeply buried in his unconscious, had a private association dating from childhood, linking sunrises and lobsters. Yet Coleridge, by definition, says that fancy "must receive all its materials ready made from the law of Association." [18]

We could also question the example which Coleridge gives of fanciful writing. Is any very different faculty involved in

> And like a lobster boyl'd the Morn
> From black to red began to turn

than in

> What, have his daughters brought him to this pass?

We could, becoming the devil's advocate for the moment, say whatever it is in the human mind invents, invents. Both passages are results of human invention, and we may as well call the power that invented the lines, imagination in either case. The *Lear* passage is greatly superior in dignity, seriousness and tragic implication—granted. But by what right do we deny imagination to the boiled lobster simile? Imagination was certainly involved in creating it, for it is a daring and inventive mind that links objects so diverse as lobsters and sunrises by the common quality of turning from black to red. In fact, it is an excellent example of that intellectual wit shot with imagination for which the metaphysicals are famous. That Samuel Butler's purpose is satiric does not invalidate his claim to imagination in the least.

We find support for our contention in T. S. Eliot, who has usually been cool to Coleridge's distinction between imagination and fancy; he never has bitten on it with any enthusiasm. In one of the finest of his critical essays, that on Andrew Marvell (1921), he observes, "The difference between imagination and

[18] *Biographia,* I, 202.

fancy, in view of the poetry of wit, is a very narrow one. Obviously, an image which is immediately and unintentionally ridiculous is merely a fancy . . . But the images in the *Coy Mistress* are not only witty, but satisfy the elucidation of Imagination given by Coleridge." [19]

In a later essay, Eliot takes two passages for analysis and comparison. " The first is from Dryden's *Preface to Annus Mirabilis*:

> The first happiness of the poet's imagination is properly invention, or the finding of the thought; the second is fancy, or the variation, deriving, or moulding of that thought, as the judgment represents it proper to the subject; the third is elocution, or the art of clothing and adorning that thought, as found and varied, in apt, significant, and sounding words; the quickness of the imagination is seen in the invention, the fertility in the fancy, and the accuracy in the expression.

The second passage is from Coleridge's *Biographia Literaria*:

> Repeated meditation led me first to suspect . . . that Fancy and Imagination were two distinct and widely different faculties, instead of being, according to the general belief, either two names with one meaning, or, at furthest, the lower and higher degree of one and the same power. It is not, I own, easy to conceive a more opposite translation of the Greek *phantasia* than the Latin *imaginatio*; but it is equally true that in all societies there exists an instinct of growth, a certain collective, unconscious good sense working progressively to desynonymize those words originally of the same meaning, which the conflux of dialects supplied to the more homogeneous languages, as the Greek and German . . . Milton had a highly imaginative, Cowley a very fanciful mind." [20]

Eliot's comparison of the two passages follows:

> The way in which the expression of the two poets and critics is determined by their respective backgrounds is very marked. Evident also is the more developed state of mind of Coleridge: his

---

[19] *Selected Essays*, 256.
[20] *The Use of Poetry and the Use of Criticism*, 18-19.

greater awareness of philology, and his conscious determination to make certain words mean certain things. But what we have to consider is, whether what we have here is two radically opposed theories of Poetic Imagination, or whether the two may be reconciled after we have taken account of the many causes of difference which are found in the passage of time between Dryden's generation and Coleridge's.[21]

Eliot understands " that Dryden's ' invention ' includes the sudden irruption of the germ of a new poem, possibly merely as a state of feeling. His ' invention ' is surely a finding, a *trouvaille*. ' Fancy ' represents the conscious elaboration of the original *donnée*." [22] And he adds:

> I am not sure that Coleridge has made as satisfactory an analysis as that of Dryden. The distinction is too simple. The last sentence, " Milton had a highly imaginative, Cowley a very fanciful mind," should be enough to arouse suspicion. It represents a course of argument which is specious. You assert a distinction, you select two authors who illustrate it to your satisfaction, and you ignore the negative instances or difficult cases. If Coleridge had written, " Spenser had a highly imaginative, Donne a very fanciful mind," the assumed superiority of imagination to fancy might not appear quite so immediately convincing. Not only Cowley, but all the metaphysical poets had very fanciful minds, and if you removed the fancy and left only the imagination, as Coleridge appears to use those terms, you would have no metaphysical poetry. The distinction is admittedly a distinction of value; the term " fancy " is really made derogatory, just applicable to clever verse that you do not like.[23]

Eliot's concern to defend metaphysical wit is obvious. He does not like Coleridge's use of fancy in a pejorative sense, if fancy is to be made equivalent to wit, for serious wit (when combined with imagination, as in the intellectual figure of Donne's compasses) is a quality in poetry that Eliot values highly.

[21] *Ibid.*, 19-20.   [22] *Ibid.*, 48.   [23] *Ibid.*, 50 51.

Since Coleridge's distinction between imagination and fancy is open to criticism, we shall, at this point, offer our own distinction. We are not now interpreting Coleridge, but offering our own theory, for which we accept full responsibility. We like Coleridge's remark on the psychological study of poetry, " According to the faculty or source from which the pleasure given by any poem or passage was derived, I estimated the merit of such poem or passage," [24] and we propose to apply it. Any combination, simile, or metaphor that is, as we say, " fanciful," trivial, arbitrary, or artificial, that appears to be the froth of wit rather than drawn from any profound level of thought united to feeling, is the product of fancy. Fancy has nothing to do with deep unconscious processes. This is not to say that many of the products of fancy—Emily Dickinson's grasshopper, for example— are not very amusing. Whereas any passage of poetry that is serious, appealing to our sense of psychological, moral, or spiritual reality that the experience as related is, in fact, so—" What, have his daughters brought him to this pass? "—; any successful treatment of human dramatic situation in poetic medium, as in Shakespeare—is the product of another faculty called imagination.

Whether poetry is formed by the fusion of conscious and unconscious, whether the poet calls on the deeper levels of his mind, whether, in a given line or lines, he uses the precipitate of his whole life's experience, governed by the control of conscious intellect at the moment of writing—or whether the verse is lightly skimmed off the surface of consciousness, like froth off a glass of beer—is our test whether the poetry or prose is work of the imagination or work of the fancy. We feel that, as now stated, the distinction is not only valid, but a critical tool of value to the practicing critic, who should not hesitate to apply it. In our distinction, we are not applying any stigma to serious

[24] *Biographia*, I, 14.

wit, nor are we implying that the conscious is necessarily the superficial. Not at all. We are saying that conscious, intellectual control, united to deep levels of experience, may be profound in its results; [25] fancy we define as the frivolity of the mind, the colt that kicks up its heels in the spring meadow. It blows the froth off the top; it has the value that all releases and safety-valves have.

We make the distinction, too, with the reservation that there is a danger in using terms like fancy and imagination for specific powers of the mind, of reviving the old faculty psychology. It should be borne in mind that such terms are convenient metaphors and that even the term imagination itself is doubtless no more than a convenient metaphor. Thus, there is no isolable faculty of the mind which creates poetry, a faculty which can be fenced off and separated from the rest of the mind. The poet, in writing poetry, is not using an isolated part of his mind labeled "imagination," but as Coleridge saw in the celebrated account of "the poet, described in *ideal* perfection," [26] he is using all the powers of his mind at once.

Commenting on Coleridge's distinction between imagination and fancy,[27] Eliot says:

> I have read some of Hegel and Fichte, as well as Hartley (who turns up at any moment with Coleridge), and forgotten it; of Schelling I am entirely ignorant at first hand, and he is one of those numerous authors whom, the longer you leave them unread, the less desire you have to read. Hence it may be that I wholly fail to appreciate this passage. My mind is too heavy and concrete for any flight of abstruse reasoning. If, as I have already suggested, the difference between imagination and fancy amounts in practice to no more than the difference between good and bad poetry, have we done more than take a turn round Robin Hood's barn? [28]

---

[25] Especially when, as with a great poet, it is combined with mastery of symbol.

[26] *Biographia*, II, 12.   [27] *Biographia*, I, 202.

[28] *The Use of Poetry and the Use of Criticism*, 68-69.

To this we answer, that to condemn an author unread is a practice no critic should boast about. Since Eliot is confessedly ignorant of Schelling, his opinion as to how much Schelling contributed to Coleridge's theory of imagination is, till he corrects that ignorance, worthless. But this is by the way. To the main point, we answer that any tool that helps to distinguish between kinds of poetry, for distinguishing is essentially the critic's business, is useful. If the distinction between imagination and fancy is correctly drawn, as we have suggested, it helps to distinguish between froth and genuine metal. And this is not simply to take another turn around Robin Hood's barn.

Coleridge, we said, caused a confusion when he identified fancy—which seemed, as he defined it, to be an activity of conscious wit, accompanied by the click of billiard balls or the clack of counters ("fixities and definites")—with the silent semi-conscious or unconscious workings of association. He made another assumption which, as we hope to show, cannot be accepted, when he assumed that the associative power is "mechanical."

Mechanical is the last word that would occur to us to describe it. It is one of the most organic processes that could be imagined. The original drinking-in of experience at the sensuous level is a natural process, none more so. The emotional linking of one experience to another through subtle similarities in nervous response is a natural process, none more so. And the sea-change that the experience suffers in the chambers of memory is a natural process, none more so. One would have thought that association would be ideally adapted to an organic theory of the imagination.

It should have been. But Coleridge, we know, was reacting to the rationalist eighteenth-century. Association in his mind had become stuck, with limpet-like suction, to the notion of mechanism. And Coleridge hated the guts (if a robot can be said to have guts) of the mechanist psychology. It was, as we have shown, the warfare of his life.

No doubt exists that Coleridge uses mechanical fancy (to which he links association) in a depreciatory or pejorative sense. His own words prove it. Fancy is not really creative. It receives all its materials " ready-made." The house of fancy is a pre-fabricated house. Compared to the creative imagination it is distinctly second-rate.

Coleridge was depreciating the power to which he owed his black, not to speak of his white, polar magic. How he came to do so is easy to see. His theory of imagination suffered because he reacted from Hartley too violently. There are three ways in which he failed to profit from or to apprehend Hartley. First, his high-flying transcendental theory of imagination failed sufficiently to, though it did partly, take account of the physiological basis of the mind, which Hartley saw so clearly. Second, he made Hartley's theory out to be much more mechanical than it actually was. Third, in despising the " fancy," which he always associated with the " mechanical " Hartleian associating power, Coleridge failed to see, although he did partly see, how important that despised power really is in works of the creative imagination.

We believe that Coleridge impoverished and weakened his theory of imagination by resolutely denying the associative power to the imagination and by confining it to the fancy. While we think that the reconciliation of active and passive powers in the creative act is Coleridge's deepest insight on that subject, and while we agree that association should be included among the passive powers, we feel that confusion is avoided if imagination is used as the over-all term to cover all that takes place in the creative process. Then the assimilative process, the unconsciously-made or passive associations, and the active creative act are all housed under the inclusive term imagination. Wordsworth was undoubtedly sounder than Coleridge on the particular point at issue. Coleridge, so great was the prejudice he had acquired against the Hartleian "mechanical" association, was throwing away one of the most valuable aids of the imagination. To be sure, he was not throwing it very far, for the fancy was supposed to come to the aid of the imagination anyhow; yet it makes a very much more effective theory of the imagination to have all the functions of the mind that cooperate in creation working together inclusively and harmoniously under the one name imagination. And it is obvious that association does help the imagination, even if it is only in a relatively humble ancillary way. Association helps; so do dissociation, unequal fading, and the peculiar tricks of memory; so do the transpositions or trans-formations that sometimes occur unconsciously. All these con-tributory powers should be grouped under the one all-inclusive creative power, i. e. imagination, which is really only a name for *the whole mind when it creates*, and Coleridge was only weakening his theory by throwing to the despised and "mechani-cal" fancy powers so important.

"Dissolves, diffuses, dissipates in order to recreate." [29] This is a good description of what actually happens in the intermediary stage (the incubation stage) between assimilation and creation. The material in the memory suffers what we have called a "sea change" or process of "uneven fading," whereby, as Ribot has shown in his excellent book on imagination, the very defects of memory from a technical standpoint are in league with the imagination. Some sort of dissociation or breaking up is neces-sary ("Memory emancipated from the order of time and space"),[30] and also it is necessary that only the salient or significant be preserved, while the insignificant details fall away, if the material is to be reformed creatively. It is this sort of

[29] *Biographia*, I, 202.   [30] *Ibid*.

transforming that is imagination's function, and if the passive or associative power is in league with the more active creative force in this matter, the poet does not stand to be the loser. " All objects (as objects) are essentially fixed and dead ";[31] these are the " fixities and definites," the dominoes and chessmen, that fancy can combine but cannot transform. At the very least, if it cannot effect a re-creation, the imagination " struggles to idealize and to unify."[32] The materials cannot be left unactivated or quite unchanged if imagination has touched them at all.

The curious thing is that Coleridge, when not controversially engaged, was perfectly well aware both of association and the unconscious as valuable aids to creation, as we have shown in chapter V. Why he admits association into his official theory somewhat grudgingly and touched by the tar-brush of the " mechanical " fancy we have shown to be due to the special circumstances of his intellectual history. And, in spite of his awareness of association and the unconscious as potential allies of the poet, he seriously underestimated the power of memory and the " deep well " to effect a sea change. For a man who profited by it so much, he was strangely ungracious concerning the alchemy of the unconscious.

To be sure, he admitted the fancy as an ally and servant of the imagination: " Imagination must have fancy, in fact the higher intellectual powers can only act through a corresponding energy of the lower."[33] Nevertheless, though a point to be borne in mind, this admission is not wholly satisfactory. Coleridge had used fancy, as we have seen, almost in a pejorative sense, especially when he compared it with imagination; he is banishing association to the basement, the servants' quarters. True, the house could not run without the servants; nonetheless, the servants must keep their place. The whole fault lies really with an antiquated psychology, an hierarchical view of the mind as

---

[31] *Ibid.*   [32] *Ibid.*   [33] *Table Talk*, April 20, 1833.

composed of various faculties, some " higher," some " lower," instead of a modern unified view of the mind in which it is seen as
a highly specialized complex of the nervous system.[34]

In any event, Coleridge can only be blamed gently, not
harshly, he can only be taken to task in a very mild way, in view
of his recognition of both association and the unconscious in the
creative process, and in view of his supreme insight into the
alliance of active and passive in the creative act. Our strictures
are slight; the flaws and confusions of his theory are only minor.

A theory of poetic creation should not exist in a vacuum, as
an abstract aesthetic structure. In the two following sections
Coleridge's theory will be checked empirically against his own
practice and that of Shakespeare. The testimony of many other
poets besides that of the two chosen could have been taken.
Walt Whitman, for example, felt that beyond the energy of
his possessed and conscious intellect the poet could draw on
deeper resources " and a new energy (as of an intellect doubled
on itself)" and Robert Frost has recorded how " step by step
the wonder of unexpected supply keeps growing." [35] Yet he
has also cautioned against " giving way to undirected associations
and kicking ourselves from one chance suggestion to another in
all directions as of a hot afternoon in the life of a grasshopper." [36]
To avoid misunderstanding it should be said that Coleridge's
theory of imagination is not regarded as limited in its application, as standing or falling on its agreement with his own particular practice; it is regarded as a theoretic structure of great
interest and perpetual relevance to genuine poets of all times and
all countries, and to all persons interested in the criticism of
poetry and the arts generally.

[34] Coleridge, while he would accept this definition of the mind in terms
of I. A. Richards, would never agree that this is all the mind is.
[35] " The Figure a Poem Makes," *Collected Poems of Robert Frost* (New
York, 1942). The brief introductory essay has no pagination in this edition.
[36] *Ibid.*

iv

Shakespeare's Unconscious

Although this may be counted somewhat of a digression, since the present discussion has to do with Coleridge's theory of the imagination, not his practice, yet, as we have just stated, since it is always wise to check theory against practice, we think it justified at this time to touch on the topic of association and the unconscious at work in the "quick forge" of Shakespeare's imagination and Coleridge's too. If it can be shown beyond cavil—and very few will be found to cavil with the idea nowadays—that association and the unconscious were indispensable to the creative work of those poets, then it follows that a theory which fails to take them into full account is, to the extent that it fails to do so, failing to correspond to what really happens in creation.

Walter Whiter, "an alcoholic clergyman," [37] was the critic who pioneered the examination of unconscious links in Shakespeare. Whiter is interested in the Lockean kind of irrational association.[38] The mind, he says, is passive in admitting the original associations and "often totally unconscious" [39] of the force of their union. The great triumph of Whiter's method is his comment on lines from *Antony and Cleopatra*, IV.xii (as amended by Hanmer in 1744):

> The hearts
> That spaniel'd me at heels, to whom I gave
> Their wishes do discandy, melt their sweets
> On blossoming Caesar.

Parallel passages are cited from *Hamlet, Timon, I Henry IV,*

---

[37] John Ralston Caldwell, *John Keats's Fancy* (Ithaca, 1946), 60.
[38] His book is entitled: *A Specimen of a Commentary on Shakespeare . . . An Attempt to Explain and Illustrate Various Passages, on a New Principle of Criticism, Derived from Mr. Locke's Doctrine of the Association of Ideas*
[39] *Ibid.*, 68.

and the *Tempest.* Whiter perceived that Shakespeare had an image-cluster or cluster of associations which may be called the dog-fawning-melting-candy association; it involves a distaste for flattering courtiers (from an obvious resemblance between them and fawning dogs), and it also includes the idea of "dogging" a person's heels. This dog-fawning cluster is the most famous of all Shakespeare's image-clusters, and Whiter was the first to notice it.

Miss Caroline Spurgeon devotes a large portion of her chapter on "Association of Ideas" in her *Shakespeare's Imagery* [40] to this very cluster which Whiter had first disclosed. She adds little, except that she gives a fuller account of the table manners of Elizabethans and the habits of dogs. One valuable point, however, Miss Spurgeon makes: the interchangeability of the images. The chain reaction may start or be touched off by any one of the series. The remarkable thing is the way Shakespeare's imagination, through seeing resemblances, can find connections with things that do not strictly belong to the dog-fawning-melting-candy association, with things that are foreign to it, yet are magnetized to it and brought within its field of force. In the quotation from *Timon* which is the climax of Miss Spurgeon's series illustrating this particular cluster, it is to be noted that the cold brook is "candied with ice." [41]

It is fascinating to watch the play of Shakespeare's mind: we seem to catch it at work in the very flow and movement of his writing. The conscious control exerted by him is busy with the business of the immediate scene, and his attention to what the action requires is seldom relaxed. But beneath the thought-connections, the imagery, the symbols that Shakespeare's intellectual imagination is shaping for the purpose of the play, from deeper levels of his psyche come those hidden connections of

[40] New York and Cambridge, England, 1935.
[41] *Timon,* IV.iii.225.

which he himself was very likely unaware. We see once more
a reconciliation of opposites. As Coleridge puts it, " In Shakespeare's poems the creative power and the intellectual energy
wrestle as in a war embrace."[42] We could not ask for a better
corroboration of Coleridge's theory of the active and passive
powers whose interaction is necessary to the creative act.

By far the most thorough treatment of Shakespeare's associative imagination is the extraordinary book by a Cambridge
naturalist, Edward A. Armstrong's *Shakespeare's Imagination*,
subtitled *A Study of the Psychology of Association and Inspiration*. Coming to Shakespeare as a naturalist and bird-lover, he
has made an exhaustive collection of the bird-images and bird-
references in Shakespeare, but his book has a much wider
interest than that. It is, as a matter of fact, a through-going study
of associative links of all kinds in Shakespeare; the author has
uncovered a very large number that Spurgeon had not noticed.
The net result of both Spurgeon's and Armstrong's studies is to
show that there were imaginative links in Shakespeare's mind
of great persistence and tenacity; however, Armstrong has been
able, not only to find many more image clusters than Spurgeon,
but to penetrate to their inner meaning.

Some of the other linkages discovered by Armstrong are the
kite-warming-pan-bed, the goose-disease [43] and the jay-paint.
These sound esoteric until they are explained, but once explained
are not recondite. Once we know that jay was the Elizabethan
term for harlot or prostitute, the connection with paint becomes
obvious. Another cluster, noticed by Spurgeon is " death, can-
non, eye-ball, eye-socket of skull (a hollow thing), ears, vault,
mouth (sometimes teeth), womb and back to death again."[44]

[42] *Biographia*, II, 19.
[43] The Bishop of Winchester owned property in Southwark which included
houses of ill fame. " Winchester goose " therefore means prostitute.
[44] Spurgeon, *Shakespeare's Imagery*, 191-92.

This association, though noticed by Spurgeon, is better interpreted by Armstrong, who gets the Freudian implications of
tomb and womb.

Let us comment for a minute on one of the candy passages,
the one from Hamlet:

> No, let the candied tongue lick absurd pomp
> And crook the pregnant hinges of the knee
> Where thrift may follow fawning.[45]

The words are pat to the character of Hamlet—timed exactly
right to the situation, they express Hamlet's disgust with courtiers
of the Rosencrantz and Guildenstern variety. The meaning is
patent—do not waste good licking where it will do no good, but
bend your knees pregnantly—and how pregnant the word "pregnant" is in this connection—where the sucking up to the source
of bounty will produce state office and revenue from broad
lands. Shakespeare's mind is ever alert, but underneath the
muscular surface are the unconscious links of the dog-fawning-
melting-candy cluster, unobtrusively ready to proffer their services.
The collaboration of active and passive could not be smoother
or more impressive in its artistic results.

We have produced evidence, and could have produced a great
deal more, to show that Shakespeare possessed an associative
imagination. The point is not in doubt. Be it observed that he
had an associative imagination, not fancy only. The examples
we have quoted (and we could have quoted many more) show
that associations helped Shakespeare when his imagination was
working at the top of its power. There is no question of the
examples being fanciful, of the lutes-lobsters-seas-of-amber variety
that Coleridge objected to. Yet Coleridge specifically said that
the passive associative power was confined to the fancy. We
can only conclude from the light of the evidence that he was

[45] *Hamlet*, III.ii.55.

wrong. The human being is seldom omniscient, and Coleridge, as even the most gifted human beings often have, had his blind spots and his prejudices.

Regrettable, but true. If anyone doubts that Coleridge had prejudices, let him read Coleridge sounding off against the French encyclopedists in _The Friend_. Anything French was likely to be detestable, or immoral, or both. Coleridge, we remember, had an almost personal animus against the _passive_ associative fancy. But why should being passive be an offense? To one who had a theory of organic growth in art, being passive should have been a recommendation. The passivity with which the secret processes of the imagination work, the assimilative and associative processes, which like almost everything most worth while take place quietly, is the virtue of them. But Coleridge, as we have shown, had acquired a strong prejudice against the associationism of Hartley, which had fallen under opprobrium through the glib label "mechanical" and was apparently thereafter not open to re-examination. We are the losers because of this, for we can imagine what Coleridge, if let loose upon Shakespeare with the tools Spurgeon, Armstrong and others would have put into his hands, could have accomplished. He, with his almost photographic memory, his intimate knowledge of Shakespeare's plays, his sensitiveness to nuances of meaning, his extraordinary psychological subtleties could have lit up for us many of Shakespeare's darkest places. But it is idle to linger fondly over might-have-beens.

To be sure, it should be added by way of correction of the above strictures, Coleridge had a sunny and luminous, which is to say, an assured insight into the creative workings of Shakespeare's mind. He was not blind to linkage of imagery in Shakespeare, to the suggestibility that one image has of another, so that like the "begats" in the Bible, one goes on begetting the next. He once observed that Shakespeare's imagery is "a series and never-broken chain." [46] In the same vein he once said: " In Shakespeare one sentence begets another naturally: the meaning is all inwoven. He goes on kindling like a meteor through the dark atmosphere." [47] Here Coleridge has appreciated " the great versatility of Shakespeare's powers of association " and " what has been called the ' streaminess ' of his thought." [48]

I. A. Richards has a passage which certainly fits as a description of " the quick forge " which was Shakespeare's imagination:

> He [the poet or artist] is pre-eminently accessible to external influences and discriminating with regard to them. He is distinguished further by the freedom in which all these impressions are held in suspension, and by the ease with which they form new relations between themselves. The greatest difference between the artist or poet and the ordinary person is found, as has often been pointed out, in the range, delicacy, and freedom of the connections he is able to make between different elements of his experience. " All the images of nature were still present to him," says Dryden, with felicity, of Shakespeare, " and he drew them not laboriously, but luckily." It is this available possession of the past which is the first characteristic of the adept in communication, of the poet or the artist. [49]

The same is said in a more interesting way by T. S. Eliot in his essay on " The Metaphysical Poets ":

> A thought to Donne was an experience; it modified his sensibility. When a poet's mind is perfectly equipped for its work, it is constantly amalgamating disparate experience; the ordinary man's experience is chaotic, irregular, fragmentary. The latter falls in love, or reads Spinoza, and these two experiences have nothing to do with each other, or with the noise of the typewriter [" the typist, home at tea-time "] or the smell of cooking; in the mind of the poet these experiences are always forming new wholes. [50]

---

[46] *Biographia*, II, 15.   [47] *Table Talk*, April 7, 1833.
[48] Armstrong, *Shakespeare's Imagination*, 117.
[49] *Principles of Literary Criticism*, 181.
[50] *Selected Essays*, 247.

We would add that the formation of these new wholes is partly due to having an active mind (the conscious intellectual emphasis is always that of the classicist), and partly due to the fortunate possession of interesting fish in the aquarium of memory.

In this connection, another comment by Coleridge shows insight into Shakespeare's creative power at work. He says, " Shakespeare's intellectual action is wholly unlike that of Ben Jonson or Beaumont and Fletcher. The latter see the totality of a sentence or passage, and then project it entire. Shakespeare goes on creating and evolving, B out of A, and C out of B, and so on, just as a serpent moves, which makes a fulcrum out of its own body and seems forever twisting and untwisting its own strength." [51] The serpent image is of considerable interest, for it should be connected with that other image of the water insect propelling itself forward with alternate spurts of rest and motion. Coleridge insisted that in the creative act there was a balance or reconciliation of powers active and passive; we wish that, for the sake of the record, he had added, " conscious and unconscious," for that is what it amounts to.

This survey or examination that we have conducted as to Shakespeare's imagination and the probable way in which he composed, has only convinced us the more how shrewd and accurate Whiter was when he wrote in 1794: " I define therefore the power of this association over the genius of the poet to consist in supplying him with words and ideas which have been

---

[51] *Works,* ed. Shedd, VI, 503. Beethoven's creative power in music worked in the same way that Coleridge saw in Shakespeare. For instance, the tremendous evolution in the final movement of the *Eroica Symphony* grows organically out of an almost piffling little tune that any street arab could play on a penny whistle, but what majesty and power Beethoven manages to elicit from it! One movement of his musical thought develops out of another, theme playing against counter-theme, in the mighty proliferation of thematic development.

suggested to the mind by a principle of union unperceived by himself." [52]

It becomes all the more extraordinary that Coleridge made so little of this fruitful suggestion, when—whether he had ever chanced to read Whiter or not—he was well aware of the streamy nature of the mind and of the associations that dart within the stream. Besides, he had so full an intuition of the way Shakespeare's mind worked, with one idea growing out of another, B out of A, C out of B, *et cetera*. It can only be set down, once more, to the unfortunate distaste he had acquired for Hartleian association, that he failed to make the connection between association and Shakespeare's imagination in its unconscious profundities which was so nearly within his grasp.

Be that as it may, what this survey proves is the rightness of Coleridge's insight into the collaboration of active and passive in the creative act.

v

Coleridge's Unconscious

Turning from an examination of Shakespeare's creative process to that of Coleridge himself, we wish to inquire whether association aided him in the composition of "The Rime of the Ancient Mariner" and "Kubla Khan."

If one thesis more than another emerges from a re-reading of Professor Lowes's *The Road to Xanadu*, it is this: one half of Coleridge's creative activity in his making of "The Rime" was nothing but associations and subtle mergings which he had stowed away in his unconscious, the other, and more decisive, half being the selection exercised by the will and the fitting of images and remembered material into the master design, which

[52] Whiter, *A Specimen of a Commentary on Shakespeare*, 68.

Lowes calls the great arc or curve of the voyage. Lowes's mention of association is continuous throughout the book. Though he declines to concern himself with psychoanalysis, from the first he admits the existence of an unconscious and attributes to it magical powers of transmutation. For instance, he speaks of "that thronging and shadowy mid-region of consciousness which is the womb of creative energy"[53] and soon refers to "that heaving and phosphorescent sea below the verge of consciousness."[54]

He credits Coleridge with a polarizing power in his reading;[55] the poet in his reading magnetized or absorbed into his memory whatever was latent or potential poetry. "We have to do," he continues in that passage which we quoted at the outset of this study, "with one of the most extraordinary memories of which there is record, stored with the spoils of an omnivorous reading, and endowed into the bargain with an almost uncanny power of association."[56] It all amounts to the fact that Coleridge, having ransacked navigation, had netted one of the richest hauls on record, all salted away in his unconscious for future use. Lowes notes, too, the copiousness of supply: "at moments of high imaginative tension associations, not merely in pairs but in battalions, are apt . . . to stream together and coalesce."[57]

If we abstract from *The Road to Xanadu* the source-hunting and the detective-tracking of Coleridge's reading, which forms so fascinating a part of it, we find that the entire book is built on the thesis that association forms an indispensable part of the creative process. Lowes, having quoted Coleridge's phrase from *The Friend* about "the hooks-and-eyes of memory" says, "The enterprise now before us is to follow . . . a singular series of impressions, its members equipped with open and palpable

[53] *The Road to Xanadu*, 13.
[54] *Ibid.*, 31.
[55] *Ibid.*, 34.
[56] *Ibid.*, 43.
[57] *Ibid.*, 44.

hooks and eyes, from books which we know Coleridge to have read." He adds that, if he is correct in his supposition, "they will lead us to the very alembic of the creative energy." [58]

To give one instance of Lowes's method is to give the key to his procedure throughout. He quotes the famous stanzas from "The Ancient Mariner" about the water-snakes; [59] he then collects from the logs of various voyages a dazzling array of descriptions of luminous or blue-green snakes. The coalescence of the various images from the voyages into Coleridge's definitive and magical stanzas on the water-snakes is due to "the inter-locking of originally quite distinct impressions into one." [60] And this process is "the key to the genesis not only of the two remarkable stanzas before us [the stanzas about the watersnakes], but also of the poem as a whole." [61]

That being so, Lowes is driven to the admission of unconscious association as part of Coleridge's creative process. He warns his reader, "We shall have to sound our dim and perilous way through chartless tracts. . . . No synthesis based on mere mnemonic joiners-work will, in my judgment, serve." [62] In other words it is not just mechanical linking that does the work, or carpentry like the dovetailing of mortice and tenon. The vital power of imagination, which fuses many onto one, works with unconscious wizardry, blending as the blurred edge of cloud into cloud, or as tributary into river.

Lowes, though, does not regard the whole process as passive; the floating elements are there, in a welter; passive association no doubt accounts for some of the juxtapositions, or, rather, fusions; but imagination works the final synthesis. He quotes Coleridge: "the imagination . . . the true inward creatrix, in-stantly out of the chaos of elements or shattered fragments of

[58] *Ibid.*
[59] *Ibid.*, 42.
[60] *Ibid.*, 50.
[61] *Ibid.*
[62] *Ibid.*, 55.

memory, puts together some form." [63] His gloss is, " That comment bares, as it happens, the secret springs of ' Kubla Khan.' Waiving for the moment its dream psychology, it is no less relevant to those workings of the imagination which underlie ' The Ancient Mariner.' " [64]

Lowes's theory of poetic creation could be accurately described as Gerard's theory of the preternaturally rapid and subtle associations of genius with the conception of the unconscious added. For instance, Lowes speaks of " the enhanced and almost incredible facility with which in the wonder-working depths of the unconscious the fragments which sink incessantly below the surface fuse and assimilate and coalesce." [65] Intellectual activity (reading) starts the process and intellectual activity (composing the poem) must finish it off. " But interposed between consciousness and consciousness is the well." [66]

It would be tedious to follow Lowes through all the windings of his investigation. His method once established, we know what to expect. We find a continual recurrence to the theme of association. For instance, he speaks of " tentacles of association," " darting and prehensile filaments of association," " two cluster-points of the sleeping images," " power of striking through confused masses of recollections to the luminous point upon which they all converge," " ' a sort of nucleus in the reservoir of the soul '; upon which ' cluster point on cluster points ' of reminiscences converged," " an eminently Coleridgean association of ideas," " another star-cluster of associations," " weaving shuttles of association," " subliminal cluster of associations," " masses of associations," " memories of those obscure sensations," " thronged precincts of the unexpressed," " many folds of recollection," " images [which] do not stream up in utter nakedness," " play of association," " whirl of association," " preternaturally

---

[63] *Ibid.*, 56. Cf. *Anima Poetae*, 206.
[64] *Ibid.*

[65] *Ibid.*, 60.
[66] *Ibid.*

agile associative faculty," "prehensile associative faculty," and the "amazing power of association in the dream."

Lowes preserves a level approach, however; he maintains equipoise between conscious and unconscious powers; he does not go overboard into exclusive preoccupation with either one. The balance he preserves is, indeed, one of the best features of the book. He sagely says:

> The web of creation, like the skein of life, is of a mingled yarn, conscious and unconscious inextricably intertwined. We are bound to *distinguish* (if we are ever to understand) between the constituents of any state or process worthy to be called a whole. We *divide* at the cost of our saving hold on integrality. The caution is Coleridge's, not mine; and imaginative creation, if we have learned anything at all from the strange phantasmagoria which we are studying, is one process, and not two—an infinitely complex process, in which conscious and unconscious jointly operate.[67]

It is on the basis of the evidence of his study that Lowes thinks Coleridge's distinction between imagination and fancy to be largely artificial. Association is or may be at work in all creative activity of the mind. " I have long had the feeling," Lowes says, " which this study has matured to a conviction, that Fancy and Imagination are not two powers at all, but one. The valid distinction which exists between them lies, not in the materials with which they operate, but in the degree of intensity of the operant power itself. Working at high tension, the imaginative energy assimilates and transmutes; keyed low, the same energy aggregates and yokes together." [68] In a work like Coleridge's " Destiny of Nations " " instead of a miracle we get marquetry." [69]

The ideal work, " The Rime of the Ancient Mariner," represents an equal collaboration between conscious and unconscious powers. In the " Destiny of Nations " " for the most part con-

[67] *Ibid.*, 65.   [68] *Ibid.*, 103.   [69] *Ibid.*

sciousness is playing a lone hand." [70] In "Kubla Khan," "the unconscious is playing its game alone—as it happens, with conspicuous and perhaps unique success." [71]

Conscious control alone produces prose, not poetry. On the other hand, uncontrolled association can be a cause of embarass-ment—*embarras de richesse*. As Lowes puts it, "that aimless flow of association from the ' the twilight realms of conscious-ness ' is, when uncurbed, the bane of all those who, like Cole-ridge himself, are what he called ' reverie-ish and streamy.' " [72] The problem is how to stop the sorcerer's apprentice. But in the successful poem, like "The Rime," the poet is a genuine creator or maker; the poem has a form, a pattern of energy, like the field of force radiating from a magnet, to which all the magnetized filings conform, in this case, the pattern of suffering and redemption, and the great curve of the voyage.

Lowes's investigation into the springs of Coleridge's imagina-tion is, unavoidably, perhaps, from the nature of the investiga-tion, bookish. T. S. Eliot makes the necessary correction:

> As we have learnt from Dr. Lowes's *Road to Xanadu* (if we did not know it already) memory plays a very great part in imagina-tion, and of course a much larger part than can be proved by that book; Professor Lowes had only literary reminiscences to deal with, and they are the only kind of reminiscence which can be fully traced and identified: but how much more of memory enters into creation than only our reading! Mr. Lowes has, I think, demonstrated the importance of instinctive and unconscious, as well as deliberate selection. Coleridge's taste, at one period of life, led him first to read voraciously in a certain type of book, and then to select and store up certain kinds of imagery from those books. And I should say that the mind of any poet would be magnetized in its own way, to select automatically, in his reading (from picture papers and cheap novels, indeed, as well as serious books, and least likely from works of an abstract nature, though

---

[70] *Ibid.*, 104.   [71] *Ibid.*   [72] *Ibid.*, 92.

even these are aliment for some poetic minds), the material—
an image, a phrase, a word—which may be of use to him later.
And this selection probably runs through the whole of his sensitive
life. There might be the experience of a child of ten, a small boy
peering through sea-water in a rock-pool, and finding a sea-
anemone for the first time: the simple experience (not so simple,
for an exceptional child, as it looks) might lie dormant in his
mind for twenty years, and re-appear in some verse context charged
with great imaginative pressure.[73]

Eliot, then, no less than Lowes, agrees to "the importance of
instinctive and unconscious, as well as deliberate selection." This
is a handsome tribute from a classicist who scouts personal
emotion and insists on conscious intellectual control, *i. e.*, on
form. The result of Lowes's massive investigation is the triumphant vindication of Coleridge's insight into the alliance of
active and passive. Lowes shows a perfect correspondence between Coleridge's practice and Coleridge's theory. Indeed, one
of the best features of Lowes's book is his constant use of certain
insights of Coleridge into the imaginative process, key phrases
like: "the imagination . . . the true inward creatrix instantly
out of the chaos of elements or shattered fragments of memory
puts together some form . . .";[74] "the streamy nature of association which thinking curbs and rudders";[75] or "a confluence
of our recollections" through which "we establish a centre,
as it were, a sort of nucleus in [this] reservoir of the soul."[76]
The net result of Lowes's book is to prove how right Coleridge
was.

The contemporary American critic who has followed up
Lowes's terminology of associative links and clusters in studying
Coleridge's creative process is Kenneth Burke. Burke, fortun-

[73] *The Use of Poetry and the Use of Criticism*, 69-70.
[74] Lowes, 56 (*Anima Poetae*, 206).
[75] *Ibid.*, 72 (*Anima Poetae*, 46).
[76] *Ibid.*, 55 (*Biographia Epistolaris*, II, 182).

ately, is without Lowes's inhibitions and timidities; he is not at all afraid of psychoanalysis; above all, he can read and interpret symbols. He has, therefore, pushed the analysis much further than Lowes did. He runs the risk of his boldness, of course; at times his reading may be extravagant or silly, but his penetrative guesses often hit the mark.

Burke finds that Coleridge had anything but a simple mind; he agrees, too, in finding a working partnership between conscious and unconscious:

> . . . the work of every writer contains a set of implicit equations. He uses " associational clusters." And you may, by examining his work, find " what goes with what " in these clusters . . . And though he be perfectly conscious of the act of writing, conscious of selecting a certain kind of imagery to reinforce a certain kind of mood, etc. he cannot possibly be conscious of the interrelationships among all these equations. Afterwards, by inspecting his work " statistically," we or he may disclose by objective citation the structure of motivation operating here . . . At present I am attempting such a " symbolic " analysis of Coleridge's writings. His highly complex mind makes the job of charting difficult. The associational interweavings are so manifold as to present quite a problem in bookkeeping.[77]

We cannot follow Burke too far in his investigation, because that would take us into the exegesis of " The Ancient Mariner." In passing we may say that Burke deserves great credit for observing that " the Mariner suffered his punishments under the aegis of the Sun, and his cure was effected under the aegis of the Moon." [78] He has priority over Robert Penn Warren in pointing out the significance of the sun and moon symbolism. But it will be sufficient to notice the secret emotive links, the " clusters " that he finds in Coleridge.

One of the principal clusters that Burke finds recurring is

[77] Burke, *The Philosophy of Literary Form*, 20-21
[78] *Ibid.*, 24.

the " guilt, Sun at noon, problem of marriage " [79] equation. The sun, as in Yeats's system, symbolizes objective reality; the moon symbolizes imagination. The Mariner undergoes an imaginative redemption, *via* the sympathy with and blessing of the water-snakes. Imagination redeems through love and sympathy, through projection into the condition of another; it has all the ethical as well as aesthetic power that it has in Shelley's *Defence of Poetry*. The sun is like " God's own head "; it is the all-seeing eye; it lights up the objective world of duty. Why guilt feelings should be connected with it is not hard to see.

But why drag in marriage? Burke thinks that Coleridge had duty-feelings towards his wife, Sarah; he establishes this point in his reading of " The Aeolian Harp." [80] Even at this early stage of his marriage, at the time of the composition of " The Ancient Mariner," friction had developed in Coleridge's relations with Sarah; guilt-feelings would be natural, therefore, and could also be occasioned by his early struggles with the drug. Burke (right or wrong; it is an interesting suggestion) finds Sarah and the Albatross in the same emotional cluster. The snakes, especially in the passage " the very deep did rot, O Christ " are connected with opium guilt. Burke also finds another emotional cluster: " the sunny mist "=" luminous gloom "=" Plato." [81]

Coleridge could not possibly himself have been conscious of all this. But there were undoubtedly within him deep-buried feelings and curious associations which played their part un-known to him while he was consciously at work on the symbolic structure of the poem. The British critic D. W. Harding supposes that " the fiction Coleridge produced made a special appeal to him and could be handled with special effectiveness

[79] *Ibid.*   [80] *Ibid.*, 71-72 and 93-94.

[81] *Ibid.*, 74-75. In criticism of Burke it should be said that it is highly unlikely that Coleridge had guilt-feelings with regard to taking the drug as early as 1797-98.

because its theme and incidents allowed highly significant though partly unconscious concerns to find expression." [82]

Robert Penn Warren thinks that the limitation of Lowes's interpretation is a failure to get the symbolic content. We agree that this *is* Lowes's limitation and it appears most strikingly in his literalist view of the crime and punishment (the punishment is totally out of proportion to the crime) and his insistence that the poem is pure phantasy. [83] The failure of Lowes, however, to penetrate the symbolic content of the poem does not invalidate his findings with regard to the associational process at work within the greater and more important symbolic activity of Coleridge's imagination. [84]

Warren in his speculation as to how a poem in general or "The Ancient Mariner" in particular came to be written rightly puts the emphasis on what he calls "the symbolic potential":

> Actually the creation of a poem is as much a process of discovery as a process of making. A poem may, in fact, start from an idea . . . Or a poem may start from a phrase, a scene, an image, or an incident [in the case of "The Ancient Mariner" it started from a dream] which has, for the poet, a suggestive quality—what, for him in the light of his total being and total available experience, we may call the symbolic potential . . . Or the original item may lead *by some more or less obscure train of association* [85] to another item which will become the true germ of the poem, and whose symbolic potential may supplant that of the first item.

---

[82] D. W. Harding, "The Theme of 'The Ancient Mariner,'" *Scrutiny*, IX (March, 1941), 342.

[83] Lowes, *Road to Xanadu*, 300.

[84] In the same way the researches of Whiter, Spurgeon and Armstrong, *et al.* into obsessive imagery in Shakespeare supplement far more important studies, such as that into the symbolic structure of *Lear* by Heilman. The secret links in Shakespeare were submarine activities of his mind which aided, perhaps in unexpected ways and places, the great dramatic and symbolic structure of the plays. The interesting feature of an unconscious association is that it may pop up at any time.

[85] Italics mine.

However the process starts, it is, of course, enormously complicated. The degree of effort may vary from instance to instance
(the poet may dream up his poem in a flash or it may be laboriously
accreted like coral), and the degree of selfconsciousness may vary
from instance to instance (the poet may or may not in the process
of creation interlard his symbolical thinking with discursive and
critical thinking). As Coleridge said, and as many other poets and
even scientists have said, the unconscious may be the genius in
the man of genius. But this is not to define the process as an
irrational process. What comes unbidden from the depths at the
moment of creation may be the result of the most conscious and
narrowly rational effort in the past.[86] In any case, the poet always
retains the right of rejecting whatever seems to violate his nature
and his developing conception of the poem. And the process of
rejection and self-criticism may be working continually during
the composition of a poem. In the case of *The Ancient Mariner*
we have good evidence that the poet was working in terms of
a preconceived theme, and we know that the original composition
required some months and that the process of revision required
years.[87]

We are not sure that Warren does not make the process out
to be more complicated than it really is. Granted that the various
interweavings of association may be "enormously complicated,"
yet the complexities of the telephone exchange of association are
unconscious, and the unconscious is by definition the not consciously known, and what is not consciously known the poet
does not have to worry about. Fortunately, for him, the poet's
worry is the shaping of language to fit his intuition, when intuition and appropriate language do not snap together in a
moment of insight. The poet's worry is the conscious architecture
of the poem—or its thematic arrangement, if he is creating a
music of ideas. But, in any event, Warren does not contradict
what has already been said; he has simply found a long way of

[86] On this point see the testimony of the mathematician Henri Poincaré
quoted in Lowes, 62-63.

[87] Warren, prefatory essay in *The Rime of the Ancient Mariner*, 114-15.

saying, in his able and detailed analysis, that the conscious and unconscious have agreed signals, throw passes, and in general, collaborate together, though consciousness is the brain, the dominant partner.

We wonder if "the sad ghost of Coleridge"—the phrase is Eliot's—could be brought from the wings once more upon the stage what he would make of the critical ingenuity that has been lavished upon the poem. How far had he consciously intended all that elaborate symbolism of the sun and the moon which Warren finds—and it is undoubtedly *there* when it is pointed out? And the slimy deep rotting, was that consciously for him a symbol of *acedia*, the stagnancy of the mind? Were the freshening breeze and the life-giving rain symbols for creative release? Was Sarah, yoked to him in unhappy marriage, round his neck, like the albatross? Were the snakes symbols for a feeling of opium-guilt?

Probably such speculations are of little value, since whatever emotional charge the symbols may privately have had for the poet, their validity in the public poem depends on whatever they may convey as universals of human experience. We wager that Coleridge himself would register surprise at some of the symbolical meaning found in the poem.[88]

Obviously, there are no easy answers as to how a poem gets written; there will always be fringes of mystery and deep reaches of the unexplored. And this is as it should be. We have no wish to claim too much for the "star-clusters of associations," for we would agree with Coleridge that it is not the fact of

[88] Very likely his experience would be similar to that of the contemporary poet, John Malcolm Brinnin, who wrote to the editor of *Poetry*: "I can only acknowledge with wonder your almost necromantically exact analysis of my poem 'Speech of the Wedding Guest.' You not only brought out conscious intentions, but made subconscious ones manifest; as a result my reading of the exegesis [in *Poetry: A Critical Supplement*, February, 1950], which began as a sort of checking-up, ended as a process of learning."

the existence of the associations, but rather what he called the "polarity" of the imagination which is the marvel.[89] Further, what is of highest importance is the *selection* that the poet makes from the images that throng up on the thresholds of consciousness, and the *use* that he makes of the nuclei or polar fields of force among the associations in a symbolic context.

vi

A Further Evaluation

Evidence has been presented from the researches of Whiter, Spurgeon and Armstrong in Shakespeare's works, and from the researches of Lowes into Coleridge's creative activity, which proves beyond reasonable doubt that association, possibly unconscious on the part of the poet himself, does play a real if minor part in the greatest works of the imagination.

This being so, why does Coleridge not frankly admit it? Why is he so niggardly in the part assigned to association? Why does he block off fancy from imagination and assign to fancy exclusively the tricks of association, which he regards at best as poor mechanical shuffling? To sharply oppose conscious and unconscious, active and passive, was certainly right; to assign association to the passive or "night" side of the mind was right also. But to belittle the association, since so many of the associations of the poet are unconscious, is to belittle the unconscious itself. And Coleridge was as great a beneficiary of the unconscious as any poet who has ever lived. It seems like being ungrateful to the hand that fed him.

The curious paradox is, as we said above, that Coleridge was perfectly well aware all the time that the unconscious helped

[89] Lowes, 192.

the poet. We may recall a few of the key phrases. "There is in genius itself an unconscious activity; nay, that is the genius of the man of genius."[90] "Shakespeare himself . . . [directed] self-consciously a power and an implicit wisdom deeper than consciousness."[91] Very important, too, is Coleridge's remark concerning man, "how much lies *below* his own consciousness."[92] The "caves of ice" in "Kubla Khan" also hint at unconscious depths in the mind, cave being a common symbol in Shelley and other poets for mysterious or unconscious regions of the mind. Wordsworth with his "unknown modes of being"[93] was, like his brother poet Coleridge, aware of an unconscious. Coleridge possessed this knowledge in common with Novalis, Wordsworth and other poets of his time. We are struck afresh by the discrepancy between the always-luminous insights in Coleridge's notebooks, and in his lectures on Shakespeare, where the rôle of the unconscious is recognized, and the official statement of his theory, in which fancy, so to say, is discriminated against, as a crude power, only capable of playing with a child's blocks ("fixities and definites"). It is the more remarkable since Coleridge himself had nothing but contempt for crude and half-baked conceptions of the mind, involving blocks or "bricks and mortar."

Three reasons may be offered for this partial occlusion of Coleridge's vision. The first is the dislike he had acquired for the whole school of Locke and Hartley; he therefore distrusted, though he did not dismiss, association, half blind to the possibilities of its unconscious linkings assistant to the imagination. The second is that Coleridge, like Kant, possessed, as we have seen, a traditional hierarchical psychology; this made it easy for him to box off fancy and imagination, even while admitting

[90] *Biographia*, II, 258.
[91] *Miscellaneous Criticism*, ed. Raysor, I, 224.
[92] *Anima Poetae*, 25.
[93] *Prelude*, I, 420.

that the lower faculty helped the higher. The third reason is that Coleridge always insisted upon the first place being given to the sovereign Reason and the active will. He says that " Shakespeare [directed] *self-consciously* a power and an implicit wisdom deeper than consciousness." [94]

His position on the unconscious, though this may surprise some people, is very close to the position of Freud. Coleridge thought that " all things that surround us, and all things that happen to us " should promote " the increase of consciousness in such wise that whatever part of the *terra incognita* of our nature the increased consciousness discovers, our will may conquer and bring into subjection to itself under the sovereignty of reason." [95] Freud, though not over-optimistic concerning the ultimate rationality of human beings, entertained the same hope.[96] The reason for this coincidence is that both Coleridge and Freud belonged to the great European intellectual tradition, in which reason had traditionally been assigned the highest place.

In the opinion of a recent critic " the only thing that kept Coleridge from achieving full-blown psychological criticism was the same thing that prevented Aristotle, the quantitative and qualitative inadequacy of the psychology. Coleridge actually anticipated the unconscious . . . , but he was so far in advance of his time as to be unable to do anything with the discovery." [97]

[94] *Coleridge's Shakespearean Criticism*, ed. Raysor, I, 224.

[95] *Statesman's Manual*, Appendix B.

[96] In his book *The Future of an Illusion* Freud's rationalism is most explicit. He says: " We may insist as much as we like that the human intellect is weak in comparison with human instincts and be right in doing so. But nevertheless there is a something peculiar about this weakness. The voice of the intellect is a soft one, but it does not rest until it has gained a hearing. Ultimately after endlessly repeated rebuffs it succeeds. . . . The primacy of the intellect belongs to a very distant but probably not a wholly unattainable future." (London, 1928), 93.

[97] Stanley Edgar Hyman, *The Armed Vision* (New York, 1948), 151.

Looking forward, for a brief moment, from Coleridge's time, along that fascinating road that leads from Xanadu to *Finnegans Wake*, may we not raise the question, has the place of the reverie and the unconscious in our mental life received recognition in literature? Overwhelmingly so. The road, if pursued, would lead from Coleridge, *via* the chapter on the stream of consciousness in the *Principles of Psychology* by William James,[98] to the first stream of consciousness novel, *Les Lauriers sont Coupés*,[99] to Virginia Woolf's *Mrs. Dalloway* and *To the Lighthouse*, to Joyce's *Ulysses* and *Finnegans Wake*.

The association of ideas has not been so fashionable in the twentieth century as it was in Coleridge's day, chiefly because the intriguing region of the unconscious has been the one which every real or amateur psychologist has wanted to explore. But the association of ideas, too, has not gone altogether unrecognized.[100] Links of association and re-instatement of earlier experience through some sensory stimulus or reminder are essential to the method of Marcel Proust's *A la recherche du temps perdu*. Such phenomena occur often in the stream-of-mind both of Stephen Dedalus and of Leopold Bloom in Joyce's *Ulysses*. To take one obvious and banal example of association: in the cemetery scene, Bloom is reminded of his main business concern of the day, to place an advertisement of Alexander Keyes's store, by seeing the keys of the caretaker. Indeed, Richard Kain who has given *Ulysses* exhaustive and microscopic study, affirms that " most common of the mental laws which Joyce demonstrates is

---

[98] " The Stream of Thought," I, 224-38.

[99] By Eduard Dujardin (1887).

[100] Association of ideas is constantly found in dreams; it is essential to Freud's interpretations of dreams and the therapeutic techniques of psychoanalysis. Freud noticed compulsion towards association in neurotic patients, but the kind of association he uncovered has led to revision of the concepts of the old non-dynamic association psychology.

that of association." [101] The truth is, the reading of Joyce's
Ulysses requires as good a memory as is required for a professional
listening to a symphony: the work is a maze of associations and
recurrent themes.

Does the method of free association play any part, not merely
unconsciously in the writing of poetry by modern poets, but as
a technique of verse composition? Probably, rather little, outside
the admittedly free-association techniques like the surrealistic
verse of André Breton. But it is generally felt that such experi-
ments, though stimulating, are too chaotic and want form. A
rather general impression exists that the difficulty of much
modern poetry is due to free association or private associations
of the poet. For instance, an interpreter of modern poetry to
the public says of Eliot's *Waste Land*, "The poem has served
as a poetic milestone to many poets; its method of free association, of hazily expressed thoughts, has been a model for their
own writing." [102] Eliot, most meticulous of poets, is never guilty
of hazy expression. If we take as typical of modern poems his
"Prufrock" and *The Waste Land*, the organization of these
poems is anything but loose and free-associational, with the
exception, perhaps, of a passage or two where reverie is indulged
in character, as dramatically appropriate; the organization is,
not logical, but psychological, a logic of images and the imagination, and thematic, play of theme and counter-theme, as in a
sonata. It was an inspired comment by I. A. Richards who first
observed that *The Waste Land* is "a music of ideas." [103]

What confirms Coleridge's sagacity as to the necessity of
balance is the fact that "free association"—the idling or free-
wheeling of the mind—in twentieth-century poetry has produced
no master work. No serious poet relies wholly on helping him-

[101] Richard M. Kain, *Fabulous Voyager* (Chicago, 1947), 131.
[102] Rica Brenner, *Poets of Our Time* (New York, 1941), 187.
[103] Richards, *Principles of Literary Criticism*, 293.

self to the smorgasbord of rich imagery; as a modern British poet puts it, " the poet cannot farm out to his unconscious the labour of craftsmanship." [104] Poets like Eliot, Lorca, and Valéry have a strong distaste for relying on the gush of dream-images without check or control. Paul Valéry, for instance, has stated, " If I were to write, I would infinitely rather write something weak, in full consciousness and in complete lucidity, than give birth to a masterpiece in a state of trance." [105]

To conclude, then, this section of our inquiry: the unconscious and association of ideas were of magical value in the composition of "The Ancient Mariner" and "Kubla Khan," though they were not the whole story in the former and probably not in the latter. Coleridge was half percipient and half impercipient; he admitted the collaboration of conscious and unconscious powers in the act of composition, in the water-insect image, in the snake image, and in the passage on the reconciliation of opposites. But he would never admit that fancy, with its laws of association, was more than a robot. He failed to unite association with the unconscious, making it mechanical instead of charging it with the potency of the deep well. He did not see that the secret unconscious felicities of association, like Jason's fleece, could be invested with magic or symbolic significance. Had he done so, he would have ridden the wave of the future. But he was prescient in many ways and never more so than in his statement of the balance or reconciliation of opposites.

[104] C. Day Lewis, *The Poetic Image* (New York, 1947), 145.
[105] *Lettre Sur Mallarmé, Variéte* II. Quoted by Elizabeth Sewell, *Paul Valéry* (New Haven, 1952), 13-14.

~~~~~~

7

COLERIDGE, CRITICS,

AND THE FUTURE

How has Coleridge's theory of the imagination fared at the hands of modern criticism? What value is his theory of imagination thought to have? Particularly, how has he fared at the hands of the new critics? Naturally, it will not be possible to answer these questions in any extended way (for that would be to write another book), but a few attitudes can be indicated, and the reception his theory has received, particularly where his theory touches upon association and the unconscious, or the distinction between fancy and imagination, can be noted.

That Coleridge is immensely influential as a critic nobody doubts. As Professor C. D. Thorpe has said:

For over a century the literary theory of the Romantic period has been the dominant force in English criticism. And of the English Romantic critics none has been more influential than Coleridge. Indeed, one of our prominent contemporaries, with distinct reservations of his own about the Romanticists, has credited a single chapter of the *Biographia Literaria*—the XIVth.—with having been " the background of the criticism of poetry for more than a hundred years." [1]

---

[1] Allen Tate, *Reason in Madness* (New York, 1941), 45. Quoted by

Yet, with the reaction that set in against Romanticism in the twentieth century, Coleridge as critic and theorist of the imagination has been regarded with considerable suspicion. Perhaps such suspicion was inevitable in the late Irving Babbitt, who preferred Coleridge's "Aristotelian chapters on Wordsworth" to "the foggy metaphysics of the imagination which precedes them."[2] Since his examination of Coleridge's theory is "quite perfunctory,"[3] it is possible that his judgment is rather less than completely objective.

Further evidence of contemporary condescension towards Coleridge is found in the writing of F. L. Lucas, of Cambridge, England. Lucas finds that Coleridge's statements about the imagination are "obscure and contorted,"[4] his classifications barren,[5] his judgments nonsensical,[6] his theories windy, cloudy, mysterious.[7] Lucas is clever but picayune in his pin-prick criticisms, however; he shows no real grasp or insight into the philosophical and theoretical issues involved.

Another Cambridge critic, F. R. Leavis, in a grudging and curmudgeonly essay on Coleridge as critic [8] dismisses Coleridge's

Thorpe, "Coleridge as Aesthetician and Critic," *loc. cit.*, 387. Cf. the claim that Coleridge "is, with the exception of Aristotle, certainly the most important progenitor of modern criticism"—Hyman, *The Armed Vision*, 11.

[2] René Wellek, "Coleridge's Philosophy and Criticism," *The English Romantic Poets: A Review of Research*, ed. T. M. Raysor (New York, 1950), 115.

[3] *Ibid.* Cf. Irving Babbitt, "Coleridge and Imagination," *Nineteenth Century and After*, CVI (1929), 383-98. Reprinted in *On Being Creative and Other Essays* (Boston, 1932), 97-133.

[4] F. L. Lucas, *The Decline and Fall of the Romantic Ideal* (New York, 1936), 163.

[5] *Ibid.*, 180.

[6] *Ibid.*, 187.

[7] *Ibid.* These particular criticisms by Lucas are picked out by Thorpe, "Coleridge as Aesthetician and Critic," *loc. cit.*, 387.

[8] F. R. Leavis, "Coleridge in Criticism," *Scrutiny*, IX (1940), 57-69. Reprinted in *The Importance of Scrutiny*, ed. Eric Bentley (New York, 1948).

aesthetics as "nuisance" and is of opinion that his "currency as an academic classic is something of a scandal."

The two most influential critics of the twentieth century are I. A. Richards and T. S. Eliot. We shall take them in that order. And first, how has I. A. Richards reacted to Coleridge's theory?

In the main, very favorably. Richards constantly refers to Coleridge in his *Principles of Literary Criticism* [9] and has devoted a whole book to the subject, his *Coleridge on Imagination.* [10] For instance, quite early in the Principles he refers to the fourteenth chapter of *Biographia Literaria* as "that lumber-room of neglected wisdom which contains more hints towards a theory of poetry than all the rest ever written upon the subject." [11]

When it comes to Coleridge's great principle of the collaboration of active and passive powers in the act of creation, Richards backs it up. He observes, concerning Coleridge's description of the poet "in ideal perfection," that "as so often, Coleridge drops the invaluable hint almost inadvertently. The wholeness of the mind in the creative moment is the essential consideration, the free participation in the evocation of the experience of all the impulses, conscious or unconscious." [12]

Fundamentally, however, though agreeing with Coleridge on this exertion *of the whole mind* in creating poetry, Richards has a very different philosophical position. He takes exception to the transcendental mysticism of Coleridge's theory: "There is nothing peculiarly mysterious about imagination. It is no more marvellous than any other of the ways of the mind. Yet it has so often been treated as an arcanum that we naturally approach it with caution. It is desirable at least to avoid part

[9] London, 1924; 2nd ed., with appendices, 1926; reprinted, New York, 1950.
[10] London, 1934.
[11] *Principles of Literary Criticism* (1926), 140.
[12] *Ibid.*, 189.

of the fate which befell Coleridge and our account will be
devoid of theological implications." [13] Yet Richards, aware that
he has paid Coleridge a somewhat backhanded compliment,
adds, as if hastily to make amends, in a footnote (after quoting
Coleridge's famous dictum: *The primary* IMAGINATION *I hold
to be . . . a repetition in the finite mind of the eternal act of
creation in the infinite* I AM [14]), "the luminous hints dropped by
Coleridge in the neighborhood of this sentence would seem to
have dazzled succeeding speculators. How otherwise explain
why they have been overlooked?" [15]

Richards makes a distinction, much as Coleridge does, between
a passive and an active imagination. Richards calls the passive
imagination "repetitive" and the active imagination "formative." [16] Once more he adds a note: "Coleridge's distinction
between IMAGINATION and fancy was in part the same as this.
But he introduced value considerations also, Imagination being
such a combination or fusion of mental elements as resulted
in certain valuable states of mind, and Fancy being a mere
trivial playing with these elements." [17] Already we see Richards
sustaining Coleridge's distinction.

When, a little later, Richards comes to comment once more
on Coleridge's passage on "that synthetic and magical power"
which reveals itself in "the balance or reconciliation of opposite
or discordant qualities," [18] he calls it "Coleridge's greatest contribution to critical theory." [19] He feels that the formulation of
the theory in this passage is original, Coleridge's very own,
adding, "Coleridge's debt to Schelling has been overestimated.
Such borrowings as he made were more hampering to him than
helpful." [20] Setting aside Coleridge's transcendentalism, he is

[13] *Ibid.*, 191.
[14] *Biographia*, I, 202.
[15] *Principles*, 191n.
[16] *Ibid.*, 192.

[17] *Ibid.*, 192n.
[18] *Biographia*, II, 12.
[19] *Principles*, 242.
[20] *Ibid.*, 242n.

of opinion that "there is enough in this description and in the many applications and elucidations scattered through *Biographia* and the *Lectures* to justify Coleridge's claim to have put his finger more nearly than anyone else upon the essential characteristic of poetic as of all valuable experience." [21]

Richards has a psychological theory of value; to him an experience is valuable if by it our impulses are harmoniously organized. "The conduct of life is throughout an attempt to organize impulses so that success is obtained for the greater number or mass of them . . ." [22] He praises "the increased organization, the heightened powers of combining all the several effects of formal elements into a single response, which the poet bestows. To point out that 'the sense of musical delight is a gift of the imagination' [23] was one of Coleridge's most brilliant feats. It is in such resolution of a welter of disconnected impulses into a single ordered response that in all the arts imagination is most shown." [24]

Turning from Richard's *Principles* to his other book, a decade later, *Coleridge on Imagination*, we find, from the first, "Coleridge's great merit as a critic—a merit unique among English critics—is the strenuous persistence with which he reflected philosophically upon criticism." [25]

Richards, unlike T. S. Eliot, supports Coleridge's distinction between imagination and fancy. He finds that "an observable and definable difference between Fancy and Imagination is the

[21] *Ibid.*, 242-43.
[22] *Ibid.*, 46.
[23] *Biographia*, II, 14.
[24] *Principles*, 245.
[25] *Coleridge on Imagination*, 5. John Crowe Ransom, referring to Richards' *Coleridge on Imagination*, says (*The World's Body*, New York, 1938, p. 163): "The new work is an attempt to recover, defend, and recommend to the modern critics the doctrine of imagination which Coleridge propounded." He, earlier, says (*Ibid.*, 74): "Richards' appropriation of Coleridge is quite a chapter of intellectual history. Coleridge assimilates Richards to himself, as the Chinese are said to assimilate their conquerors . . ."

central point of Coleridge's critical theory." [26] He further finds that "the difference is not only observable but describable and of use in many branches of psychology. In fact his distinction is one of the few which have yet been made that are of use in comparing forms of growth and changes of structure in the mind. It is not a distinction introduced *ad hoc* for literary purposes." [27]

Quite a large part of the book is taken up with the discussion and explication of Coleridge's distinction. Richards brings to bear on the illustrative examples of fancy and imagination, used by Coleridge, particularly those from *Venus and Adonis*, that instrument of elaborate analysis which his disciple, Empson, developed even further.

Since Richards is a student of psychology, and known primarily as a psychological critic, his endorsement of Coleridge's psychological insight must carry weight. He finds that "there can be little doubt that Coleridge as against Associationism of the Hartley-Condillac type was right all along the line." [28] And, further, "When he kept to psychology, he often showed a very curious prescience of the developments to come." [29]

One of the passages in which Richards most strongly endorses Coleridge's psychological insight is this:

These are utterances [30]—and the collection could be greatly extended—that seem to make Coleridge anticipate much that is most fruitful in recent psychology. In contrast to theories of association by which a state of mind is represented as a cluster or composition of revived impressions fished up from a mental storehouse and arranged around a sensation given to a passive mind—the whole offered like a deck of cards to a self or will standing over against it and able at best to approve or veto or rearrange it—his conception of the mind as an active, self-forming, self-realizing system is plainly an immense improvement. As an instrument for exploring

---

[26] *Ibid.*, 31-32.   [28] *Ibid.*, 67.
[27] *Ibid.*, 34.   [29] *Ibid.*
[30] He has been quoting Coleridge on the stream of consciousness.

the most intricate and unified modes of mental activity—those in poetry—its superiority seems overwhelming.[31]

Richards' book is open to two criticisms. The first is that he dismisses the whole Schelling question too airily. The second is that, to a considerable extent, it is Richards on imagination rather than Coleridge. This, however, since we find Richards stimulating, is hardly a fault.

Richards dismisses the whole Schelling question, as he had previously in the *Principles*, with the remark which we quoted above, " Coleridge's debt to Schelling has been overestimated. Such borrowings as he made were more hampering than helpful." [32] To be sure, Coleridge's debt to Schelling *has* been overestimated, but that does not excuse the critic, as we suspect to be the case here, for brushing off Schelling unread or for neglecting to arrive at a true estimate of Coleridge's indebtedness to Schelling's philosophy. For some indebtedness there definitely was. Undoubtedly Coleridge could and did work out for himself a theory of imagination as vital, as a living process; as a unifying and esemplastic power; as a reconciler of opposites; as a combiner of active and passive. But Schelling supplied the notion of subject-object, reconciliation of conscious-subject and unconscious-object in the act of consciousness, *a fortiori* in the act of creation. This notion of the unconscious was that which caused all the elements of Coleridge's theory to fly together into place as at a magic touch. It is obvious that the chapters of *Biographia* which are Schelling transcribed by Coleridge (however they may have been privately useful to Coleridge in preparing the ground of his theory) have no claim to originality, but the places where Coleridge writes from himself, as in the definition of imagination and the description of the poet " in ideal perfection " are original and of the highest value. He would

[31] *Ibid.*, 69.   [32] *Principles*, 242n.

be a hardy man who would affirm that Schelling contributed nothing at all (along with the other influences) which shaped the great statement of the reconciliation of opposites.[33]

Richards' position is that he accepts Coleridge's psychology, while rejecting his transcendentalism. For Richards, not having Coleridge's faith in a living God, has substituted for it a religion of the imagination. No doubt the greatest chapter in what is throughout a great book is the chapter on myth. Richards' view is original and interesting, for to him Science itself—with its abstract schematization—is another myth-making activity. With the great, and indeed, saving value that Richards places on imagination and myth, he rates Coleridge's theory of imagination very high indeed. Yet he cannot accept the metaphysical matrix from which the theory arose. Thus he cuts out the heart of Coleridge's theory—" the One life within us and abroad " from which the principle of organic unity proceeded—and having performed that cardiac operation (very delicately, for Richards is a skillful operator), thumps it on the back and says, Go forward into the world with my blessing. We wonder though, with so vital an organ removed, whether the patient would have long to live.

Eliot is just as sceptical as Richards is of the value of Coleridge's German borrowing. He says, " Nor am I sure that Coleridge learned so much from the German philosophers, or earlier from Hartley, as he thought he did; what is best in his criticism seems to come from his own delicacy and subtlety of insight as he reflected upon his own experience of writing

[33] Richards is a scrupulous reader but sometimes misleads us. In *Coleridge on Imagination*, for example, he attributes several passages to Coleridge which are actually translations from Schelling. These are the quotations from *Biographia*, I, 168; I, 172 (Richards, 61); the capitalized quotation (Richards, 63, middle); *Biographia*, I, 178 (Richards, 64, middle). True, he finally admits (65): " Most of these formulations of doctrine Coleridge drew from Schelling."

poetry." [34] While we are in hearty agreement with this last remark, it seems to us that Coleridge's prestige does not suffer in the least from the frank admission that his theory of imagination is eclectic, in the best sense, forming into Coleridge's own compound the best of Plotinian, Hartleian, Schellingian and other sources, united to his own experience.

The work in which Eliot most carefully considers Coleridge's distinction between imagination and fancy is the one from which we have just quoted. He (with perhaps less of Richards' psychological interest and training) wonders whether the distinction is worth making. Indeed, Coleridge's distinction between fancy and imagination commits what would today be called the genetic fallacy. By what divining rod can the critic know from what mysterious reach of the poet's mind did this particular passage originate? If the poem is to be objectively judged "as poem and not as another thing," genesis becomes less important than the effectiveness of this or that line or passage as part of an aesthetic structure.

Though Eliot considers Coleridge "perhaps the greatest single figure in Shakespeare criticism down to the present day," [35] in

[34] *The Use of Poetry and the Use of Criticism*, 71. Coleridge himself wished he had developed his thought independently: " As my opinions were formed before I was acquainted with the schools of Fichte and Schelling, so do they remain independent of them, though I con- and profess great obligations to them in the development of my thought, and yet seem to feel that I should have been more *useful* if I had been left to evolve them without knowledge of their coincidence." *Letters*, II, 683. Richards (*Coleridge on Imagination*, 3-4) is critical of Eliot's remark; his point is that Coleridge's critical insights were sharpened by philosophical speculation.

[35] Eliot, " Shakespearean Criticism: I—From Dryden to Coleridge " in *Companion to Shakespeare Studies*, eds. Harley Granville Barker and G. B. Harrison (Cambridge, England, 1934), 287-99. Cf. " Coleridge was perhaps the greatest of English critics, and in a sense the last. After Coleridge we have Matthew Arnold; but Arnold—I think it will be conceded—was rather a propagandist for criticism than a critic . . . ," Eliot, " The Perfect Critic," in *The Sacred Wood* (London, 1934), 1.

his first essay in *The Sacred Wood*, "The Perfect Critic," he pokes fun at Coleridge's "metaphysical hare-and-hounds," [36] and he concludes his series of Harvard Lectures with the words, "The sad ghost of Coleridge beckons to me from the shadows." [37] Allen Tate is concerned to some extent with the famous distinction, observing of Coleridge that

> the distinction between Fancy and Imagination is ultimately a psychological one: he discusses the problem in terms of separate faculties, and the objective poetical properties, presumably resulting from the use of these faculties, are never defined, but are given only occasional illustration. (I have in mind his magnificent analysis of "Venus and Adonis," the value of which lies less perhaps in the critical principles he supposes he is illustrating, than in the perfect taste with which he selects the good passages for admiration.[38])

But with Tate this is not the main consideration. With him the main lines of battle are drawn over the question whether Coleridge valued poetry for aesthetic pleasure only (as did Poe), or whether Coleridge valued poetry as a mode of knowing truth equal in its own way to philosophical or scientific modes of cognition. According to Tate, Coleridge was ambiguous on this issue, and bequeathed to later generations a "fatal legacy" of indecision.[39] He says:

There can be little doubt that Coleridge's failure to get out of

---

[36] *The Sacred Wood*, 12-13.

[37] *The Use of Poetry and the Use of Criticism*, 149. This is the last sentence in the book and is no more than a humorous valedictory, a caution to the poet against too much theorizing. Eliot, however, rates Wordsworth as a critic higher than Coleridge (*Ibid.*, 71-72: "Of the two poets as critics, it was Wordsworth who knew better what he was about: his critical insight, in his one Preface and the *Supplement*, is enough to give him the highest place."

[38] "Literature as Knowledge," *Southern Review*, VI (1940-41), 649.

[39] *Reason in Madness*, 51.

the dilemma of Intellect-or-Feeling has been passed on to us as a fatal legacy. If the first object of poetry is an effect and that effect is pleasure, does it not necessarily follow that truth and knowledge may be better set forth in some other order altogether? It is true that Coleridge made extravagant claims for a poetic order of truth, and it is upon these claims that Mr. I. A. Richards has based his fine book, *Coleridge on the Imagination*: Mr. Richard's own testimony is that the claims were not coherent. The coherent part of Coleridge's theory is the fatal dilemma that I have described.[40]

Coleridge should not be blamed for the duality of the imagination; its duality is incurable. To blame Coleridge for it would be like blaming Tate for the double population in the South. Imagination can, when it creates organic wholes, give exceeding aesthetic pleasure ("a sense of musical delight"). But to limit it, as Poe did, to the creation of "beauty" (the realm of aesthetic pleasure) is to train one's telescope on only one side of the moon. Imagination, perhaps by virtue of its power of creating organic wholes, is an instrument of cognition, a mode of knowing reality. Knowledge as tested by pragmatic or positivistic tests compared to the full imaginative understanding of a reality is as a phone book with its list of names to a knowledge of the lives and histories of the persons there listed.

The opinion of Ransom is perhaps typical of that of the new critics, an attitude of respect mingled with distrust and accompanied by reservations: "Coleridge is probably the best practitioner of criticism that we have in the classics of our language, and his interest in ubiquitous, but we have the greatest difficulty in capturing and consolidating any set methods or principles out of his vagaries of speculation, and few of us would care to underwrite the immortality of his fantastic language."[41]

[40] *Ibid.*
[41] "Strategy for English Studies," *Southern Review*, VI (1940-41), 229.

Ransom sees the characteristic act of the creative imagination according to Coleridge as the formation of metaphor:

> Coleridge's specific theory of poetry has do with the act of the Secondary Imagination in composing the poetic metaphor, and with its consequence, the noblest poetic object which we can experience. . . . Coleridge in his doctrine is very close to Hegel's theory of poetry. He is continually talking about poetic imagination as an "esemplastic" faculty, reconciling opposites into a unity. Its work is a "coadunation"; and also furnishes a kind of "inter-animation" between the opposed parts of the metaphor, which are, as Richards would say, the tenor and the vehicle.[42]

We accept this account by Ransom as accurate enough, though it is curious that Hegel should be mentioned rather than Schelling. The reconciliation of thesis and antithesis in a synthesis runs throughout post-Kantian philosophy. The schema occurs both in Fichte and Schelling, as well as in Hegel. Ransom should have added that the characteristic act of imagination in the theory of Coleridge is not only the creation of metaphor but also (and more importantly) of symbol.

Ransom himself has developed a theory of poetry as knowledge, and I am in hearty agreement with him that poetry *is* a mode of cognition. To him both science and poetry are modes of cognition, but the description of reality given by science is abstract, consisting of laws or formulae, while poetry sees "things in their thinginess, or *Dinge* in their *Dinglichkeit*."[43] "It is not by refutation," he says, "but by abstraction that science destroys the image. It means to get its 'value' out of the image, and we may be sure that it has no use for the image in its original state of freedom. . . . It is thus that we lose the power of imagination, or whatever faculty it is by which we are able

[42] *The New Criticism* (Norfolk, Conn., 1941), 76.
[43] "Poetry: A Note in Ontology," from *The World's Body*, reprinted in *The Great Critics*, eds. J. H. Smith and E. W. Parks (New York, 1951), 770

to contemplate things in their rich and contingent materiality." [44]
Though the definition of imagination here offered is not Coleridge's, yet one can see a Coleridgean reconciliation of opposites
in Ransom's union of structure and texture in the poem, and
Ransom is in the Coleridge tradition as a powerful defender of
the imagination.

Cleanth Brooks, that determined hunter of paradoxes, is inevitably impressed by the *paradox* (reconciliation of active and
passive, more than usual state of emotion with more than usual
order) in Coleridge's theory. He connects Donne's imagination
and Coleridge's. Donne, he finds, was obsessed with the problem
of unity: how lovers become one, how the soul becomes one
with God:

> Frequently . . . one type of union becomes a metaphor for the
> other. It may not be too far-fetched to see both as instances of,
> and metaphors for, the union which the creative imagination itself
> effects. For that fusion is not logical; it apparently violates science
> and common sense; it welds together the discordant and contra-
> dictory. Coleridge has of course given the classic description of
> its nature and power. [Here he quotes the passage on "the balance
> or reconcilement of opposite or discordant qualities."] It is a
> great and illuminating statement, but it is a series of paradoxes.
> Apparently, Coleridge could describe the effect of the imagination
> in no other way.[45]

The two of Coleridge's principles which have proved most
fruitful in modern criticism are organic unity and reconciliation
of opposites. The distinction between organic and mechanic
form which he introduced into English criticism from Germany
is still operative. For example, Cleanth Brooks has stated: "One
of the critical discoveries of our time—perhaps it is not a discovery
but merely a recovery—is that the parts of a poem have an organic

[44] *Ibid.,* 772.
[45] *The Well-Wrought Urn* (New York, 1947), 17.

relation to each other . . . The parts of a poem are related as are the parts of a growing plant." [46] The examination of a poem as symbolic structure, all the parts related to one another in an organic whole, is the method of his book, *The Well-Wrought Urn.* Then, too, Herbert Read shows a manifest preference for organic as opposed to geometric designs in Chapter I of his book, *Art and Society.* And G. Wilson Knight, perhaps the most Coleridgean of modern critics, is perpetually referring to works of art in organic terms.

Coleridge's other principle, that of the reconciliation of opposites, has proved equally vital. It is, indeed, the principle of creativity; the great poet, in composing the poem, holds in equilibrium his "negative capability" and his creative will.

I. A. Richards has developed a theory that tragedy is the reconciliation of the opposite impulses of pity and terror. Coleridge's principle is also the basis of the theory of metaphor: the two halves of metaphor (tenor and vehicle) are reconciled in a higher third. Just as in the system of Hegel, thesis and antithesis are reconciled in a synthesis which is more than the sum of the two but an interfusion of both, so the lovers and compasses are both seen in a new light, the paradox of union-in-separation or twoness-in-oneness receiving a luminousness that neither separately could achive. The principle, too, lies at the root of the theory of mature poetry developed by I. A. Richards and Cleanth Brooks. Poetry of that order is a poetry of irony and paradox which takes into account the discordant and unpleasant aspects of experience in a reconciliation or balance which is the poem.

Having shown the reactions of Richards, Eliot, Tate, Ransom and Brooks to Coleridge's theory, we should now be in a position to make some generalization with regard to the reception of

[46] "Irony and 'Ironic' Poetry," *College English,* IX (1948), 231-32. See also his "The Poem as Organism," *English Institute Annual* (1940), 20-41.

Coleridge by the new critics. René Wellek has thus summarized the impact of Coleridge on the new criticism:

> . . . crucial critical concepts have come from Germany through the mediation of Coleridge and have profoundly influenced modern anti-romantic English and American criticism: " organistic " aesthetics (whatever its antecedents in antiquity), the view of imagination as a reconciliation of opposites, the use of irony, paradox, and tension as poetic principles. But in contemporary criticism these terms are shorn of their metaphysical implications and are taken out of their context, which in Coleridge and Schelling, is that of a justification of art as the mediator between man and nature. This difference is well brought out in Ronald S. Crane's attack on Cleanth Brooks, " The Bankruptcy of Critical Monism " (*Modern Philology*, 1948). The discussion of Coleridge's conceptions there is one of the clearest expositions of his central critical concepts which I know.[47]

Wellek is entirely right in his observation of the influence of Coleridge on the new critics; they take from Coleridge that which suits their own theories of poetry, but they one and all show a devastating unconcern with German philosophy in its greatest period, that of Kant, Schelling, and Hegel. They understand Coleridge's theory in parts, but seem incapable of understanding it *in toto*. They take it by itself, disassociating it from the philosophy and metaphysics from which it grew. And that is a mistake.

One difference may be pointed out in the reception of Coleridge's theory by Richards and that by Eliot, Tate and Ransom. Richards, with his eclectic interest in psychology, at once pounces on the psychological insights in Coleridge's theory of the imagination as a creative power. The other critics mentioned are more concerned with Coleridge as a philosophical critic, that is, as one who applies philosophical principles, Aristotelian or other, to particular literary judgments.

[47] " *Coleridge's Philosophy and Criticism*," loc. cit., 113.

A very curious critical dichotomy exists as to the value of Coleridge as practical critic and as theorist of the imagination. On the one hand he is praised to the skies for the insight of his psychological analyses, a good example of which would be his analysis of the diseased imagination in Lady Macbeth; but on the other hand as a theorist or aesthetician of the imagination, the usual critical tone adopted towards him is one of shaking the head, of regretting brilliant gifts dispelled in opium,[48] of finding, with more headshaking, if not outright boredom, his theories dark and devious, too involved in the jungle of German metaphysics for much daylight to have penetrated there. In other words, there exists the sharpest contrast between the high valuation of Coleridge as practical critic, his specific critical insights, and the low or dubious valuation of Coleridge as theorist and metaphysician. We have already quoted the scouting of Coleridge's metaphysics by Eliot and Ransom.

Raysor's devoted editorial labors on Coleridge have put all students of Coleridge in his debt and give his opinion weight. Raysor finds Coleridge's criticism and his metaphysics at variance:

> Coleridge's criticism has been justly described as philosophical; but the term carries with it implications which must be avoided before it can properly be applied to Coleridge's noblest work, since it assumes a concentration upon ideas of the most complete generalization. As an aesthetician Coleridge was indeed a philosopher in this essential sense of the word, but he was unfortunately derivative, mediocre, and, on a subject which requires system, fragmentary: he cannot be said to succeed in his occasional violent efforts to engraft his metaphysical conceptions upon his criticism.[49]

The terms "derivative," "mediocre," and "fragmentary" are harsh ones to use. We hope that the present study will prove

[48] A good antidote to this sort of thing is I. A. Richards' recent introduction to the Viking Portable Coleridge (New York, 1950).
[49] *Coleridge's Shakespearean Criticism*, I, xlviii.

a corrective to them. It is not hard to see how Raysor formed this opinion. Having discovered, in editing Coleridge, passages lifted from Schelling or Schlegel in Coleridge's lectures, he found the conclusion that Coleridge was derivative forcibly borne in upon him. But it cannot be too often said that Coleridge, sunk in opium and pressed for money, obliged to deliver public lectures, siphoning off the best of German aesthetic thought, with gay insouciance as to *meum* and *tuum*, was not Coleridge at his best, Coleridge giving us in *Biographia* the ripe fruits of a life spent in meditation upon poetry enriched with his own original insights. Besides, even in the lectures, Coleridge performed a valuable function, for the insularity of English criticism badly needed to be fertilized with German ideas.

It is rather common to regret Coleridge's involvement in German metaphysics. Raysor, for instance, says: "A good case may be made out to show that Coleridge lost rather than gained from the German influence. Not only is the material which he borrowed consistently inferior to his own criticism, but it encouraged his characteristic weakness for semi-mystical intuitionalism. This is especially true of his eccentric theory of the imagination, derived primarily from Schelling; but instances might be multiplied." [50] Raysor praises highly:

chapters xvii–xviii of *Biographia Literaria*, the great analysis of Wordsworth's theories of poetic diction; [51] but it cannot be too strongly emphasized that the general ideas even in this part of *Biographia Literaria* are inductive generalizations based upon the personal experience of poetic creation and the observation of the practice of other poets; they are not in any sense a deduction of art from a metaphysical system, like that branch of philosophy which we call aesthetics. Coleridge's unsuccessful aesthetic specu-

[50] *Ibid.*, I, xxxiii, n.
[51] Cf. Raysor, "Coleridge's Criticism of Wordsworth," *PMLA* (1939).

lations may be fairly represented by his unfortunate theory of the imagination in the first part of *Biographia Literaria*.[52]

Raysor is a scholar whose editorial competence no one can doubt. But he is a strange critic of Coleridge; with the one hand he gives and with the other he takes away. On the one hand, in several passages in his measured and excellent introduction of *Coleridge's Shakespearean Criticism* he has paid Coleridge as critic, for some of his individual insights, the very highest tribute, admitting that in perceptiveness he far surpassed Schlegel.[53] But on the other hand, as we have noted above, he has described Coleridge's theory of the imagination as " eccentric " and " unfortunate," " derived primarily from Schelling," and Coleridge himself as a " mediocre philosopher," and as an aesthetician " derivative, mediocre, and in a subject which requires system, fragmentary." As to Coleridge being a professional philosopher, we agree with Raysor that he is at best an amateur, though a gifted and inspired one. As to the derivativeness of Coleridge's aesthetic theory, and especially in the lectures, we agree again, because the evidence is incontrovertible. But that Coleridge failed to make inspired use of his borrowings we deny. Raysor's opinion that Coleridge's theory of imagination is " derived primarily from Schelling " is disputable. If he had said " derived partly from Schelling," we should be more disposed to agree. And as to Raysor's remark that Coleridge's theory

[52] *Coleridge's Shakespearean Criticism*, I, xlvii-xlviii n.

[53] *Ibid.*, I, lxi: " The unhappiness which turned inward his superb analytical powers and forced him to explore his own soul as few men ever have, created an introspective psychologist of supreme genius and gave him the basis for a knowledge of human motives which no English critic has ever surpassed. In rich ethical reflectiveness, in delicate sensitiveness of poetic imagination, and, above all, in profound insight into human nature, Coleridge is a critic worthy of his high place at the head of English criticism of Shakespeare. The greatest of English creative writers received his due tribute from the greatest of English critics."

of the imagination is " eccentric," we should dub it as itself one of the more eccentric curiosities of literary judgment.

Herbert Read cannot agree with Raysor's strictures on Coleridge's theory of imagination. He says, " I do not know from what more positive standpoint Raysor is criticizing the critic and philosopher to whom he has given such loving care; but from my own standpoint I must dissent from these strictures. Its terminology apart, I believe that Coleridge's theory of the imagination has been proved essentially sound by later and more scientific researches." [54]

To be sure, Raysor has said that he thinks Wordsworth's theory of imagination is far more valid than Coleridge's. With this in mind, we begin to see the ground of his judgment. Wordsworth had a more solid, earthbound theory of imagination rooted in eighteenth-century aesthetics and the Lockean theory of association. But we would be far from admitting the inferiority of Coleridge's theory to Wordsworth's. Philosophically, Coleridge could run circles around Wordsworth at any time. Wordsworth's theory of poetry is too recessive (to states of childhood), and his doctrine of emotion recollected in tranquillity comes near to committing the Tolstoyan fallacy of regarding art as a mere communication of affective states. Coleridge's view of the creative act, so far from being eccentric, is central. It is in the main stream of European tradition descending from the *Ion*. It makes the creative act, like a divine *fiat*, genuinely creative, an act aesthetic, an act *sui generis*, an act ordering a new symbolic content.

René Wellek finds less discrepancy between Coleridge's theory

[54] Herbert Read, " Coleridge as Critic," *Sewanee Review* " LVI (Autumn 1948), 609-10. Reprinted in book form London (Faber and Faber), n. d. The essay was Read's contribution to a symposium on the great critics at Johns Hopkins University, Baltimore, April, 1948. Read's essay is interesting because he finds in Coleridge one of the roots of existentialism.

and practice than Raysor does, but he, too, thinks that Coleridge's practical criticism is much superior to his theory:

> Surveying all these writings [he has been writing a critical bibliography] on Coleridge as aesthetician and critic, one cannot help concluding that the case for the close unity between Coleridge's theory and practice is well established. But still it would be hard to deny that Coleridge's main theoretical ideas are derivative and second-hand, and that his specific merit as a critic is in the practical application of these principles. Paradoxically, these derivative principles are those which are now most admired.[55] In a history of European criticism Coleridge can claim a high position only in virtue of his novel critical opinions and the considerable merit of being the transmitter of many aesthetic ideas from Germany to England.[56]

But the dichotomy between Coleridge the practical critic and Coleridge the theoretical critic makes very little sense. Aristotle, who gave us the critical principle that poetry is more philosophical than history because it deals with universals and the principle of catharsis, is equally strong when it comes to practical judgments, of the *Iliad*, of Sophocles' *Oedipus*. It is hard to think of any great critic who was not strong in both directions. Why should Coleridge be an exception?

Coleridge's practical criticism is acknowledged to be of a high order. For instance, his critique of Wordsworth in volume II of *Biographia* is usually conceded to be one of the finest pieces of extended analysis in English criticism. His Hamlet criticism (despite the fact that his Hamlet too much resembles Coleridge), his Shakespeare criticism generally, his delicate analysis of *Venus*

[55] Not by all critics. See *supra*.

[56] "*Coleridge's Philosophy and Criticism*," *loc. cit.*, 116-17. In his recent and valuable *History of Modern Criticism 1750-1950*, Wellek takes much the same position, allowing Coleridge credit chiefly as transmitter of German critical terminology and ideas. See Wellek's summing up in Vol. II (*The Romantic Age*), 185-87.

and Adonis, as a whole, and in individual passages (where the closeness of his reading initiates a method later carried to greater lengths by Richards and Empson), his pre-Eliot appreciation of Donne, and much else, in spite of changing fashions, will stay as part of the corpus of English criticism as long as criticism is read or studied. Is the theoretical part of his criticism merely obnoxious? Certainly not. The value of his critical principles is much more important than the question of originality. The number of basic critical principles is necessarily small. It does not often fall to the lot of a critic to introduce into critical currency three such principles as the originating quality of imagination, organic unity, and reconciliation of opposites. (We used the word *introduce* designedly, for we do not claim that Coleridge *originated* these ideas). These principles are as valid and as important as Aristotle's principle of poetry dealing with universals. These principles will last as long as criticism itself lasts.

To regret Coleridge the aesthetician, to maintain that his theory befogged his critical practice is a manifest absurdity. Until his practical criticism and his theory are studied in conjunction, either will be only partially understood. To quarrel with Coleridge's theory of imagination is to quarrel with the organ of his critical insight. It was the vitalist-organic theory which made so many of his insights into Shakespeare possible. Without his lifelong interest in psychology, without his principle of living organic beauty, most of Coleridge's Shakespeare criticism would be dead, or still-born, or non-existent.

That Coleridge tunneled deep into unwholesome mines of metaphysics may be, and surely is, a matter of regret so far as his poetry is concerned. It stifled a gift.[57] Most commentators

---

[57] We do not mean that a study of metaphysics is necessarily bad for a metaphysical poet. The point is, that an exclusive concern with metaphysics is a diversion of energy away from poetry. This is bad on the principle that the unused limb will eventually wither up and die.

agree that there was something *emotional* in Coleridge's pursuit of metaphysics; [58] he wove a cocoon about himself, he formed about himself a kind of womb. But that he read metaphysics is our gain so far as his criticism is concerned. Whatever we may think of Coleridge's metaphysics *per se*, of the manuscript philosophy that he bequeathed to his devoted disciple Green, or of the Kantian and post-Kantian philosophy in which he immersed himself, it is no matter of regret, it is a matter of congratulation, that he read German aesthetic theory. For this was the golden age of German aesthetic theory, the age of Lessing, of Herder, of Winckelmann, of Goethe, of Schiller, of the Schlegels, of Schelling, of Novalis, of Hegel. It was a point of the highest good fortune that Coleridge stayed in Germany at the turn of the eighteenth century and that he kept in touch thereafter with German literature and aesthetic. The reading that he did in German aesthetics—added to his own keen native sensibility—was partly responsible for the acuity of his critical perceptiveness.

So far, then, from there being a disparity between Coleridge as practical critic, Coleridge as aesthetician, and Coleridge as metaphysician, the strength of any one of his concerns was due to interplay with the other two. We cannot say, for example, that there was any discontinuity between Coleridge's theory of imagination and his metaphysics, for what could better fit into his Neo-Platonic and somewhat Buddhistic view of the totality of life as unity of being, all life one gigantic organic unity, than a theory of imagination as organic, and producing organic unity? The German aesthetics are not an excrescence upon Coleridge's earlier Plotinian view of the imagination, but are integrated with it in an organic manner; this very delicate and perfect shading of the one into the other was not difficult, for Goethe, Schelling, the

[58] Coleridge himself furnished the hint in "Dejection: An Ode."

two Schlegels and Hegel were concerned with the same problems as Coleridge was (mediating function of art between intellect and nature, union of conscious and unconscious, the concrete-universal) and belonged in aesthetics to the same Neo-Platonic tradition. Coleridge's practical criticism would have consisted in isolated and fragmentary judgments, were it not for his organic theory of imagination which informed them all with life and meaning, made them part of an organized body of critical thought.

The critics who have studied Coleridge most closely in a specialized way all seem to concur in the agreement between his theory and his practice. Enrico Pizzo, in an article in *Anglia* as far back as 1916, first expounded the intimate connection between them.[59] "Miss Alice Snyder's thesis on the *Critical Principle of the Reconciliation of Opposites as Employed by Coleridge* (Ann Arbor, 1918) tried to show how closely Coleridge's theory and practice are integrated, and how fruitful this critical principle was in Coleridge's hands, especially in the details of the Shakespearean criticism . . . She perceived the essential unity of Coleridge's thought."[60] The same can be said of Gordon McKenzie's *Organic Unity in Coleridge*.[61] He shows the principle of organic unity at work in Coleridge's criticism of many of Shakespeare's plays. Wellek's criticism that McKenzie makes too much of the distinction between reconciliation of opposites and organic unity is justified, however, for actually the two are inseparable halves of one view of the imagination.

The latest discussion of Coleridge's theory of imagination is that by Bate.[62] Bate's essay is valuable for drawing attention

[59] Wellek, "Coleridge's Philosophy and Criticism," *loc. cit.*, 109.
[60] *Ibid.*, 109.
[61] University of California Publications in English, 1929.
[62] Bate, "Coleridge on the Function of Art," *loc. cit.*

to other definitions of the imagination by Coleridge than the standard one in *Biographia*. He rightly says that Coleridge's theory of the imagination is only to be understood as part of Coleridge's psychology: "Coleridge's conception of the imagination can be approached only as a necessary concluding hypothesis in his theory of the mind."[63] He criticizes the belief that Coleridge's theory of imagination is central in Coleridge's criticism. Bate is to be venerated for his knowledge of eighteenth-century aesthetics (the background for Coleridge's theory), but his present view is paradoxical and unsound. For the theory of imagination *is* central to Coleridge's criticism. The dynamic-organic definition of the imagination is the heart of Coleridge's aesthetics; the principle of the reconciliation of opposites is the systole and diastole of that heart; theories of meter and diction and all other outlying parts of Coleridge's poetics are members and limbs, which, deprived of that heart, would be deprived of life.

Coleridge has given us a fairly complete and very valuable poetics. A practicing poet would do well to compare S. T. Coleridge's poetics with T. S. Eliot's; he would find the comparison exceedingly instructive. Coleridge's poetics needs a certain filling in, but it is sound on essentials. The gaps or the parts that need filling in are the period of gestation between the act of the primary imagination (perception) and the creative act—Coleridge says very little about this. But his most serious deficiency is not saying enough about the labor of revision; he does not give sufficient attention to the poetic discipline. Eliot has something to say about it, and on this point at any rate is a useful supplement to Coleridge.

From the particular angle of vision of the present study Coleridge's theory of the imagination is most open to criticism for an inconsistency in his, in the main, consistent position. The

[63] *Ibid.*, 141.

inconsistency that we find is in the rôle Coleridge assigns to the unconscious workings of association. When Coleridge is at his best he speaks of a reconciliation of opposites, of active and passive, of conscious and unconscious powers, in the act of composition. When he is dogmatic, he exclusively appropriates all the magic to imagination, allows "fancy" or unconscious association no magic at all, makes it dull and mechanical.[64]

No term of description is more frequently applied to the imagination by Coleridge than "modifying power." Yet he goes into little detail of the manner in which the modifying occurs. It is unfortunate that he for the most part failed to see the modifying possibilities of association, for this is not always a mechanical transposition as in Coleridge's fancy; he failed to avail himself of the slipping and sliding, the uneven fading, the reintegration, the sea-change and the endless possibilities of fusion present in association, for truly this power can be imaginative, not merely fanciful, and a powerful adjutant to the imagination. Imagination connives at the secret help of association which plays into its own purposes as modifying power. Imagination is Prospero and association his tricksy Ariel. Too bad that Coleridge did not live long enough to read *The Road to Xanadu* —or, if Coleridge's ghost ever looked over Lowes's shoulder, how fascinated he would have been at the play of the hooked atoms there laid bare.

"Genius of the highest kind implies an unusual intensity of the modifying power."[65] "The rules of the IMAGINATION are themselves the very powers of growth and production."[66] The

---

[64] We are warned at this point to be on our guard against assuming that Coleridge *always* regarded it as mechanical; his wonderful phrase "the phantasmal chaos of association" (*Biographia*, I, 81) proves otherwise. Then why did he sometimes, identifying fancy with association, speak of it as mechanical? Probably for the very human reason that he had not thought the subject through quite to the bottom.

[65] *Table Talk*, May 1, 1833.   [66] *Biographia*, II, 65.

imagination "struggles to idealize and to unify. It is essentially vital, even as all objects (as objects) are essentially fixed and dead." [67] "That synthetic and magical power . . . the imagination" [68] takes the materials with which it works and "blends and (as it were) fuses, each into each." [69] Imagination is coadunative, esemplastic, the shaping power. [70] It is "the power by which one image or feeling is made to modify many others and by a sort of fusion to force many into one." [71] Here, compressed into one paragraph, is much that is essential in Coleridge's theory of imagination.

Coleridge's theory of imagination, then, in the main, is remarkably consistent. He had pondered the subject long and deeply. No doubt he had his moments of dulled vision, as we all do. His theory has certain lacunae, lacks and deficiencies. His treatment of meter, however, is more satisfactory than Wordsworth's, and this is not remarkable in one whose mastery of it in "The Ancient Mariner" and "Christabel" is little less than miraculous. His analysis of metrical effects is at all times extremely subtle; unlike Dr. Samuel Johnson, he fully appreciated the music of Lycidas. He lacks Eliot's brilliant remarks on the auditory imagination, but his theory of imagination as a power that reconciles diverse and disparate elements looks ahead to Eliot's chemical analogy of the plate of platinum (the analogy of the imagination as catalyst) in "Tradition and the Individual Talent." He anticipates Eliot's impersonal theory of poetry to a considerable extent. In his superb critique of *Venus and Adonis* he observes as one mark of Shakespeare's promise as a poet and dramatist of genius "the choice of subjects very remote from the private interests and circumstances of the writer himself." [72]

[67] *Ibid.*, I, 202.   [69] *Ibid.*
[68] *Ibid.*, II, 12.   [70] Cf. "Dejection: An Ode."
[71] Shakespeare lectures of 1818, in Smith and Parks *The Great Critics*, 545.
[72] *Biographia*, II, 14.

Then, too, Coleridge anticipates Eliot in providing for, through reconciliation of opposites, that union of intellect and feeling, the disunion of which, under his famous phrase, " dissociation of sensibility " [73] Eliot deplored. Coleridge's theory is strong in the treatment of dramatic illusion, weakest in its lack of an adequate treatment of tragedy; perhaps adequacy on this subject was impossible to a man whose favorite critical term was " genial." Since, as Richards has shown, pity is the impulse to approach, and terror the impulse to flee from, Coleridge neglected in tragedy a unique opportunity to employ the critical principle of the reconciliation of opposites. Yet, when every reservation is made, Coleridge's theory of the imagination is superior to all others in England that had preceded it, because he had a first rate poetic gift, a first rate critical insight, and a thorough basis for his theory, both psychological and philosophical. There is no modern critic of the first rank—I. A. Richards, T. S. Eliot, John Crowe Ransom, Allen Tate, Kenneth Burke, for example—who does not either acknowledge indebtedness to Coleridge or receive stimulation from his thinking.

Coleridge was the first man in the history of English criticism to have an adequate theory of the imagination. This statement is not made with any desire to disparage earlier theories on the subject, particularly those of Hobbes and Dryden, the series of papers on the imagination by Addison, or the views of Hume. It is made on the following grounds. Coleridge, for the first time in English theory, worked out an adequate account of how active and passive powers of the mind collaborate in the poetic act. Secondly, his dynamic and genuinely creative imagination is much more satisfying than the compounding power of Addison or Hume. Thirdly, and this is the most important reason of all, Coleridge's theory of imagination is really adequate because he, for the first time in English theory, made imagination the creator

[73] *Selected Essays,* 247.

of symbol, not merely the creator of figure of speech or metaphor. With Coleridge (as with Blake too) imagination is the achromatic lens to spiritual vision.

Many critics, victims, perhaps, of specialization and the intensive study of parallel passages, have been too much impressed by Coleridge's borrowings and have denied him originality. Comparing this passage and that, they say, "It is obvious Coleridge lifted his theory of imagination from Schelling." Or, looking closely at parallels which can undoubtedly be found, "How obviously Coleridge's theory is derived from Plotinus." Coleridge's theory *is* derived from Plotinus, *is* derived from Schelling, and many more. The point, however, is the original amalgam that Coleridge made, the very excellent job of smelting and welding the best elements of older theories into one. If ever a man was a genuine eclectic, that man was Coleridge. In the history of the imagination, Coleridge is the supreme and original amalgamator.

It might be worth while to see, briefly, what the elements of that amalgam are, so that, first, it can be appreciated how and why they were malleable into one, and, second, the unique quality of Coleridge's amalgam can be more justly estimated.

From Plato Coleridge learned to respect the intuitive intellect. He learned that ideas are the only realities; ideas are constitutive. Creative imagination is mysterious; it is shrouded in the numinous; inspiration is a kind of divine inebriation—such was the theory of *Ion* and *Phaedrus*. So far as poet or maker copied reality or stirred up emotion, he was unworthy of respect or admission into the republic; but insofar as he mastered divine ideas and bodied these forth in symbol or parable, he was exercising his creative function as a poet should. From Plotinus Coleridge learned that the poet's intelligence is a sort of emanation from the divine intelligence, which it attempts to realize. The poet works as God works; ideal forms shadowed forth in his imagination, he attempts to project or objectify in whatever medium he chooses. Since even the plants have an ideal form which they are trying to realize, the poet is working in unison with the organic forms of nature. All are inspired by the breath or *anima* of the One. Coleridge's neoplatonizing was only strengthened by the attraction that he felt towards the Neo-Platonism of the Renaissance,[74] and reinforced by his liking for the Cambridge Platonists. Imagination was no rearranger or copyist according to this theory; it would be impossible to be a convinced Neo-Platonist and to doubt the creativity of the imagination.

From Aristotle Coleridge learned to have respect for association of ideas, at least as stated in Aristotelian terms.[75] He learned, too, and adopted " with full faith the principle . . . that poetry . . . is essentially ideal ";[76] perhaps, it would be better to say, that poetry deals with universals. From Aristotle's psychology and from the Aristotelian tradition of the schoolmen, Coleridge learned about the *vis receptiva* or purely passive side of the mind, the reproductive imagination, which reinstated images, as opposed to the creative imagination, which created them.[77]

From Bruno and Boehme, Coleridge learned a theory of dualism, and reconciliation of opposites. This theory had similarities to the biblical myth of Jacob wrestling with the angel; the opposition or wrestle between the " fell incensed points " was eminently creative. This theory proved of great value when Coleridge came to state his theory of reconciliation between

[74] Coleridge: " The early study of Plato and Plotinus, with the commentaries and the THEOLOGIA PLATONICA of the illustrious Florentine [Marsilius Ficinus]; of Proclus, and Gemistius Pletho "—*Biographia*, I, 94.

[75] Coleridge states his conviction that where Hartley differed from Aristotle, he differed " only to err "—*Biographia*, I, 73.

[76] Coleridge (*Biographia*, II, 33): " I adopt with full faith the principle of Aristotle, that poetry as poetry is essentially *ideal*, that it avoids and excludes all *accident* . . ."

[77] He refers to the *vis receptiva*, *Biographia*, I, 70.

active and passive powers of the mind. Bruno's and Boehme's dialectic of opposites is almost the essential core or kernel of his theory.

From Leibniz Coleridge acquired the first adumbration of the notion of an unconscious. From Herder and other eighteenth-century thinkers he imbibed the notion of organic unity. From Kant Coleridge learned that the Hartleian theory of association was inadequate as a theory of mind. It came to him from Kant, as a great Copernican revolution, that the mind is a creator of its own forms by which it apprehends the world. Even in scientific research, the mind is creative, for *it must ask the right questions*, or it will never learn the right answers, or wrest from nature her secrets. The Kantian imagination was too tied down as a mediator to the understanding for it to appeal to Coleridge,[78] yet Kant's aesthetic theory made him aware that in creation the imagination has free play, not being tied down by memory to the order of time or place. The general effect of Kant was a liberation from the psychologies of seventeenth and eighteenth century mechanists, from which Coleridge was looking for the way out. Yet it is to be suspected that even the mechanists contributed their quota; from Hartley, for instance, Coleridge must have learned increased awareness of association, and his belief that association is fundamentally reducible to one law.

From Fichte and Schelling, Coleridge learned about the reconciliation of subject and object. This conciliation conformed to what he had already learned from Bruno and Boehme, and it doubtless helped him to the statement of conciliation of active and passive in the act of creation. Schelling reinforced the thought of Plotinus. Both Schelling and Plotinus believed that

[78] Thorpe, " Coleridge as Aesthetician and Critic," *loc. cit.*, 398: " Coleridge was not content . . . to stop with Kant's idea of the work of imagination as merely continuous with that of the understanding, with no power to penetrate to truth beyond that of the sensory manifold."

art (the work of imagination) is the product of an intelligence akin to divine intelligence. The difference is this: for Schelling nature is dumb or dumbly striving, unconscious that she is reaching towards consciousness, whereas for Plotinus the divine mind is working within nature's forms to realize its ideas. From Schelling Coleridge learned that art (the work of imagination) is the reconciler of the unconscious (nature) and conscious intelligence. From Schelling, and from German philosophy of the eighteenth century, Coleridge learned the notion of the unconscious, which was the missing piece, the one piece needed, to complete his theory of imagination. The next step was obvious: to combine the intuitive conscious creative intelligence of Plotinus with the dark obscure forces of the unconscious in the creative wrestle or fruitful balance of imagination.

The coincidence of the paths traced by Coleridge's mind and by Schelling's—or, if not coincidence, certainly the parallelism— is astonishing. Both went to Plotinus, as to a chief source; both were influenced by Bruno and Boehme. To reconcile Schelling's ideas on the imagination with the rest of Coleridge's system would not be difficult, since many of Schelling's leading ideas were already domiciled in Coleridge's mind. The absorption would require no shock at all.

In Wordsworth Coleridge early learned to admire " the union of deep feeling with profound thought; the fine balance of truth in observing, with the imaginative faculty in modifying the objects observed." [79] The key words here, as Thorpe points out,[80] are *union* and *balance*. Here is already suggested a theory involving balance or reconciliation of opposites. And what did Coleridge learn from his own practice as a poet? Chiefly, certitude and assurance. He could write knowingly of imagination, for who could know better than Coleridge?—that there was in

---

[79] *Biographia*, I, 59.
[80] Thorpe, " Coleridge as Aesthetician and Critic," *loc. cit.*, 411.

the process something conscious and designed, but also there was that unaccountable artesian well out of which rumbled or bubbled up a "Kubla Khan." Unfortunately, it could not be counted upon, as could Old Faithful, to well up at regular intervals.

Coleridge, then, achieved the most balanced theory of the imagination that had heretofore been achieved in English theory; moreover, he achieved the first theory to date in England in which the integration of conscious and unconscious powers was maintained. To be sure, hints of an unconscious had been thrown out by Dryden—" a confused Mass of Thoughts, tumbling over one another in the Dark: When the Fancy was yet in its first Work, moving the Sleeping Images of Things towards the Light " [81]—but it cannot be claimed that Dryden had a theory of conciliation of opposites.

Bate, whom we quoted above, has a few words about Coleridge's position in the history of European criticism. He says:

> Coleridge occupies a unique position not only in English but in European romantic criticism as a whole: he represents, that is, a suggestive and in some respects challenging attempt to unite the traditional rationalistic values of classicism with the organic vitalism to which the romantic movement aspired, and to substantiate and rest this union upon an ultimate metaphysical base. One may grant that it was only an attempt, and both the fragmentary results and the aim itself may be variously viewed. But it must not be forgotten that, from his hope of achieving such a synthesis, Coleridge's writings possess their only unity.[82]

This statement is too pale. It leaves one with the feeling that Coleridge attempted, but only imperfectly achieved, a synthesis, an integrated theory of imagination. It may well be that in the field of philosophy Coleridge had pollen fingers and was simply

---

[81] Dryden, dedication of *The Rival Ladies* to the Earl of Orrery, *loc. cit.*, I, 1.

[82] Bate, " Coleridge on the Function of Art," *loc. cit.*, 154.

the fertile introducer of other men's ideas; in that field, it may be, he achieved no synthesis. But in the field of imagination Coleridge was king; and we like very much better than Bate's comment, the remark by Thorpe, that Coleridge "was first of all a master of synthesis"[83] and that "the key words to his achievement are catholicism, reconciliation, and integration."[84] We like better Thorpe's comment that

> in his metaphysics certain old and venerated truths contained in Platonic and Plotinian writings found a place, along with Aristotelian concepts and such notions as the *natura naturans* behind the *natura naturata* of the Stoics and Scholastics, in a synthesis which contained elements from the newer theories of the Cambridge Platonists, of Spinoza, Leibniz, Kant, and Schelling and of the dominant empirical philosophy of Hobbes, Locke, and their eighteenth-century disciples—but all in a new form, because all had passed through the alembic of his powerful creative mind.[85]

Thorpe further says that Coleridge achieved a "blend of idealisms" and that "in the sense that his integration is the most comprehensive, come the nearest to reconciling the many diverse and complex elements of his heritage of any aesthetic theory of modern times, Coleridge may be called the Aristotle of his age."[86]

To be sure, Coleridge cannot be likened to Aristotle without serious reservations. He resembled Aristotle, or Goethe, in the breadth of his interest in politics, in science, in psychology, in philosophy and ethics. No Englishman of his day had a profounder grasp of philosophic problems. Yet to be likened to Aristotle in any true sense he would have to have an ordered system of thought; a lucid series of treatises in many related fields, such that all subsequent thought for centuries would hinge upon them. Coleridge occupies no such commanding position in the history of thought. Even in his own chosen field of

---

[83] Thorpe, "Coleridge as Aesthetician and Critic," *loc. cit.*, 389.
[84] *Ibid.*   [85] *Ibid.*, 390.   [86] *Ibid.*, 391.

aesthetics, Aristotle probably commands more authority than Coleridge, for Coleridge produced no such organized treatise as the *Poetics*. Yet to dismiss Coleridge as a man merely of scattered insights and marginalia would be a mistake. In one department he surpassed Aristotle, for Aristotle on the subject of the creative imagination is thin and meagre.

Coleridge really did achieve an integrated theory of imagination. He was not fitting together pieces from this philosophy and from that—here a piece from Plotinus, there a piece from Berkeley, there a piece from Schelling as though it were a Chinese puzzle; the integration he achieved was of a different order. He took from each philosophy that which was pertinent to a living view of the imagination; the union was that of cell with cell, as in a living organism. It was an organic theory of imagination that he produced: "The rules of the IMAGINATION are themselves the very powers of growth and production." Perhaps it need not be observed that he must have had a remarkable intuitive gift always to pick the vital element relating to imagination from every philosophy he touched.

The conclusion of this study is that Coleridge's theory of imagination is one of the great theories that will always be taken into account, whatever future discoveries are made. It is great because it stands the test of practice, because it corresponds to the way the creative mind really works. It is great because not an isolated insight, but part of a psychology and a philosophy. It is part of a transcendental world view—a view that is too much discredited nowadays when more pragmatic ideas are the fashion. Though this view had its idealistic weaknesses, an organic and creative, even if pre-evolutionary, way of looking at the world is not laughable or ridiculous. When the sentimental mists are wiped off the glass, it is a valid way of seeing things. Association of ideas—or, better—association of images as assistant to the imagination—would have fitted very snugly into this organic view. It is a pity Coleridge did not give it a more honored place. But aside from the slight astigmatism, which we have many times noticed, every review of Coleridge's theory of imagination leaves us with fresh wonder at the depth and clarity of his insight. The razor's edge did indeed become the saw to the armed vision.

BIBLIOGRAPHY

PRIMARY SOURCES

Addison, Joseph. *The Spectator.* Edited by G. Gregory Smith. Everyman's Library edition. 4 vols. London: J. M. Dent, 1907.

Akenside, Mark. *The Pleasures of Imagination.* London: Printed for R. Dodsley, 1744.

Alison, Archibald. *Essays on the Nature and Principles of Taste.* London: Printed for J. J. G. and G. Robinson; Edinburgh: Bell and Bradfute, 1790.

Allen, Walter (ed.). *The Writer on His Art.* New York: McGraw-Hill Book Company, 1949.

Allsop, Thomas (ed.). *Letters, Conversations, and Recollections of S. T. Coleridge.* London: Moxon and Company, 1836.

Aquinas, St. Thomas. *Basic Writings of Saint Thomas Aquinas.* Edited by Anton C. Pegis. 2 vols. New York: Random House, 1945.

Aristotle. *Aristotle, On the Art of Poetry.* Edited and translated by Ingram Bywater. Oxford: at the Clarendon Press, 1909.

————. *The Art of Rhetoric.* Translated by John Henry Freese. London: William Heinemann, 1926.

————. *Aristotle's Psychology: A Treatise on the Principle of Life (De anima and Parva naturalia).* Translated with introduction and notes by William A. Hammond. London: Swan Sonnenschein and Co.; New York: The Macmillan Company, 1902.

————. *De anima.* Edited with translation, introduction, and notes by R. D. Hicks. Cambridge: at the University Press, 1907.

————. *The Works of Aristotle.* Translated into English under the editorship of W. D. Ross. 11 vols. Oxford: at the Clarendon Press, 1908-1937.

————. *Basic Writings.* Edited by Richard McKeon. New York: Random House, 1941.

Armour, Richard W. and Raymond F. Howes (eds.). *Coleridge the Talker: A Series of Contemporary Descriptions and Comments.* Ithaca, New York: Cornell University Press; London: Oxford University Press, 1940.

Augustine, St. *The Confessions.* Translated by E. B. Pusey, D. D. Mount Vernon: Peter Pauper Press, n. d.

Bacon, Francis. *The Works of Francis Bacon.* Edited by James Spedding, Robert Leslie Ellis, and Douglas Denon Heath. 8 vols. London: Longmans and Company, 1879.

————. *Selections* [including *The Advancement of Learning*, published in 1605]. Edited by Matthew Thompson McClure. New York: Charles Scribner's Sons, 1928.

Beattie, James. *The Minstrel: or, The Progress of Genius.* Edinburgh: James Ballantyne, 1803.

Berkeley, George, Bishop of Cloyne. *Complete Works.* Edited by Alexander Campbell Fraser. 4 vols. Oxford: at the Clarendon Press, 1901.

——. *A New Theory of Vision.* And other select philosophical writings. Edited by A. D. Lindsay. London: J. M. Dent, 1910.

——. *Philosophical Commentaries,* generally called the *Commonplace Book.* An *editio diplomatica* edited by A. A. Luce. London: Thomas Nelson and Sons, 1944.

Boehme, Jakob. *The Signature of All Things.* Introduction by Clifford Bax. London: J. M. Dent; New York: E. P. Dutton, 1912.

Campagnac, E. T. (ed.) *The Cambridge Platonists:* being selections from the writings of Benjamin Whichcote, John Smith and Nathaniel Culverwel. Oxford: at the Clarendon Press, 1901.

Carlyle, Thomas. *The Works of Thomas Carlyle.* Centenary edition. Edited by Henry Duff Traill. 30 vols. London: Chapman and Hall [1895?-].

Coleridge, Samuel Taylor. *Aids to Reflection.* Edited by Henry Nelson Coleridge. London: William Pickering, 1839.

——. *Anima Poetae.* Edited by Ernest Hartley Coleridge. London: William Heinemann; Boston: Houghton Mifflin Company, 1895.

——. *The Best of Coleridge.* Edited with an introduction and notes by Earl Leslie Griggs. New York: Thomas Nelson and Sons, 1934.

——. *Biographia Epistolaris.* Edited by A. Turnbull. 2 vols. London: G. Bell and Sons, 1911.

——. *Biographia Literaria.* Edited by J. Shawcross. 2 vols. Oxford: at the Clarendon Press, 1907.

——. *Christabel.* Edited by Ernest Hartley Coleridge. Facsimile of the Ms. Published under the Direction of The Royal Society of Literature. London: Henry Frowde, 1907.

——. *Coleridge on Logic and Learning.* Edited by Alice D. Snyder. New Haven: Yale University Press, 1929.

——. *Coleridge's Miscellaneous Criticism.* Edited by T. M. Raysor. Cambridge, Mass.: Harvard University Press, 1936.

——. *Coleridge's Shakespearean Criticism.* Edited by T. M. Raysor. 2 vols. London: Constable and Company; Cambridge, Mass.: Harvard University Press, 1930.

——. *Coleridge's Treatise on Method.* Edited by Alice D. Snyder. London: Constable and Company, 1934.

——. *Collected Letters of Samuel Taylor Coleridge.* Edited by Earl Leslie Griggs. 2 vols. Oxford: at the Clarendon Press, 1956.

——. *The Complete Poetical Works of Samuel Taylor Coleridge.* Edited by Ernest Hartley Coleridge. 2 vols. Oxford: at the Clarendon Press, 1912.

———. *The Complete Works of Samuel Taylor Coleridge*. Edited by W. G. T. Shedd. 7 vols. New York: Harper and Brothers, 1884.

———. *Confessions of an Inquiring Spirit*. Edited from the author's ms. by Henry Nelson Coleridge. London: William Pickering, 1840.

———. *Essays on His Own Times*. Edited by His Daughter [Sara Coleridge] 3 vols. London: William Pickering, 1850.

———. *Essays and Lectures on Shakespeare*. Everyman edition. London: J. M. Dent; New York: E. P. Dutton, 1907.

———. *The Friend*. A Literary, Moral, and Political Weekly Paper, Excluding Personal and Party Politics and the Events of the Day. Conducted by S. T. Coleridge, of Grasmere, Westmorland. No. 1, June 1, 1809 to No. 27, March 15, 1810. Penrith, 1809-1810.

———. *The Friend*. 3 vols. London: Printed for Rest Fenner, Paternoster Row, 1818.

———. *Hints towards the Formation of a More Comprehensive Theory of Life*. Edited by Seth B. Watson. London: John Churchill, 1848.

———. *Inquiring Spirit: A New Presentation of Coleridge from His Published and Unpublished Prose Writings*. Edited by Kathleen Coburn. New York: Pantheon Books, 1951.

———. *Letters from the Lake Poets*, Samuel Taylor Coleridge, Wordsworth, and Southey to Daniel Stuart, editor of the *Morning Post* and the *Courier*. London: West, Newman and Company, 1889.

———. *Letters of Samuel Taylor Coleridge*. Edited by Ernest Hartley Coleridge. 2 vols. Boston: Houghton Mifflin Company, 1895.

———. *The Literary Remains of Samuel Taylor Coleridge*. Edited by Henry Nelson Coleridge. 4 vols. London: William Pickering, 1836-1839.

——— and William Wordsworth. *Lyrical Ballads*. Bristol: Printed for Biggs and Cottle for T. N. Longman, Paternoster Row, London, 1798. Noel Douglas Replicas. London: Noel Douglas, 1926.

——— ———. *Memorials of Coleorton*. Edited by William A. Knight. 2 vols. Edinburgh: David Douglas, 1887.

———. *Miscellanies Aesthetic and Literary*. Edited by T. Ashe. London: G. Bell and Sons, 1892.

———. *The Philosophical Lectures of Samuel Taylor Coleridge: Hitherto Unpublished*. Edited by Kathleen Coburn. London: Pilot Press, 1949; New York: Philosophical Library, 1949.

———. *The Poems of Samuel Taylor Coleridge*. Edited by Ernest Hartley Coleridge. London: Oxford University Press, 1912.

———. *The Poetical Works of Samuel Taylor Coleridge*. Edited with a biographical introduction by James Dykes Campbell. London: Macmillan & Company, Ltd., 1925.

———. *The Rime of the Ancient Mariner*. Illustrated by Gustave Doré. New York: Harper and Brothers, 1877.

————. *Seven Lectures on Shakespeare and Milton.* With an introduction by J. Payne Collier. London: Chapman and Hall, 1856.

————. *Statesman's Manual.* London: Printed for Gale and Fenner, Paternoster Row, 1816.

————. *The Table Talk and Omniana of Samuel Taylor Coleridge.* London and New York: Oxford University Press, 1917.

————. *Unpublished Letters of Samuel Taylor Coleridge.* Edited by Earl Leslie Griggs. 2 vols. New Haven: Yale University Press, 1933.

Cottle, Joseph. *Early Recollections of Samuel Taylor Coleridge.* 2 vols. London: Longmans, Rees and Company, 1837.

————. *Reminiscences of S. T. Coleridge and Robert Southey.* New York: Wiley and Putnam, 1847.

Cowl, R. P. (ed.). *The Theory of Poetry in England.* London: Macmillan & Company, Ltd., 1914.

Cudworth, Ralph. *The True Intellectual System of the Universe.* 3 vols. London: T. Tegg, 1845.

Dante. *The Divine Comedy.* Translated by Carlyle-Wickstead. Introduction by Professor C. H. Grandgent of Harvard University. New York: Random House, 1932.

————. *Hell (L'Inferno).* Translated by Dorothy L. Sayers. Harmondsworth, Middlesex, England: Penguin Books, 1949.

————. *The Portable Dante.* Edited by Paolo Milano. New York: The Viking Press, 1947.

Dennis, John. *The Grounds of Criticism in Poetry.* London: Printed for Geo. Strahan and Bernard Lintott, 1704.

De Quincey, Thomas. *The Collected Writings of Thomas De Quincey.* 14 vols. Edinburgh: A. and C. Black, 1889-90.

————. *Confessions of an English Opium-Eater.* New York: Hurst and Company [1900].

————. *Recollections of the Lake Poets.* With an introduction by Edward Sackville-West. London: John Lehmann, 1948.

Descartes, René. *The Philosophical Works of Descartes.* Edited and translated by Elizabeth S. Haldane and G. R. T. Ross. 2 vols. Cambridge: at the University Press, 1931.

Donne, John. *The Poems of John Donne.* Edited by H. J. C. Grierson. London: Oxford University Press, 1933.

Dryden, John. *Essays of John Dryden.* Edited by W. P. Ker. 2 vols. Oxford: at the Clarendon Press, 1926.

Duff, William. *Essay on Original Genius: and its Various Modes of Exertion in Philosophy and the Fine Arts, Particularly in Poetry.* Second edition. London: Edward and Charles Dilly, 1767.

Eckermann, J. P. *Gespräche mit Goethe.* Edited by Adolf Bartels. 2 vols. Jena: E. Diederichs, 1908.

Emerson, Ralph Waldo. *The Complete Works of Ralph Waldo Emerson.* Edited by Edward Waldo Emerson. 12 vols. Cambridge, Mass.: The Riverside Press, 1903-4.

Garrod, H. W. (ed.). *Coleridge: Poetry and Prose with Essays by Hazlitt, Jeffrey, De Quincey, Carlyle.* Oxford: at the Clarendon Press, 1925.

Gay, John. " Concerning the Fundamental Principles of Virtue or Morality." Appeared at first anonymously as the preface to the translation by Edmund Law of Archbishop King's Latin *Essay on the Origin of Evil* (1731). In *The English Philosophers from Bacon to Mill*, edited by Edwin A. Burtt. New York: Random House, 1939.

Gerard, Alexander. *An Essay on Genius.* London: Printed for W. Strahan; T. Cadell; etc., etc., 1774.

———. *An Essay on Taste.* Edinburgh: J. Bell and W. Creech, 1780.

Gilbert, Allan H. (ed.). *Literary Criticism: Plato to Dryden.* New York: American Book Company, 1940.

Gillman, James. *The Life of Coleridge.* 2 vols. London: William Pickering, 1838.

Goethe, Johann Wolfgang. "Wilhelm Meister's Critique of Hamlet." *Goethe's Literary Essays.* Edited by J. E. Spingarn. London: Oxford University Press, 1921.

Greever, Garland (ed.). *A Wiltshire Parson and His Friends*: the correspondence of William Lisle Bowles together with four hitherto unidentified reviews by Coleridge. Boston: Houghton Mifflin Company, 1926.

Hartley, David. *Observations on Man, His Frame, His Duty, and His Expectations.* 2 vols. London: Samuel Richardson, 1749.

Hawthorne, Nathaniel. *The Complete Works of Nathaniel Hawthorne.* Fireside edition. 13 vols. Boston and New York: Houghton Mifflin Company, 1909.

Hazlitt, William. *The Complete Works of William Hazlitt.* Edited by P. P. Howe. 21 vols. London and Toronto: J. M. Dent, 1930-1934.

Hedge, Frederic Henry. "Coleridge," in *The Transcendentalists: An Anthology.* Edited by Perry Miller. Cambridge, Mass.: Harvard University Press, 1950.

Hegel, G. F. W. *The Introduction to Hegel's Philosophy of Fine Art.* Translated with notes by Bernard Bosanquet. London: Kegan Paul, Trench and Company, 1886.

Hobbes, Thomas. *The English Works of Thomas Hobbes of Malmesbury.* Edited by Sir William Molesworth. 11 vols. London: John Bohn, 1839-45.

Hume, David. *A Treatise on Human Nature.* Edited by T. H. Green and T. H. Grose. 2 vols. London: Longmans, Green and Company, 1875.

———. *Enquiry Concerning Human Understanding.* Edited by L. A. Selby-Bigge. Oxford: at the Clarendon Press, 1902.

————. *Essays, Moral, Political, and Literary*. Edited by T. H. Green and T. H. Grose. 2 vols. London: Longmans, Green and Company, 1875.

Iamblichus of Chalcis. *Iamblichus on the Mysteries of the Egyptians, Chaldeans, and Assyrians*. Translated from the Greek by Thomas Taylor. Second edition. London: Bertram Dobell, 1895.

Johnson, Samuel. *The Critical Opinions of Samuel Johnson*. Edited by Joseph Epes Brown. Princton: Princeton University Press, 1926.

————. *The Lives of the English Poets*. Edited by George Birkbeck Hill. 3 vols. Oxford: at the Clarendon Press, 1905.

Kames, Henry Home, Lord. *Elements of Criticism*. Edited by Abraham Mills. New York: Sheldon and Company, 1876.

Kant, Immanuel. *Critique of Aesthetic Judgment*. Edited and translated by James Creed Meredith. Oxford: at the Clarendon Press, 1911.

————. *Critique of Pure Reason*. Translated by F. Max Müller. 2 vols. London: Macmillan & Company, Ltd., 1881.

————. *Critique of Pure Reason*. Translated by F. Max Müller. Second edition, revised. New York: The Macmillan Company, 1949.

————. *Critique of Pure Reason*. Translated by Norman Kemp Smith. London: Macmillan & Company, Ltd., 1929.

Keats, John. *The Letters of John Keats*. Edited by Maurice Buxton Forman. London: Oxford University Press, 1935.

Lamb, Charles. *The Works of Charles Lamb*. Edited by E. V. Lucas. 6 vols. New York: The Macmillan Company, 1913.

Locke, John. *An Essay concerning Human Understanding*. Edited by Alexander Campbell Fraser. 2 vols. Oxford: at the Clarendon Press, 1894.

Longinus, Cassius. *Longinus On the Sublime*. Translated by W. Rhys Roberts. Second edition. Cambridge: at the University Press, 1907.

Leibniz, Gottfried Wilhelm. *New Essays Concerning the Human Understanding*. Translated from the original Latin, French and German by Alfred Gideon Langley. New York: The Macmillan Company, 1896.

Lessing, Gotthold Ephraim. *Laocoön: An Essay upon the Limits of Painting and Poetry*. Translated by Ellen Frothingham. Boston: Little, Brown and Company, 1910.

Mill, John Stuart. *Dissertations and Discussions*. 3 vols. Boston: William V. Spencer, 1865.

More, Henry. *Philosophical Writings of Henry More*. Edited with introduction and notes by Flora Isabel MacKinnon. New York: Oxford University Press, 1925.

Morgann, Maurice. *Essay on the Dramatic Character of Sir John Falstaff*. Edited by William A. Gill. London: Henry Frowde, 1912.

————. [Anon.] *Essay on the Dramatic Character of Sir John Falstaff*. London: Printed for T. Davies, 1777.

Pico della Mirandola. *On Imagination*. Edited by Harry Caplan. New Haven: Yale University Press, 1930.

Plato. *The Dialogues of Plato*. Translated into English with analyses and introductions by Benjamin Jowett. 4 vols. New York: Charles Scribner's Sons, 1895.

Plotinus. *The Ethical Treatises*. Being the Treatises of the First Ennead with Porphyry's *Life of Plotinus*. Translated from the Greek by Stephen MacKenna. London and Boston: The Medici Society, 1926.

——. *Psychic and Physical Treatises*; Comprising the Second and Third Enneads. Translated from the Greek by Stephen MacKenna. London: Medici Society, 1921.

——. *On the Nature of the Soul*, Being the Fourth Ennead. Translated from the Greek by Stephen MacKenna. London: Medici Society, 1924.

——. *On the Divine Mind*, Being the Treatises of the Fifth Ennead. Translated from the Greek by Stephen MacKenna. London: Medici Society, 1926.

—— *On the One and the Good*, Being the Treatises of the Sixth Ennead. Translated from the Greek by Stephen MacKenna and B. S. Page. London: The Medici Society, 1930.

——. *Treatises of Plotinus*. Translated by Thomas Taylor. London: Thomas Taylor, 1834.

Reid, Thomas. *Essays on the Intellectual Powers of Man*, in *The Works of Thomas Reid*. Edited by Sir William Hamilton. Edinburgh: Maclachlan and Stewart, 1863.

Reynolds, Sir Joshua. *Discourses on Art*. (With this is bound *Longinus On the Sublime*: An English Translation by Benedict Einarson, The University of Chicago.) With an introduction by Elder Olson, The University of Chicago. Chicago: Packard and Company, 1945.

Richardson, William. *Essays on Shakespeare's Dramatic Characters*. The Sixth edition. London: Printed for Samuel Bagster, 1818.

Robinson, Henry Crabb. *Henry Crabb Robinson on Books and their Writers*. Edited by Edith J. Morley. 3 vols. London: J. M. Dent, 1938.

——. *Blake, Coleridge, Wordsworth, and Lamb: Reminiscences of Henry Crabb Robinson*. Edited by Edith J. Morley. Manchester, England: at the University Press, 1922.

——. *The Correspondence of Henry Crabb Robinson with the Wordsworth Circle*. Edited by Edith J. Morley. 2 vols. Oxford: at the Clarendon Press, 1927.

Robinson, Herbert Spencer (ed.). *English Shakespeare Criticism in the Eighteenth Century*. New York: H. W. Wilson, 1932.

Ruskin, John. *Complete Works*. Edited by E. T. Cook and Alexander Wedderburn. 39 vols. London: George Allen; New York: Longmans, Green and Company, 1903-1912.

Shakespeare, William. *Twenty-Three Plays and the Sonnets*. Edited by Thomas Marc Parrott. New York: Charles Scribner's Sons, 1938.

Schelling, F. W. J. von. *Sämtliche Werke, 1792-1850*. 14 vols. Stuttgart, 1856-1861.

Schiller, Friedrich. *Aesthetical and Philosophical Essays*. New York: National Library Company, 1902.

———. *The Esthetic Letters, Essays, Including Letters on the Esthetic Education of Mankind*. Translated by J. Weiss. Boston: Little, Brown and Company, 1845.

Schlegel, Augustus Wilhelm von. *Lectures on Dramatic Art and Literature*. Translated by John Black. Second edition, revised by Rev. A. J. W. Morrison. London: G. Bell and Sons, 1914.

Shelley, Percy Bysshe. *The Poetical Works*. Edited by Edward Dowden. London: Macmillan & Company, Ltd., 1913.

———. *Shelley's Literary and Philosophical Criticism*. Edited by John Shawcross. London: Oxford University Press, 1932.

Smith, D. Nichol (ed.). *Eighteenth Century Essays on Shakespeare*. Glasgow: James MacLehose and Sons, 1903.

Spinoza, Benedictus de. *Chief Works*. Translated from the Latin by R. H. M. Elwes. 2 vols. London: Bohn's Philosophical Library, 1883-84.

Tucker, Abraham. *The Light of Nature Pursued*. 2 vols. London: Henry G. Bohn, 1852.

Vives, Ludovicus. *Vives on Education*. Edited by Foster Watson. Cambridge: at the University Press, 1913.

Warton, Thomas, Joseph and Thomas. *The Three Wartons. A Choice of Their Verse*. Edited by Eric Partridge. London: The Scholartis Press, 1927.

Whiter, Walter. *A Specimen of a Commentary upon Shakespeare*. London: Printed for T. Cadell in the Strand, 1794.

Wordsworth, Dorothy. *The Journals of Dorothy Wordsworth*. Edited by Ernest de Selincourt. 2 vols. New York: The Macmillan Company, 1941.

Wordsworth, William. *The Poetical Works of Wordsworth*. Edited by Thomas Hutchinson. London: Oxford University Press, 1932.

———. *The Prelude or The Growth of a Poet's Mind*. Text of 1805. Edited by Ernest de Selincourt. London: Oxford University Press, 1933.

———. *Wordsworth's Literary Criticism*. Edited by Nowell C. Smith. London: Henry Frowde, 1905.

——— and Dorothy Wordsworth. *The Letters of William and Dorothy Wordsworth*. Edited by Ernest de Selincourt. 6 vols. Oxford: at the Clarendon Press, 1935-39.

Young, Edward. "Conjectures on Original Composition in a Letter to the Author of 'Sir Charles Grandison,'" (1759). In *Criticism: The Foundations of Modern Literary Judgment*. Edited by Mark Schorer, Josephine Miles and Gordon McKenzie. New York: Harcourt, Brace and Company, 1948.

NAME INDEX

Abrams, Meyer H., 140n.
Addison, Joseph, 50, 53n., 84–88, 96, 128, 136, 138, 192, 217, 280
Aeschylus, 192
Akenside, Mark, 53–54, 56n., 88, 89
Alison, Archibald, 87, 163
Aquinas, 33
Aristotle, 32, 33, 34, 35, 45, 46, 51, 63, 64, 65, 66, 72, 91, 121, 134n., 139, 140, 158, 192, 206, 250, 255, 255n., 268, 273, 274, 282, 286–87
Armstrong, Edward A., 231–32, 233, 245n., 248
Arnold, Matthew, 173n., 174, 262n.
Auden, W. H., 95
Augustine, 42, 99, 168

Babbitt, Irving, 64n., 255
Bacon, Francis, 63, 169
Basler, Roy B., 214n.
Bate, Walter Jackson, 51n., 55n., 91, 121, 129n., 201, 276–77, 285–86
Baudelaire, Charles, 188, 200, 203
Beatty, Arthur, 12
Beccaria, 59
Beethoven, Ludwig van, 235n.
Belsham, William, 16
Benziger, James, 140n.
Bergson, Henri, 38
Berkeley, George, 18, 19, 21, 22, 23, 24n., 63, 71, 76, 78, 80–81, 161, 169, 287
Blair, Hugh, 87
Blake, William, 59, 67n., 97, 131, 152, 204, 209, 281
Bodkin, Maud, 179, 209
Boehme, Jacob, 71, 72–73, 76, 84, 89, 131–33, 282, 283, 284

Bowles, William Lisle, 18, 195
Bowra, C. M. (Sir Maurice), 124n.
Boyle, Robert, 169
Bredvold, Louis I., 94
Brenner, Rica, 252
Breton, André, 252
Brett, R. L., 23n., 31n., 74n., 107
Brinkley, Roberta F., 200n.
Brinnin, John Malcolm, 247n.
Broad, C. D., 176n.
Brooks, Cleanth, 86, 167, 203, 266–67
Bruno, Giordano, 76, 79, 131, 282, 283, 284
Buddha, 275
Bullitt, John, 55n., 129n.
Bundy, M. W., 128n.
Burke, Edmund, 87
Burke, Kenneth, 181n., 185n., 242–44, 280
Burnet, Bishop, 180
Butler, Samuel, 218–19
Byrom, John, 89

Caldwell, John Ralston, 229n.
Carlyle, Thomas, 188, 207, 208
Carlyon, Clement, 25, 26n.
Carritt, E. F., 85
Carver, P. L., 138n.
Cassirer, Ernst, 38, 200
Chew, Samuel C., 153n.
Cicero, 191
Cimarosa, 190
Coburn, Kathleen, 37, 59n., 102, 104, 175
Coleridge, George, 16n.
Coleridge, Hartley, 20n., 159, 214
Coleridge, Samuel Taylor. See Subject Index

297

SUBJECT INDEX

Aesthetics, 5, 14, 29, 30–31, 44, 84–85, 98, 120–21, 147, 213; "organistic," 268; Coleridge's, criticized by Raysor, 269; Tolstoyan fallacy in, 272; Coleridge as transmitter of German ideas on, 273; Coleridge's, defended, 274–277; value of German theories of, 275

Allegory, contrasted with symbol, 204

Association of ideas, Coleridge's interest in, 9–12, 28–29, 31, 32–39; Hartley's theory of, 12–16, 20, 108; Wordsworth's interest in, 24; Hazlitt's interest in, 25, 31; Mackintosh, Sir James, lectures on, 26; Kant's theory of, 29–30; Aristotelian theory of, 32–34; Coleridge's law of, 35; Bergson and, 38; Cartesian theory of, 42; Hobbes' theory of, 44–47; Locke's theory of, 47–48; Hume's theory of, 48–51; Malebranche and, 48; Addison and, 50; Akenside and, 53–54; Duff and, 55; Sharpe and, 55; Gerard and, 56–57; Condillac and, 58, 105, 108, 259; emotional, 153, 162, 166; Coleridge's theory of, criticized, 224–28, 277–78; Coleridge's criticism of Hartley-Condillac theory of, 259–60

Associative linking, 5, 113–114; and foci of association, 154–55, 242; unconscious, in Shakespeare, 163–66, 229–36; uncontrolled, 228, 241; unconscious, in Coleridge, 236–44; Lowes on, in Coleridge, 237–40; Warren on, 245; as contributing to creation, 248; in Proust, 251; in

Joyce's *Ulysses*, 251–52; in modern poetry, 252–53; in "The Ancient Mariner" and "Kubla Khan," 253

Borrowdale, 182

Broad Church Movement, 111

Calne, Wiltshire, 32, 103

Cambridge Platonists, the 74–76, 88, 168, 282, 286

Catalyst, Eliot's, power of forming new wholes, 234, 279

Christian Platonism, 73–74, 111

Christ's Hospital, 66–67

Clevedon, Somerset, 70

cogito quia sum, 100

Coleridge's criticism, grounded in psychology, 215; grounded in philosophy, 258, 285; of Shakespeare, 262, 271; practical, contrasted with his theoretic, 269–76; of Wordsworth, 270

Coleridge's theory of imagination, 1–8; vital sources of, 60–99 *passim*; ultimate source of, 68; first adequate account of imagination as symbolic power, 211; based on transcendental world-view, 212–13; coherent, 213; based on a psychology, 214–17; compared to earlier theories, 217; evaluation of, 248–53; criticized by Richards, 256–61; criticized by Eliot, 261–63; eclectic, 262, 281, 286–87; Raysor calls, "unfortunate," 271; Read considers, "essentially sound," 272; defended, 279–88

Coleridge's writings *cited*: "The

Date